**W9-AOD-725**

# CRITICAL PERSPECTIVES ON JEAN RHYS

# CRITICAL PERSPECTIVES ON JEAN RHYS

*Edited by Pierrette M. Frickey*

An Original by Three Continents Press

*A Three Continents Book*

Published in the United States of America by
Lynne Rienner Publishers, Inc.
1800 30th Street, Boulder, Colorado 80301

Copyright © By Three Continents Press 1990
of Cover Art of Max K. Winkler

Library of Congress Cataloging-in-Publication Data:

Critical perspectives on Jean Rhys / edited by Pierrette M. Frickey — 1st edition
    p.  cm. — (Critical perspectives: 14)
    Includes bibliographical references.
    ISBN 0-89410-058-0: $25.00. — ISBN 0-89410-059-9 (pbk.) $15.00
    1. Rhys, Jean — Criticism and interpretation.  I. Frickey,
Pierrette M.  II. Series.
PR6035.H96Z625  1990                                     90-11062
823' .912 — dc20                                              CIP

# ACKNOWLEDGMENTS

With pleasure and gratitude I acknowledge the following individuals and associations who have granted permission to quote copyrighted material:

Wallace Literary Agency, Inc., agents for the estate of Jean Rhys, for the quotations which appear throughout the essays included in this collection and which were taken from the works of Jean Rhys.

"Making Bricks without Straw. " Credit Jean Rhys. Reprinted from *Harper's Magazine (July 1978)* by permission of Wallace and Shiel Agency.

"A Conversation with Jean Rhys, 'the best English novelist'" from *Mademoiselle* 79 (October 1974). Credit Mary Cantwell. Courtesy *Mademoiselle.* Reprinted by permission of The Condé Nast Publication Inc.

"The Hole in the Curtain." Credit Jan van Houts. Printed by permission of Jan van Houts.

"A Gloomy Child and Its Devoted Godmother: Jean Rhys *Barred, Sous les Verrous* and *In de Strik."* Credit Martien Kappers -den Hollander. Reprinted by permission of Martien Kappers-den Hollander. The article appeared previously in *Autobiographical and Biographical Writing in the Commonwealth,* (Proceedings of the European Association of Commonwealth Language and Literature), Ed. Doireann MacDermott, Editorial AUSA, Sabadell, Barcelona, Spain 1984, and in *Jean Rhys Review* 1, 2 (Spring 1987), Ed. Nora Gaines. Also appeared in *Commonwealth Literature - Mostly Canadian,,* ed. Th. L. D' Haen a.o., Amsterdam, Free University Press, 1986.

"Without a Dog's Chance" Credit V.S. Naipaul. Reprinted from *New York Review of Books* 18 (18 May 1972) by permission of Gillon Aitken.

"Reflections of Obeah in Jean Rhys' Fiction." Credit Elaine Campbell. Reprinted from *Kunapipi* 4,2 (Winter 1982) by permission of Elaine Campbell and Anna Rutherford, Editor of *Kunapipi.*

"Jean Rhys and the Genius of Impressionism." Credit Todd K. Bender.

Reprinted from *Studies in the Literary Imagination* 11,2 (Fall 1978) by permission of Paul Blount, editor of *Studies in the Literary Imagination*.

"Whispers Outside the Room: The Haunted Fiction of Jean Rhys. Credit Colette Lindroth. Reprinted from *The Review of Contemporary Fiction 3, 2 (1984)* by permission of the author and John O'Brien, editor of *The Review of Contemporary Fiction,*

"'Women Must Have Spunks': Jean Rhys's West Indian Outcasts." Credit Lucy Wilson. Reprinted from *Modern Fiction Studies* 32, 3 (Autumn 1986) by permission of Lucy Wilson and *Modern Fiction Studies*.

"The World of Jean Rhys's Short Stories." Credit A.C. Morrell. Reprinted from *World Literatuure Written in English* 18, 1 (April 1979) by permission of A.C. Morrell. An abridged version of the article was printed in *Contemporary Literary Criticism* 19 (1981).

"Characters and Themes in the Novels of Jean Rhys." Credit Elgin Mellown. Reprinted from *Contemporary Literature* 1,3 (1972) by permission of Elgin Mellown and Margaret A. Walsh, Rights and Permissions Editor of *Contemporary Literature*.

"Sun Fire — Painted Fire: Jean Rhys as a Caribbean Novelist." Credit Louis James. Reprinted from *Ariel* 8, 3 (July 1977) by permission of Cbristopher Wiseman, acting editor of *Ariel*.

"The Emergence of a Form: Style and Consciousness in Jean Rhys's *Quartet*. Credit Thomas Staley. Reprinted from *Twentieth Century Literature* 24 (Summer 1978) by permission of Thomas Staley and William McBrien, editor of *Twentieth Century Literature*.

"The Artist Emerging." Credit Helen Nebeker. Printed by permission of the author.

"Symbolic Imagery and Mirroring Techniques in *Wide Sargasso Sea*" Credit Veronica Marie Gregg. Printed by permission of the author.

"*Wide Sargasso Sea* and the Gothic Mode." Credit Anthony Luengo. Reprinted from *World Literature Written in English* 15, 1 (April 1976) by permission of Anthony Luengo and the editor of *World Literature Written in English*.

"*The Other Side:* Wide Sargasso Sea and *Jane Eyre*." Credit Michael Thorpe. Reprinted from *Ariel* 8,3 (July 1977) by permission of Ian Adam, editor of *Ariel*.

"The Wide Sargasso Sea: a West Indian Reflection." Credit John Hearne. Reprinted by permission of John Hearne.

*"Wide Sargasso Sea."* Credit Kenneth Ramchand. Reprinted from *An Introduction to the Study of West Indian Literature.* Sunbury-on-Thames: Thomas Nelson and Sons Limited, 1980. Permission by Kenneth Ramchand and Thomas Nelson and Sons, Limited.

"Dark Smile, Devilish Saints." Credit John Updike. Reprinted from *The New Yorker* 56, 82 (August 11, 1980) by permission of John Updike and *The New Yorker.* Also by permission of Alfred A. Knopf, Inc., for reprint from *Hugging the Shore: Essays and Criticism* (1983) by John Updike,

I am grateful to André Deutsch Ltd. for use of the photograph of Jean Rhys (page viii), published in *Jean Rhys Letters 1931-1966,* © 1984.

I am grateful to Francis Wyndham for his permission to reprint Jean Rhys's letter to her daughter.

# TRANSCRIPT OF LETTER BY JEAN RHYS

. . . them.
As to the truth and the whole
truth—it is very rare (?) And
never one sided.

A novel is not truth (must
continue in pencil pen given out)
but there is a good deal of truth
in writing—more than in the
mean and prejudiced lies that
so many believe.
Perhaps the worst thing about
being old is that the effort
to answer them is too great and
prejudice too deeply rooted

# PREFACE

The mounting popularity of Jean Rhys, particularly in the past five years, is such that the sheer number of articles written about all aspects of her fiction made the selection process for this collection a difficult task. To simplify matters, three major factors guided the choice of articles for this *Critical Perspectives on Jean Rhys*: the representation of West Indian and European/American criticism, since Jean Rhys is an author claimed by both England and the Caribbean ; the selection of essays that offer a balance between analyses of content, style, and structure; the consideration of specific works within the two genres used by Rhys, the novel and the short story, as well as perspectives on her entire fiction.

For the serious reader and/or researcher of Rhys, who may be familiar with much of the work done on her, this collection affords a convenient way of reviewing the major trends in the criticism of Rhys's fiction and of accessing an up to date, comprehensive bibliography of this criticism.

The general reader and/or student of Jean Rhys will find in this volume essays addressing issues important to the understanding of her fiction and useful information about her life through what she herself chose to reveal rather than from speculation.

# TABLE OF CONTENTS

# INTRODUCTION

Jean Rhys's response to the reception of the W. H. Smith Award in 1967 was that "the honor had come too late. . ." (Turner 56). Indeed, Rhys remained practically unnoticed until the end of her life. Only one year before her death in 1979, when she was little known outside Great Britain, she was invited to Buckingham Palace by the queen to receive the prestigious Council of Great Britain Award for Writers for her contribution to literature. And it was not until the publication of her fifth and last novel that she was finally acknowledged as a West Indian writer by her Caribbean compatriots. The sudden revival of interest in the almost forgotten Jean Rhys started with the 1966 publication of *Wide Sargasso Sea*, which won her the W.H. Smith Literary Award and the Heinemann Award of the Royal Society of Literature. The mysterious author, "the inscrutable Miss Jean Rhys" who for some "went into hiding" and for others simply had died following the 1939 publication of *Good Morning, Midnight*, suddenly resurfaced to command attention after more than twenty years of obscurity. Her first four novels were reprinted, and she was proclaimed in the *New York Times Book Review* "the best living English novelist" (Alvarez 6). There followed an outpouring of interviews, articles, reviews, and the publication of twelve books on Jean Rhys (Angier, Codaccioni, Davidson, Gardiner, Given, Harrison, Hemmerechts, James, Nebeker, O'Connor, Staley, Wolf). Elgin Mellown's 1984 two-hundred page bibliography and the number of more recent publications attest to the extent of her international acclaim.

Rhys's double identity as a writer—European because four of her novels are set exclusively in Europe where she lived most of her life, and West Indian since she was born in and wrote about the Caribbean in *Wide Sargasso Sea*—is responsible for the polarization of criticism. In claiming Rhys as their own, Caribbean critics call worldwide attention to the uniquely West Indian character of her entire work while European and American critics tend to focus upon the plight of the Rhysian heroine in a society alien to her and to the modernism of Rhys's fiction. This book includes both critical perspectives. But of common concern to all is the life of Jean Rhys about which there are more speculations than accurate facts.

Since no biography of Rhys will be written unless her will is violated (Wyndham 9), the temptation of interpreting her autobiographical novels as a literal transcription of her life has led to the kind of speculations which upset Rhys during her life (MBWS 71). Only the unfinished autobiography, *Smile Please*, and her correspondence edited by Francis Wyndham tell her story accurately. *Smile Please*, written shortly before she died, to set the record straight and correct the lies told about her (9), concerns mainly her childhood in Dominica and her life in Europe prior to her meeting Jean Lenglet. *Jean Rhys Letters 1931-1966* covers the period between the death of her second husband, Leslie Tilden Smith, and her own in 1979. This carefully edited collection of letters affords an unprecedented insight into Rhys, the woman and the writer whose meticulous craftsmanship is evident in her account of the composition of *Wide Sargasso Sea*. Also of interest is the description of Rhys's writing relationship with her first husband, Jean Lenglet, in Martien Kapper-den Hollanders' articles, "The Dutch Connection" and "A Gloomy Child and Its Devoted Godmother: Jean Rhys, *Barred, Sous les Verrous* and *In de Strik*."

In addition to what Jean Rhys wrote about herself, there are a number of informative interviews, a few included in this work. In "Making Bricks Without Straw," Rhys made plain her resentment of any inquiries about her private life and her outrage at the lies printed in the transcripts of these meetings; for this reason, she tended to repeat pat answers to get rid of unwanted visitors, a factor explaining the repetitive nature of many of the reports. Yet, her attitude toward those she considered her friends because they showed genuine interest in her work produced a few excellent interviews. Among these is Jan van Houts' account of his visit to her cottage in Cheriton-Fitzpaine, an especially revealing piece since it uncovers a side of Rhys too seldom noticed, that of a fun-loving, witty companion. Its value lies, however, in the comparision that can be made between Jan van Hout's report of that brief encounter with Jean Rhys's own version of it in "Who Knows What's Up in the Attic?" (SIOL 160).

What we know about Jean Rhys's life is that she was born Ella Gwendolen Rees Williams in Dominica, an island in the Lesser Antilles, in 1890. Her father had come from Wales to practice medicine there and had married Minna Lockhart, a third-generation creole whose family had owned a plantation, burned in 1830 after the Emancipation Act. At seventeen, after having completed her schooling at a Catholic school in Roseau, Rhys left for England to live with her aunt Clarice. In London, she studied at the Royal Academy of Dramatic Art until, shortly thereafter, her father died. Unable to stay with her aunt, the young girl found herself alone without any means of financial and moral support in an alien society. For a time, she worked as a chorus girl and as part-time model, living the errant life described in *Voyage in the Dark* in order to support herself. To make matters worse, a significant first love affair with a man older than she ended abruptly, leaving her emotionally wrecked and, as Francis Wyndham points out, marked for life by a sense of doom regarding any future love relationships (11). For the rest of her life, this former lover, whose identity she never revealed, continued to be her benefactor. In 1919, she married Jean Lenglet (pen name, Edouard de Nève), a French-Dutch songwriter and journalist who performed as "chansonnier" in Montmartre and later would write *Sous les Verrous*, a novel about his emprisonment and his relationship with Jean Rhys at the time. From their union was born a son who died shortly after birth and a daughter, Maryvonne, entrusted to the care of her father after his divorce from Rhys. The couple lived in France for a time, then left for Vienna, where Lenglet worked for Japanese government officials as part of an international mission administering post-war Vienna. After their return to Paris, Lenglet was arrested for illegal entry into France and financial irregularities. Following this incident and Rhys's affair with Ford Madox Ford, the couple divorced. In her letters, Rhys shows a life-long affection for Jean Lenglet and a profound love for their daughter whose regular visits she treasured.

Eventually Jean Rhys returned to England where she lived with and later married Leslie Tilden Smith, a literary agent and editor for several publishing houses including Hamish Hamilton. Jean went to Paris to write, and in 1936 visited Dominica in company of her husband. Before returning to England the couple made a short visit to New York. Rhys's second marriage was far from being idyllic because of constant money problems aggravated by Jean's drinking and her fragile health. Rhys, who had by then published a book of short stories, *The Left Bank and Other Stories* (1927), and four novels, *Quartet* (1928), *After Leaving Mr. Mackenzie* (1930), *Voyage in the Dark* (1934), *Good Morning, Midnight* (1939), vanished from the public eye for a decade. She resurfaced in 1949 when she answered an announcement in *The New Statemen* asking the whereabouts of the author thought dead by many.

Not until the publication of her correspondence in 1984 did we learn what happened to Jean Rhys during the period of silence which mystified her readers. These were difficult years for Rhys. Two years after the death of Leslie Tilden Smith in 1945, she married Max Hamer, Leslie Tilden Smith's cousin. During that third marriage, she experienced renewed financial difficulties, frequent movings to less than satisfactory rented hotel rooms and cottages, and poor health. Max Hamer was involved in financial irregularities and consequently in trouble with the law, a repeat of what had happened to Jean Lenglet. World War II caused a tragic separation from her daughter, Maryvonne, who spent time in a concentration camp. Yet, and in spite of the customary depiction by many of a weak, helpless, and passive woman surrendering to a tragic fate, Rhys managed to survive physically and emotionally and to write, no small feat considering the circumstances of her life, most accurately described by herself in her correspondence. This is the hallmark of her heroines, whose passivity and fatalism, so often commented upon by critics, is paradoxically matched by a stubborn will to live and the kind of tenacity common to survivors.

During what may have been her most troubled years, Rhys worked on her masterpiece, *Wide Sargasso Sea*, and published short stories, some of which would appear later in *Tigers are Better Looking* (1968) and *Sleep It Off, Lady* (1976). *Wide Sargasso Sea* would remain her crowning achievement and a symbolic journey home. With this last novel and her unfinished autobiography published after her death, she completed the voyage begun in *Voyage in the Dark*. Would she have written were it not for the circumstances of her life? This question is partly answered by her statement to interviewers that she wrote to relieve herself of the enduring pain which characterized her life. But she also acknowledged in one of her letters three major factors affecting her decison to write: Mrs. Adams, the wife of *The Times* correspondent in Paris, who showed Rhys's writings to Ford; Ford himself, and Paris, of which she kept the fondest memories ( JRL 65).

Ford Madox Ford, whom Rhys described as "a down to earth, business-like snob, grimly determined to get on," played, nevertheless, a vital role in her career (Plante 260). In spite of her realization that Ford had taken advantage of her, as he had of other women, Rhys acknowledged his contribution ". . . Ford helped me more than anybody else: 'Do this! 'Don't do that.' He insisted on my reading French books and I think they helped me a lot. They had clarity" (Vreeland 226). Ford helped launch Rhys's career. He printed her story, "Vienne" in *The Transatlantic Review*, which he edited, wrote the preface to *The Left Bank and Other Stories*, and introduced her to Leslie Tilden Smith, who became instrumental in having *Quartet* published by Jonathan Cape (Plante 264). It is evident, however, from Ford's preface to *The Left Bank and Other Stories* that the novice came to him already a confirmed writer with definite ideas about what her writing ought to be, "I tried. . .very hard to induce the author of the *Left Bank* to introduce some sort of topography of that region . . . into her sketches. . . . But would she do it? No! . . . Her business was with passion, hardship, emotion. . . . She is probably right. Something human should, indeed, be dearer than all the topographies of the world" (LB 26). Rhys was already a gifted writer, impressive enough to share with D.H. Lawrence Ford's attention and to enlist his help in finding publishers for her works. ".. . Miss Rhys sent in several communications with which I was immensely struck, and of which I published as many as I could. What struck me on the technical side . . . was the singular instinct for form possessed by this young lady, an instinct for form being possessed by singularly few writers" (LB 24-25). Even Stella Bowen, Ford's common-law wife, in her begrudging report of the Ford-Rhys affair, concedes Rhys's "gift of prose . . . her needle-quick intelligence" (166-167).

There were others who had a similar impact on Rhys's career. After Selma Vaz Dias had located Rhys in 1949 for the purpose of adapting *Good Morning, Midnight* to a radio show, admirers of her early novels encouraged her to continue to write. Her letters, published in 1984, indicate the major role played by Francis Wyndham, a devoted friend, and Diana Athill, her editor; both provided her the support she needed to continue to write in spite of the odds against her. The correspondence makes clear, however, that even when faced with incredible odds, Jean Rhys not only continued to write, but never compromised her ideas of what writing ought to be about. Never do we have the impression that the physically weak Rhys described by David Plante in *Three Difficult Women* had relinquished any of her principles about authorship and her intention to write.

Jean Rhys wrote in order to rid herself of pain, as she repeatedly said to her interviewers, but also simply because she was meant to write. She speaks of this commitment in *Smile Please*: "I must write. If I stop writing my life will have been an abject failure. It is that already to other people. But it could be an abject failure to myself. I will not have earned death" (163). Long before her meeting with Ford, she had experienced the calling which may have well begun her career. It happened after the disappointment of a first broken love affair described in *Voyage in the Dark*: "I passed a stationer's shop where quill pens were displayed . . . . I went into the shop and bought a dozen. Then I noticed some black exercise books on the counter. . . . I bought several of those, I didn't know why, just because I liked the look of them. I got a box of J nibs, the sort I liked, an ordinary pen-holder, a bottle of ink and a cheap inkstand. It was after supper that night . . . that it happened. My fingers tingled, and the palm of my hands. . . . I wrote until late into the night, till I was so tired that I couldn't go on, and I fell into bed and slept" (SP 128,129). The subject which she chose to write about was what she knew best, herself (Bernstein 40, Cantwell 206).

Yet, if the term autobiographical writing often evokes a sentimental cathartic outpouring, Jean Rhys earned the accolade of "best living English novelist" for more than a confessional talent (Alvarez 6). The answer to her success lies in the way she viewed the act of writing: "It's hard to explain how, when and where a fact becomes a book. I start to write about something that happened or is happening to me, but somehow or other things start changing. It's as if the book had taken possession. Sometime a character will run away from me, like Grace Pool, the nurse in *Wide Sargasso Sea* and get more important than I intended. It happened beyond my will" (Cantwell 171). Through writing, Rhys imposed her will over her fate, giving shape to a life otherwise formless and making sense out of it (Bernstein 41). By distancing herself from reality, she assumed control over it. In this sense, writing exorcised the pain. And, too, she achieved greater objectivity in rendering the truth while avoiding the kind of sentimentality she thought had no place in a serious work of art. As Veronica Gregg puts it, "What the writer seems to be proposing in her autobiographical writings is the construction of a fictive self through which she can impart the 'truth' of her perceptions, sensibility, and intellect" ( 42).

Her manuscripts, notes, and her journal, now all a part of the Rhys Collection at the University of Tulsa, reveal the story of that transformation from the raw material of life into art. Today, it receives increasing attention from critics and warns against the danger of taking too literally Rhys's admission of writing about herself. Teresa O'Connor's recent "*Jean Rhys*, Delphine Chartier's, "Jean Rhys: L'Auto-censure créatrice. Analyse des versions successives de la nouvelle 'Rapunzel, Rapunzel,' " and Veronica Gregg's "Jean Rhys and Modernism: A Different Voice" are examples of this recent interest.

The works she left as testimony of her life's achievement rather than a straight report of her personal experiences fall into two phases. To the first belong the four novels set exclusively in Europe, *Quartet, After Leaving Mr. Mackenzie, Voyage in the Dark*, and *Good Morning, Midnight*. The second consists of *Wide Sargasso Sea*, Rhys's only novel set in the West Indies, and *Smile Please,* which for the most part recounts her childhood in Dominica. Her three volumes of short stories, *The Left Bank and Other Stories*, *Tigers Are Better Looking*, and *Sleep It Off, Lady* include ten West Indian stories while thirty-six are set in Europe.

Among Rhys's novels, *Quartet* is the object of most of the unfounded speculations about Rhys's personal life because it is based on the stormy relationship of the ménage-à-trois (Rhys, Ford, and Ford's common-law wife, Stella Bowen) while Jean Lenglet, Rhys's first husband, was in jail. The story is made even the more attractive to those wishing to elaborate on Rhys's marriage and her relationship to Ford because each member of the trio wrote his own version of the story, Ford in *When the Wicked Man*, Bowen in her autobiography, *Drawn from Life*, and Lenglet in *Barred*. Yet in a letter to Francis Wyndham, Rhys warns against making false assumptions: ". . . it wasn't autobiography, as everyone seems to imagine though some of it was lived of course" (JRL 171). At any rate, whether Rhys wrote *Quartet* to avenge herself of her callous lover, Ford, remains far less important than the writing connection among Ford, Rhys, and Lenglet. Martien Kappers den Hollanders' articles, "The Dutch Connection" and "A Gloomy Child and Its Devoted Godmother: Jean Rhys, *Barred*, *Sous les Verrous*, and *In de Strik* " help correct the inaccuracies written about Rhys.

Marya, the heroine of *Quartet*, is as alone and destitute in Paris as was Anna in London. Soon after her arrival in the French capital, her husband, Stephan Zelli, is jailed for fraudulent art deals, and she ends up living with an odd couple, Heidler, a writer, and his common-law wife, Lois. The novel tells how she fulfills the needs of the callous pair, who find in her an easy prey. Lois' determination to keep Heidler from leaving her by allowing him to have a fling conveniently at home and Heidler's insatiable sexual appetite for attractive, talented and also vulnerable women are satisfied. The novel ends, as the others, in disillusion and hopelessness. Marya loses both, a husband who, knowing of her affair with Heidler, rejects her when he comes out of prison, and a lover ready to end one more relationship. Marya's violation of accepted social norms is not the issue as much as the imperatives of survival. As Thomas Staley notes, "She is vulnerable but she is not a victim of her own moral code of behaviour. Survival and protection are the motivating force behind her actions. . . " ( 39).

Although *Quartet* was the first published novel, *Voyage in the Dark* was written earlier. The novel came from Rhys's journal begun shortly after her arrival in England. The work is significant as it begins the saga which will take the heroine of *Quartet*, *After Leaving Mr. Mackenzie*, and *Goodmorning, Midnight* through England and France, in quest of something better in life before the final return home in Rhys's last novel, *Wide Sargasso Sea*. Anna, the seventeen year old girl who left her island for a romanticized England, the land of wisteria, romance and pretty ladies (SP 64-65), finds herself disappointingly alone and without money in a world totally alien to her. Not only has she lost the most significant person in her life, her father, but she soon loses her first lover, a man much older than she who gave her love and security. The novel ends with her abortion and the doctor's comment, "She'll be all right . . . . Ready to start all over again in no time, I've no doubt." And Anna is ready to start "all over again, all over again. . . (VID 159). The artistic merit of *Voyage in the Dark* and the other novels of Jean Rhys, is their modernity as they put to the test the concepts of morality and normality. As Todd Bender points out in his "Jean Rhys and the Genius of Impressionism," all depends upon the reader's bases for judgment. To understand the Rhysian heroine's reaction to the circumstances of life, one must switch sides and see things the way she does (52).

Rhys's last two continental novels, *After Leaving Mr. Mackenzie* and *Good Morning, Midnight*, continue the saga of the West Indian woman whose fortune has not changed since she came to England in *Voyage in the Dark*; although Rhys gave her a different name in each novel, she is the composite whose consciousness records experience. In *After Leaving Mr. Mackenzie,* her name is Julia Martin. Like Anna and Marya, she drifts, this time from Paris to London. Her ex-lover, Mr. Mackenzie, leaves her, ending the regular weekly three hunded francs allowance with a final payment of fifteen hundred francs. With this, she buys expensive pretty clothes and then she goes to London after being encouraged to do so by her new lover, George Horsfield, "a decent Englishman," modeled after Jean Rhys's second husband, Leslie Tilden Smith, according to Rhys's stepdaughter, Phyllis Smyser. In London she meets her former lover, W. Neil James, who gives her money. But it is from Uncle Griffiths, whom she next visits, that she expects the kind solicitude usually accorded by a relative to someone as destitute as she. Instead, astounded to see her, Griffiths declares that he has no money before being asked for some. After giving her one pound for a return ticket, he tells her, "Take my advice. You get along back as quickly as you can" (ALMM 85). While in London, Julia visits her mother, who is on her death bed, and has an unpleasant encounter with her sister, the self-sacrificing, aging Norah to whom Uncle Griffith would leave his money if he had it because she never abandoned the family. After her mother's funeral, Julia returns to Paris, where Mr. Horsfield, now back to the security of his house, "quiet and not without dignity . . . . a familiar world," tries "to put Julia entirely out of his mind" (ALMM 175). The novel ends with Julia asking a hundred francs of Mr. Mackenzie, who, prompted by "the romantic side of his nature," approaches her and offers her a drink (ALMM 190).

*Good Morning, Midnight*, the expression of a sensibility which, according to John Leonard, finds an echo in the works of modern women writers such as Doris Lessing and Joan Didion (Leonard 37), ends the series of the four novels set in Europe. It was Rhys's preferred novel and undoubtedly the most acccomplished one, excepting *Wide Sargasso Sea*. V.S. Naipaul praises it as "the most subtle and complete of the novels and the most humane" (Naipaul 30). In it, Rhys tells the story of Sasha Jensen, a once beautiful woman growing old, alone with only a gigolo for companion and Paris as a reminder of a time bygone. But Sasha has finally learned something that none of the other heroines of Rhys's previous novels have, that faced with the impossibility of changing her destiny she can choose to accept it and recognize its irony: when a young man, who had been following her, seeing her face at the light of the street lamp exclaims, " *Oh, la la* . . . . *Ah, non, alors,* " she says, "The joke's on me this time" (GMM 187). Rendered less vulnerable by this acceptance, she can now manipulate events instead of being manipulated by them. In a reversal of situation, which Elgin Mellown calls a "reversed mimicry of her own life" (462), she turns down the ouvertures of the gigolo, René, by giving him money and asking him to leave in spite of the realization that he was the only companion she could have had. And the novel ends with the symbolic affirmation of her own condition when she embraces the wretched traveling salesman, "another poor devil of a human being" who comes into her room as the gigolo leaves. In giving herself to the one who embodies her own wretchedness, she is finally reconciled with herself: "I put my arm round him and pull him down on to the bed, saying 'Yes - yes - yes . . .'" (GMM 350).

In 1967, Jean Rhys's last novel, *Wide Sargasso Sea*, was published, and it is only then that she became known as a West Indian writer. In his 1968 article, "The Road to Thornfield: An Analysis of *Wide Sargasso Sea*," Wally Look Lai notes, ". . . there can be little doubt that a serious reading will reveal *Wide Sargasso Sea* to be one of the genuine masterpieces of West Indian fiction" (38). But it is Kenneth Ramchand who, in 1970, acknowledged the novels and all previous works by Rhys as West Indian, pointing to her rediscovery as "the most spectacular turn of fortune" (*The West Indian Novel and Its Background*, XI). Still, the supreme testimony to Rhys's West Indian authenticity comes from John Hearne, who sees in *Wide Sargasso Sea* "the touchstone against which to assay West Indian fiction before and after it" (323-324).

*Jean Rhys Letters 1931-1966* gives a detailed account of her writing of *Wide Sargasso Sea*, of which she wrote three versions not counting the first, a film script she lost ( 143, 172). The novel was writen with the intention of telling her own version of Charlotte Brontë's mad woman in the attic " . . .I've never believed in Charlotte's lunatic, that's why I wrote this book. . . . The creole in Charlotte Brontë's novel is a lay figure — repulsive which does not matter, and not once alive which does. . . . I've brooded over 'Jane Eyre' for years. . . . I was vexed at her portrait of the 'paper tiger' lunatic, the all wrong creole scenes" (1296, 56, 262). Her novel is the story of a West Indian white creole, Antoinette, married for her money right out of the convent to an English man, Rochester. The work recreates the turbulent years following emancipation, the heated passions born from newly acquired freedom, and the nightmarish landscape infused with magic in which the pair are suddenly cast as lovers. It is about the struggle involved in the reconciliation of opposites when the opposites are two young people, curious about each other, and under the spell of the tropics. The novel begins with the burning of Coulibri Estate, Antoinette's home, by the ex-slaves, the ensuing madness of her mother, and the death of her child brother. It ends with Antoinettes's incarceration in Rochester's tower in England, which she sets on fire before plunging to her death from its battlement.

Although Rhys was acknowledged for a long time only as an English writer, the West-Indian character of her writings has received increasing attention since the publication of *Wide Sargasso Sea*. Of particular interest is her ability to identify with two worlds, in this case Europe and the West Indies, and with the paradox they may represent, a quality often present in the literature of exile. Jean Rhys's fiction can be said to reflect the kind of truth apparent only to those who can see both sides of this reality. Readers unable to perceive the two fail to understand, for instance, the complexity of *Wide Sargasso Sea*, in which is expressed through the marriage of the opposites, Rhys's own divided consciousness. Jean D'Costa notes, "A reader of Rhys usually puzzles over her viewpoint looking for and against both perspectives. Her insider-outsider's treatment of England, France and the Caribbean gnaws at comfortable ethnocentricism. Her characters play out pathologies of exploitation as lovers, siblings, as neighbours, as whole social groups. Looking for some kind of familiar ground the reader tries to fit Rhys into available models of contemporary fiction and fails" (391).

*Smile Please*, Rhys's unfinished autobiography, reveals to what extent Rhys internalized the contradictions inherent to the world in which she grew up. She was raised by a distant, repressed mother whom she describes as solemn and by a contrastingly free-spirited imaginative father she admits to have romanticized" (42-43,72). Her Victorian upbringing contrasted sharply with the uninhibited life of the black islanders (52). Incidentally, critics have commented on Rhys's ambiguous stance toward blacks, with whom she identified and at the same time rejected. This love-hatred complex is perhaps best explained as an ego-protective mechanism since she felt rejected by her mother, "the warm center of the world" and by blacks with whom she claims common heritage: "I would never be a part of anything. . . and I knew it, and all my life would be the same, trying to belong, and failing" ( 49, 124). Equally paradoxical is her feeling about the Dominican landscape, which she finds at once threatening and beautiful: the blue sea is treacherous; the stars are "benevolent," yet "quite indifferent; " the majestic hills are "austere, lost;" danger lurks in the sunlight ( 87, 8, 25 ). In the magic atmosphere of this island, Catholicism and voodooism share power, and the significant religious experience described by Rhys in her autobiography is shared by her intense fear of Obeah magic ( 79,29-30). This is the world Jean Rhys never forgot, an island where passions run hot, darkness is as intense as sunlight and hatred as powerful as love. It must be of significant interest to us since in it is found the essence of Jean Rhys's life and of her writings. It explains the pronouncement she made a few years before she died, " It is in myself. . . . All. Good, evil, love, hate, life, death, beauty, ugliness" (161). With this statement, Rhys not only explained herself but also her heroines, whose central consciousness records and communicates experience.

Her imaginative insights are black and white, notes Wilson Harris (146). More than this, her consciousness is at once West Indian and European, male and female, and the composite of all finds itself expressed in the Antoinette-Rochester relationship of *Wide Sargasso Sea*. In assuming Rochester's and Antoinette's point of view, Jean Rhys becomes both. With this amazing gift of understanding, she makes it clear that the truth is seldom one-sided. Today the criticism of her fiction addresses all angles of this multidimensional representation of truth, depending on the critic's perception of the message, his sensibility and values, and it is incumbent upon the serious reader of her fiction to be acquainted with all aspects of that truth. Lucy Wilson's study of the black West Indian female characters in Rhys's work demands attention equal to that given by Caribbean critics to the alienation of the white creole in the historical context of the British colonies during post-emancipation.

But to say that Rhys confined herself to problems and issues specific to any interest group would be missing the point. Her fiction explores more than the particulars of race, sex, and nationalities. John Updike points to the universal character of her prose in that it renders the sense of fragmentation, of alienation, common to the modern age (82). V.S. Naipaul, in his "Without a Dog's Chance," recognizes also in Rhys's writing many of the themes which concern us today: isolation, the lack of a sense of society or community, the impression that things are falling apart ( 29-31); and Kenneth Ramchand speaks of Rhys's ability to convey modern man's sense of alienation coming from having no roots, of belonging everywhere and nowhere (TC 236). But more specifically, the poignant saga of the Rhsyian heroine whether it be Anna, Marya, Julia or Sasha, could be that of any woman terribly alone and at the mercy of manipulative, self-serving individuals in a society alien to her. It is about survival in the face of penury, ill health, and bitter disappointments in love. What makes the telling compellingly true to us is that in it the reader recognizes his own fears and insecurities, regardless of race, age, and gender. Jean Rhys reminds us that human affections at best are transitory, that deceptions are often our lot, and that there is no place for the weak, the poor, and the old in a world where youth, power and money are revered. And in this compelling tale of one woman's misfortune, critics have found many causes served.

Until Jean Rhys was given a place among West Indian writers, European and American critics had ignored the West-Indianness of her fiction. As early as 1927, Ford Madox Ford had mentioned briefly her connection with the Caribbean in his preface to *The Left Bank* (TLB 24), as did Alec Waugh in his 1949 *The Sugar Island;* however, it was not until after the publication of *Wide Sargasso Sea* and Kenneth Ramchand's pioneer article on the novel that critics such as Thomas Staley spoke of that special quality which sets her apart from other Western writers: "It became clear to me from the first reading of her work that her background and culture not only set Rhys apart from her contemporary novelists, but also shaped a widely different sensibility and radical consciousness" (JR 1). Although non-Caribbean critics pay increasing attention to the West Indian character of Rhys fiction ( James, Campbell, O'Connor), the most serious studies of that aspect of Rhys's work still issue from West Indian criticism, which analyses Rhys's use of different types of languages, creole and standard English, and images to communicate the truth about her characters and the setting affecting their sensibilties.

Caribbean critics generally examine the alienation of the white creole in post colonial society and write about *Wide Sargasso Sea* almost exclusively. Their insight into the complex images and the language specific to Rhys's West Indian novel is valuable since it affords non-Caribbean readers an understanding of Antoinette Cosway's world and of the destructive attraction between the two lovers whose unfortunate plight is coming from two socially, historically, and geographically opposed societies. One can but agree with Ramchand's position that readers must know the West Indies or be well-informed about them in order to fully measure the impact of the Caribbean setting on the consciousness of Rhys and to understand *Wide Sargasso Sea* .

Several West Indian critics find implicit in *Wide Sargasso Sea* the attempt to reconcile differences between Europe and the Caribbean and a search for the kind of spirituality which makes the reconciliation possible. Wally Look Lai sees in the marriage of Antoinette and Rochester the meeting and relationship of Europe and the West Indies. Antoinette's leap toward the image of Tia at the end of the novel is viewed as "a return, however difficult, to the spiritual world on the other side of Wide Sargasso Sea" (27). John Hearne acknowledges in the work the revival of hopes for unity, a new expression of Plato's concept of the soul, whose divided parts hunger for reconciliation (332). In his article, "Terrified Consciousness," Kenneth Ramchand tells us that *Wide Sargasso Sea* is in part about the contrast of two worlds, a contrast which becomes as well "a lament for the divided self" ( 107). Salvation, if any, can be achieved only through visionary love and the surrendering of conventional values in a materialistic world ( 236). The novel might well represent the painful discourse between the two parts of Jean Rhys's own divided consciousness, European and West Indian.

In spite of whatever hope *Wide Sargasso Sea* might offer through Antoinette's symbolic leap and the vision it may conjure, West Indians paint a bleak picture of its forecast. For Wally Look Lai, Antoinette's final spiritual embrace of Tia is only an illusion (Look Lai 52). John Hearne tells us that hope is blighted, quoting Forster's words, " 'No, not yet . . . No, not there' " (333). And Ramchand sees the quest for unity as "a fleeting possibility" (225). For Michael Thorpe, *Wide Sargasso Sea* is a study "of tragic incompatibility retrieved from Charlotte Brontë's workshop floor" (109). Not quite so bleak is the interpretation given by a non-West Indian, Elaine Campbell, who sees the novel as "Rhys's contribution to the dissolution of social barriers grounded in racial differences" (50). The true answer lies perhaps in Lucy Wilson's pronouncement that the strength of Jean Rhys is in her honesty and in her commitment to social justice. In exposing the truth, her 'dangerous books,' cause her to be at odds with the lies perpetrated and maintained by the interest of power groups. In the aftermath of colonialism, the black characters in Rhys's fiction, unlike their white counterparts, "thrive on adversity" deriving their strength from a history of fighting against a prevailing power structure (440).

Generally, criticism of Rhys coming from England, the United States, and Canada gives attention to the movement of the "developing consciousness" central to Rhys's five novels and through which experience is sifted. It is, for instance, the essence of the articles by A.C. Morell and Elgin Mellown. Much of what is said about Rhys focuses on her rendition of the plight of the underdog, for which Ford praises her (LB 24), mainly her depiction of the lone woman in exile in a society of individuals motivated by self -interest. And some, as we have pointed out, read into this painful saga the true account of Rhys's life, failing to recognize that Rhys's heroines, except for Marya in *Quartet,* are single and that none are mothers or writers.

In the late 60's and the 70's, when feminist studies were much in demand, particularly in the United States, the Rhysian heroine came to represent the fate of the single woman in a man's world. Titles representative of this new trend read, "Of Heroines and Victim," "Women's Lot," "The Liberated Woman in Jean Rhys's Later Short Stories" (Abel, Porter, Casey). Yet Rhys denied that her works were intended to carry a feminist message (Cantwell 210, Plante 272), insisting that she wrote about life, not about propaganda (Cantwell 310). In a world of Jean Rhys's fiction, experience educates the sensibilities of men and women. In fact, in one of her letters about *Wide Sargasso Sea* she made clear that the novel is as much about Antoinette's misfortune as it is about Rochester's, both of whom she pities (JRL 269).

Critics on both sides of the Atlantic have elaborated to excess on the theme of alienation and on speculative interpretations of Rhys's fiction as facts at the expense of examining the craftsmanship which places Rhys among the best women contemporary writers. In this respect, her letters are enlightening. She wrote no less than three versions of *Wide Sargasso Sea.* But from that "slow perfectionist writer . . . who produces lucidity out of an almost incredible mass of tangled notes, drafts, all written on assorted scraps of paper" noted by her editor (Athill 378), issued a prose ruthlessly matter of fact, free of frills and of sentimental outpourings. She attributes that quality to the influence of French authors, particularly Anatole France, Maupassant, and Flaubert, whose clarity of style impressed her, and to Ford's advice to translate a passage in another language, and if the translation did not make sense to discard the passage (Cantwell 206). Many of her collected letters, particularly those included in part VI of Francis Wyndham's edition, describe her writing process and reveal how painstakingly careful a writer she was: " I know it seems stupid to fuss over a few lines or words, but I've never got over my longing for clarity, and a smooth foundation underneath. . . . I've learned one generally gets this by cutting, or by very slight shifts and changes. . ." (JRL 60). In another letter, she repeats the same concern, "Sometimes I long for an entirely new way of writing. New words, new everything — sometimes I am almost there. But no — it slides away. Besides, the old ideas, clarity, unity and so on — I can't get away from them — they are *valid"* (JRL 160). Jean Rhys's slow progress in writing *Wide Sargasso Sea* was not so much an indication of her wish to abandon writing but rather her unflinching commitment to quality (JRL 253).

If the new criticism of Jean Rhys is at all indicative of a shift towards the artistic mode in Rhys works, a far more important concern than her private life, Kristien Hemmerechts' 1986 book, *A Plausible Story and a Plausible Way to Telling It: a Structuralist Analysis of Jean Rhys's Novels* is also recommended reading. Also of significant import are Judith Gardiner's recent article in *Boundary*, "Good Morning Midnight, Good Night Modernism," Veronica Gregg's analysis of imagery in *Wide Sargasso Sea*, and Todd Bender's piece on impressionism in Rhy's fiction. The last two are featured in this volume.

Because of Jean Rhys's dedication to the art of writing, the articles selected for inclusion in this critical perspective examine the form and style of her fiction, her superb craftmanship responsible for a prose touchingly true yet artistically formal. They explain the complex pattern of images used by Rhys to communicate not only the West Indian reality but also the sense of fragmentation and loss common to modern man regardless of his origin. Also represented are the two poles of criticism, West Indian and non-West Indian, and the concerns expressed by each. In their difference of focus is found the reflection of Rhys's own double consciousness as a writer and her equal understanding of the problems inherent to whites and blacks, to the colonists and the colonized. In all, it is to Jean Rhys the writer and to her ability to grasp the truth of a moment in the drama of a life and to render it convincingly real that this critical perspective gives tribute. For this she wanted most to be remembered. "Listen to me," she admonishes David Plante, "I want to tell you something very important. All of writing is a huge lake. There are great rivers that feed the lake, like Tolstoy and Dostoevsky. And there are trickles, like Jean Rhys. All that matters is feeding the lake. I don't matter. The lake matters. . . . It is very important. Nothing else matters" (Plante 247). The essays chosen for this edition respect the will made explicit by Jean Rhys herself in the opening section of this work; they appraise the quality of her literary works and in doing so give her a rightful place among the major contemporary women writers from Europe and the West Indies.

# WORKS CITED

Abel, Elizabeth. "Women and Schizophrenia: The Fiction of Jean Rhys."
*Contemporary Literature* 20 (Spring 1970): 155-177.

Angier, Carole. *Jean Rhys.* New York: Viking Penguin Inc., 1985.

Alvarez, A. "The Best Living English Novelist." *New York Times Book
Review* 17 March, 1974: 6-7.

Athill, Diana. "Jean Rhys and the Writing of *Wide Sargasso Sea.*" *Bookseller*
3165 (20 Aug. 1966): 1378-1379.

—. Forward. *Smile Please.* By Jean Rhys. London: André Deutsch, 1979.

Bender, Todd. "Jean Rhys and the Genius of Impressionism." *Studies in the
Literary Imagination* 11. 2 (Fall 1978): 43-53.

Bernstein, Marcelle. "The Inscrutable Miss Jean Rhys." *Observer Magazine*
[Color Supplement to the Observer (London)] 1 June 1969: 40-42, 49-
50.

Blodgett, Harriet. "Tigers Are Better Looking to Jean Rhys." *Arizona
Quarterly* 32 (1976): 226-44.

Bowen, Stella. *Drawn from Life. Reminiscences.* London: Collins Brothers.
166-168.

Campbell, Elaine. "Reflections of Obeah in Jean Rhys' Fiction." *Kunapipi* 4.
2 (Winter 1982): 42-50.

Cantwell, Mary. "A Conversation with Jean Rhys, 'the best English
Novelist.'" *Mademoiselle* 79 (October 1974): 170-171, 206, 208, 210,
213.

Casey, Nancy. "The 'Liberated' Woman in Jean Rhys's Later Short Fiction."
*Revista Interamericana Review* 4 Summer 1974), 26-272.

Charpentier, Delphine. " Jean Rhys: Auto-censure créatrice. Analyse des
versions successives de la nouvelle 'Rapunzel, Rapunzel'." *Jean Rhys
Review* 1.1 (Fall 1986): 15-29.

Codaccioni, Marie-José. *L'Autre vie de Bertha Rochester.* Paris: Didier 1984,
701pp.

Davidson, Arnold. "The Dark Is Light Enough: Affirmation of Despair in Jean
Rhys's *Good Morning Midnight.*" *Ariel* 24, 3 (1983): 349-364.

—. *Jean Rhys.* New York: Ungar Press, 1985. 165pp.

Ford, Ford Madox. Preface. *The Left Bank and Other Stories.* By Jean Rhys.
London: Jonathan Cape, 1927; New York: Harper and Brothers, 1927;
New York: Arno Press, 1970. 7-27.

Gardiner, Judith Kegan. "Good Morning, Midnight; Good Night,
    Modernism." *Boundary* 11 (1-2) (Fall-Winter 1982-1983): 133-151.
—. *Rhys, Steade, Lessing and the Politics of Empathy*. Bloomington: Univer-
    sity of Indiana Press, 1989. 200 pp.
Givner, Joan. *Charlotte Brontë, Emily Brontë and Jean Rhys: What Rhys's
    Letters Show about that Relationship*. Wesport, CT. : Greenwood Press,
    1988. 350pp.
Gregg, Veronica Marie. "Jean Rhys and Modernism: A Different Voice."
    *Jean Rhys Review* 1.2 (Spring 1987): 30-46.
Harris, Wilson. "Carnival of Psyche: Jean Rhys's *Wide Sargasso Sea*." *Kun-
    apipi* 2.2 (1980): 142-150.
Harrison, Nancy. *Jean Rhys and the Novel as Women's Text*. Chapel Hill: The
    University of North Carolina Press, 1988.
Hearne , John. "The Wide Sargasso Sea: A West Indian Reflection." *Cornhill
    Magazine* 1080 (Summer 1974): 323-333.
Hemmerechts, Kristien. *A Plausible Story and a Plausible Way of Telling It:
    A Structuralist Analysis of Jean Rhys's Novels*. Frankfurt/M., Berne,
    New York: European Studies: Series 14, Anglo-Saxon Languages and
    Literature 163 (1986). 460pp.
James, Louis. *Jean Rhys*. Critical Studies of Caribbean Writers: Mervyn
    Morris, Gen. Ed. London: Longman, 1978.
Kappers- den Hollander, Martien. "Jean Rhys and the Dutch Connection."
    *Journal of Modern Literature* 2,1 (March 1984): 159-173.
— . "A Gloomy Child and Its Devoted Godmother: Jean Rhys, *Barred, Sous
    les Verrous*, and *In de Strik*." *Autobiographical and Biographical
    Writing in the Commonwealth*, (Proceedings of the European Associa-
    tion of Commonwealth Language and Literature). Ed.  Doireann
    MacDermott.Barcelona: Editorial AUSA, 1984: 1223-130. *Jean Rhys
    Review*. Ed. Nora Gaines. 1. 2 (Spring 1987): 20-29.
Leonard, John. "What men don't know about women" *New York Times* 119
    (12 May 1970): 37.
Look Lai, Wally. "The Road to Thornfield Hall. An Analysis of Jean Rhys'
    Wide Sargasso Sea." *New Beacon Review*. Ed. John La Rose. London:
    New Beacon Books Ltd., 1968.  Margary, Kevin
Mellown, Elgin W. "Characters and Themes in the Novels of Jean Rhys."
    *Contemporary Literature* 13 (Autumn 1972): 458-75; also in *Contempo-
    rary Women Novelists*, ed. Patricia Meyer Spacks. Englewood Cliff,
    N.J.: Prentice Hall, 1977. 118-36.
Naipaul, V.S. "Without a Dog's Chance." *New York Review of Books* 18 (18
    May 1972): 29-31.
Nève, Edouard de (Jean Marie Lenglet). *In de Strik*. Amsterdam: Andries
    Blitz, 1932; *Sous les verrous*. Paris: Librairie Stock, 1933; *Barred*.
    Trans. Jean Rhys. London: Desmond Harmsworth, 1932.

Nebeker, Helen. *Jean Rhys: Woman in Passage*. Montréal: Eden Press
    Women's Publication, 1981.
Morrell, A.C. "The World of Jean Rhys's Short Stories." *World Literature
    Written in English* 18 (April 1979): 235-244.
O'Connor. Teresa. *Jean Rhys: The West Indian Novels*. New York: New York
    University Press
Plante, David. "Jean Rhys: A Remembrance." *Paris Review* 76 (1979): 238-
    284. Reprinted in David Plante. *Difficult Women: A Memoir of Three*.
    New York: Atheneum, 1983.
Porter, Dennis. "Of Heroines and Victime: Jean Rhys and *Jane Eyre*." *Massa-
    chussetts Review* 17 (Autumn 1976): 540-552.
Ramchand, Kenneth. *An Introduction to West Indian Literature*. Sunburry-on-
    Thames Middlesex: Thomas Nelson & Sons Limited, 1976.
Staley, Thomas. "The Emergence of a Form: Style and Consciousness in Jean
    Rhys's *Quartet*." *Twentieth Century Literature* 24 (Summer 1978):
    202-224.
— . *Jean Rhys: A Critical Study*. Austin: University of Texas Press; London:
    Macmillan, 1979.
Thorpe, Michael. "'The Other Side': *Wide Sargasso Sea* and *Jane Eyre*."
    *Ariel* 8, 3 (July 1977): 99-110.
Turner, Alice K. "Paperbacks in the News: Jean Rhys Rediscovered: How it
    Happened." *Publishers Weekly*, 206 (1 July 1974), 56, 58.
Updike, John. " Dark Smile, Devilish Saints." *New Yorker* 56 (11 August
    1980): 82, 86, 90.
Houts, Jan van. "Het gaatje in het gordijn" *De Revisor* (1982); "The Hole in
    the Curtain" Unpublished Trans. John Rudge (1981).
Vreeland, Elizabeth. "Jean Rhys." *Paris Review*, 76 (1979), 219-237.
Waugh, Alec. *The Sugar Island. A Caribbean Travelogue*. New York: Farrar,
    Straus and Co., 1949.
Wilson, Lucy. "'Women Must Have Spunks": Jean Rhys's West Indian
    Outcasts *Modern Fiction Studies* 32.3. (Autumn 1986): 439-448.
Wolfe, Peter. *Jean Rhys*. Boston: Twayne Publishers, 1980.
Wyndham, Francis , Ed. *Jean Rhys Letters, 1931-1966*. London: André
    Deutsch, 1984.

# I. RHYS ON RHYS

# RHYS ON RHYS

If Jean Rhys had intended to keep her life private, the publication of her last novel saw to the contrary. Reporters, scholars, and curious readers, armed with cameras and tape recorders, made their way to the diminutive village of Cheriton-Fitzpaine to find Jean Rhys. There are many interviews of Jean Rhys, but a number of them are disappointingly repetitive, suggesting perhaps the possibility of plagiarism on the part of some. "Making Bricks Without Straw" gives a likely explanation for this. This witty piece by Rhys reveals the ignorance and insensitivity of those whose sole motivation for their visit was to extract a rare confession from her about personal matters. It also makes clear that such interviewers were hardly a match for the shrewd Miss Rhys. If, on the other hand, the visitor expressed a felt interest in her work and/or in Dominica, Rhys would grant a valuable interview. This happens to be the case of Mary Cantwell's "A Conversation with Jean Rhys, 'the best living English novelist,'" one among several excellent interviews of Rhys which, with Marcel Bernstein's and Elaine Campbell's, fall in this category. Cantwell's report informs the reader about Jean Rhys's own view of autobiographical writing, of what influenced most her career as author , and of the significant roles played by Dominica, her childhood and her daughter in her life. Still another revealing piece about Rhys is "The Hole in the Curtain," a translation of a story written by Jan van Houts, a Dutch secondary school teacher and writer, who spent five days with Jean Rhys in 1970 and became her friend and correspondent thereafter. "The Hole in the Curtain" is a companion piece to Jean Rhys's own version of this meeting in "What's up in the Attic," published in *Sleep It Off, Lady*. This makes for the value of Jan van Houts' piece. Not only does it contain important revelations of a side of Jean Rhys seldom explored, but it also affords an interesting comparison with Rhys's version, one which highlights Rhys's talent in transforming autobiographical material into art. The stylistic differences between the two pieces point to Rhys's accomplished impressionistic technique in rendering the truth of a moment rather than recording it.

# A CONVERSATION WITH JEAN RHYS

## by Mary Cantwell

There is a small library in the town in which I grew up and as a child I would go there two or three afternoons a week to sit at one of its old, round tables and thumb through the magazines we didn't get at home. I also took out every detective story that featured a corpse in a country house library, skimmed historical novels looking for sexy passages and became one of the few Americans under 70 who has read the complete Gene Stratton Porter. And now, whenever I am home, I still find myself in that library, still looking for detective stories and the kind of novel that's a good companion on a long, hot, New England afternoon. A few years ago I picked up one called *Good Morning, Midnight* by a woman named Jean Rhys. I took it to my house, curled up on a couch probably with a glass of beer in my hand, and proceeded to see my own reality erased. That is perhaps one test of a novel — does the writer's reality eclipse the reader's? — and it is a test Jean Rhys passes with horrifying ease. The novel, which is set in the 1930s, is about a forty-ish woman named Sasha Jansen who is revisiting Paris, a Paris which is haunted by her youth. There she has lost a child, a husband, lovers and her illusions. She has no money of her own and the common sense of a grasshopper. What she does have is self-knowledge and a stubborn ability to put one foot in front of the other, although her steps lead backwards more often than not. The novel ends tragically, but not finally; one knows, at the end, that Sasha will go on walking, and going nowhere.

Any good book about Paris can pluck you out of your chair and set you down in *Gauloise* country. But *Good Morning, Midnight* does far more. Reading it, I felt myself to be the fiction — a woman who runs a clean, well-lighted house, drinks only in moderation and has a little money in the bank — and Sasha the fact. To be precise, the fact of me. Sasha's inertia, helplessness, hopelessness were mine; that no one knew about them was, I figured, only because I hadn't been found out.

From *Good Morning, Midnight*, I went on to *Quartet* and *After Leaving Mr. MacKenzie*, both of them books about the same woman although she bears different names. In fact, the trio, along with *Voyage in the Dark*, which is out of print in this country, could be subtitled *Down and Out in Paris and London*. All were published in the '30s; then the author disappeared for 27 years, to surface again in 1966 with *Wide Sargasso Sea*, a tour-de-force about the life of Charlotte

21

Bronte's Mrs. Rochester before she is shut up in the attic at Thornfield Hall. (The success of this last novel is what led to the reissue of the others)

Because I am generous with my obsessions, I pressed my Jean Rhys novels on friends. One said reading *Good Morning, Midnight* was like lying in your own coffin listening to the nails being pounded in. Another, a veritable Robespierre of the Women's Movement, thought no one had written better about women, adding, however, that she was not one of those women. The others admitted to, though not with so pretentious a phrase, shocks of recognition.

We were a cult. Jean Rhys readers are. (The English critic Francis Wyndham, writing of those few who managed to find her out-of-print books during the 27 year silence, said they formed "a small but passionate band.") Then suddenly, this year, Jean Rhys caught on, so to speak. A. Alvarez, who wrote *The Savage God*, called her "the best living English novelist" in a long piece in *The New York Times Book Review*. Bookstores couldn't keep the new paperback editions of her novels in stock. A movie star took an option on *Good Morning, Midnight*. And Jean Rhys, about whom I knew nothing and presumed dead, turned out to be an 80-year-old ex-mannequin, ex-chorus girl who lived alone in a small village in Devon and is working on a new collection of stories. She is also an accidental recluse: that she has a reputation as a hermit is due less to voluntary isolation than to letters lost, telephones unanswered and a reluctance, during the publicity surrounding her winning a major English literary award in 1968, to being photographed when found by the local press in a beauty parlor having a shampoo. She is often lonely, she says, though never in the morning, when she feels she has the world to herself, and lives, she adds, on boiled ham. "And I used to have a good head for drink," she told me on the midsummer day I came to call, "but it's going."

To get to Jean Rhys' house, one drives along narrow lanes lined with hedges taller than the car, across a patchwork quilt of square fields — gold, green, pale green and a red like powdered brick. A taxi, mine, going through the village is so rare as to bring people to their windows, and Jean Rhys' cottage is as walled in wildflowers as Sleeping Beauty's palace is in thorns. The cottage is tiny, so is its owner, who was dressed, for the occasion perhaps, in a beige silk blouse with a blue brooch at the throat, a long black velvet skirt, and a striped black and gold jacket. Like Gloria Swanson, Elizabeth Taylor and Mrs. Onassis, however, Jean Rhys has a head a mite too big for her body. The comparison and the observation are not gratuitous: like them, she is a beauty. Seeing her, and most especially her eyes which are an enormous blue-gray, widely set and shadowed, skillfully, with dabs of more blue, one wonders if the mere fact of being remarkable-looking complicated one's life no matter how conventionally one wishes to live it. Yes, she answers unblushing, it leads to "entanglements and mix-ups. And I, unfortunately, tend to attract very odd people."

Jean Rhys was born in Dominica, a small island in the West Indies, the daughter of a Welsh doctor and a Creole — a white West Indian. She came to London when she was sixteen, enamoured with the idea of England — "When I was young," she says, "I was full of romantic ideas . . . you can't imagine. I wanted to be excited" — and quickly disillusioned. She had hoped to be an actress and studied for a term at the Royal Academy of Dramatic Art, but froze in front of an audience. She became a chorus girl. Her father dies, her mother was sick, and her sister, she says didn't like her. "Is she Norah," I asked, "in *After Leaving Mr. MacKenzie?*" "Oh yes," she replied. ("All you people who've knuckled under — you're jealous," the heroine, Julia, shouts to Norah. "D'you think I don't know? You're jealous of me, jealous, jealous. Eaten up with it." Julia is the kind of bad penny that pops up in everyone's family, the kind that emerges from God knows where every five years needing a loan. Norah is also the kind that pops up in everyone's family. She stays home, nurses the sick and lives a life steeled with propriety. Norah is "good," Julia is "bad," and there's no question about who's gotten the kicks out of life, as well as the slaps.) After marrying a Dutch poet, less out of sentiment than to get out of England, Jean Rhys spent 10 years wandering with him about the Continent. "When I came to France," she told me, "I felt as if I'd come out of prison and into the air. Then," she added, "things began to go wrong in Paris."

"What went wrong?"

"Well, that's *Quartet.*"

I had suspected, in fact assumed, that Jean Rhys had based her novels on her life. But to meet her, I discovered, was to be simultaneously introduced to Sasha, Julia, Marya, Anna, even Mrs. Rochester. Whenever I asked about one of them — Jean Rhys' women they've been called — she replied with "I."

*Quartet*, for instance, is about an English chorus girl, Marya, who marries a man named Stephen because the alternative is the continuation of "a vague procession of towns all exactly alike, a vague procession of men also exactly alike." Stephen is shady but kind. They live on money about whose origin Marya is wary but incurious ("Maybe it was ego, maybe selfishness," says Jean Rhys of her own first marriage, "but I never asked my husband where the money was coming from. Later he told me that a Frenchwoman would have been sure to find out.") and Stephen goes to jail for theft. Marya, young, pretty, broke, is taken up by an Englishman named Heidler and his wife Lois. They give her a home in their Paris studio, and Marya becomes Heidler's mistress. His wife doesn't fuss, in fact she aids and abets: if one has a husband inclined to stray, one gathers, the wise woman will arrange it so he doesn't have to stray farther than across the living room. In the end Heidler dumps Marya, as he has dumped others. So does Stephen, ostensibly because she has been unfaithful, more likely because he is bored by living with a limp dishrag.

Ford Madox Ford, the English critic and novelist, was Jean Rhys' discoverer and patron. While trying to sell translations of her husband's work, she was encouraged to send some of her own to Ford at his *Transatlantic Review.* They were published as *The Left Bank*, for which he wrote an enthusiastic introduction. Ford is also the model for Heidler.

Stella Bowen, the Lois Heidler of *Quartet*, who lived with Ford for some years and bore him a daughter, wrote in *Drawn from Life* that Jean Rhys lived in "an underworld of darkness and disorder, where officialdom, the bourgeoisie and the police were the eternal enemies and the fugitive the only hero." And she adds plaintively ". . . here I was cast for the role of the fortunate wife who held all the cards and the girl for that of the poor, brave and desperate beggar who was doomed to be let down by the bourgeoisie. I learned what a powerful weapon lies in weakness and pathos and how strong is the position of the person who has nothing to lose. . ." So Stella Bowen draws Jean Rhys, and so Jean Rhys draws Stella/Lois — "She gave a definite impression of being insensitive to the point of cruelty — or was it stupidity?" And the reader, dazzled by each performance, can only conclude that it is wiser to nurse a serpent in one's bosom than to install a writer in the hall bedroom.

"Something that haunts me," I said, "in both *After Leaving Mr. MacKenzie* and *Good Morning, Midnight* is that child who dies — the infant with the ticket around his wrist."

"My son did die. It made a terrible impression on me and I had to bring it in. I think it was Somerset Maugham who said that if you write out a thing, it goes . . . it doesn't trouble you so much. You're left with vague melancholy, but not utter misery. I suppose it's like psychoanalysis or a Catholic going to confession."

"But that kind of writing is often indiscriminate autobiographical spew. Yours has form, precision."

"I think French books helped me an awful lot there. They had clarity. Ford insisted — if you weren't sure of a paragraph or statement, translate it into another language. And if it looks utterly silly, get rid of it. Anglo-Saxon is rather messy, don't you think?"

"What did you read?"

"Contemporary French novels — I've forgotten their names. And I loved Maupassant, Anatole France, Flaubert."

"Have you ever thought of Emma Bovary as an ancestor of your women?"

"My women are so much lacking in common sense. I think Madame Bovary was more down to earth. I was never very sensible. . . Until I started to write, and concentrated on writing, it was a life in which I didn't quite know what was going to happen."

"And has most of what you wrote about happened to you?"

"It's hard to explain how, when and where a fact becomes a book. I start to write about something that has happened or is happening to me, but somehow or other things start changing. It's as if the book had taken possession. Sometimes a character will run away from me, like Grace Poole, the nurse in *Wide Sargasso Sea*, and get more important than I intended. It happened beyond my will. But the feelings . . . the feelings are always mine."

As we talked I was drinking Scotch and Jean Rhys, vermouth and soda, a light rain spat outside the minute, white-walled livingroom, and one or the other of us was forever getting up to turn on or off the electric fireplace. "England," she said, "is so cold."

Jean Rhys will probably never go back to Dominica, but the woman in *Wide Sargasso Sea*, Mrs. Rochester ("She is Creole girl, and she have the sun in her"), starved for warmth and color and scent — "that woman is like me." That morning, while I was sightseeing in Exeter Cathedral, a bridal party arrived and, deciding to be a member of the wedding, I sat through the whole ceremony. When I described the way the women were dressed, adding that it would take a stylist to outfit me for an English wedding because those hats, those flowered prints, that eye shadow are not within my ken, she laughed, still as much a foreigner in England as I.

Jean Rhys' women think a lot about their looks. So, it is safe to say, does Jean Rhys. Worried about which photograph I wanted of her, she'd say "That one makes me look like a fox, and not a very nice fox." Another she labeled "a libel." She was right. Of all of them, she said, "Sometimes I think there's a conspiracy among photographers to make me look either pathetic or mad as a hatter."

Jean Rhys' women also think a lot about their clothes. A fur coat, a nice black dress may change their lives. You're okay, the world says you're okay, if you've got a fur coat and a nice black dress. Who can touch you when you're armored in good clothes? And when I asked Jean Rhys about what her success and the money that goes with it meant to her, she said "For one thing, it would mean clothes. A really pretty suit or dress would mean a lot to me."

Money: the means to buy the really pretty suit or dress, a winter in Italy, a car to take her out of the cottage and around Devon. When Jean Rhys' daughter (by the Dutch poet), who lives in Holland and was visiting, and I were talking about the inflation that has replaced Vietnam and sex in the great American dialogue, her mother cried out "Stop, please!" We had frightened her.

Jean Rhys' women never have a cent. They live on their looks and a certain charm, trade them for the pounds and francs they promptly blow on clothes and liquor. "It's appalling, perfectly appalling," Lois Heidler says, "to think of the difference that money makes to a woman's life." Without an inheritance, without adequate jobs, they wangle money from lovers, ex-lovers, quasi-strangers: Anna Morgan in *A Voyage in the Dark* turns to part-time prostitution. "They had no alternatives, did they?" I said to Jean Rhys, referring to their economic situations. "Do you think anybody ever really does?" she answered, referring to our lives.

"I think women have been rather badly treated," she added. "A woman almost has to be twice as good as a man to be a success. I'm glad there's so much fuss about it now . . . because it wasn't really fair." But when a British television production of one of her novels was so distorted as to make the Movement the message, she was "so depressed I swore I'd never write again. I just wanted to say about life, not about propaganda."

"Yet there's a lot of rage, mostly aimed at men, in your novels." ("Sob stuff, sex stuff. That's the way men talk. And they look at you with hard greedy eyes. I [Marya] hate them with their greedy eyes.")

"However much you cut, or how careful you are, your own feeling will come through. But on the whole I'm rather sorry for everybody . . . I've reached that stage."

Sasha, Julia, Anna, Marya are angered by their lovers, their former lovers. "the species wife" ("there she was: formidable, very formidable, an instrument made exactly shaped and sharpened to one purpose. She didn't analyze: she didn't react violently: she didn't go in for absurd generosities or pities. Her motto was 'I don't think women ought to make nuisances of themselves. I don't make a nuisance of myself; I grin and bear it, and I think that other women ought to grin and bear it.'" — *Quartet*) and the safe and smug ("If all the good and respectable people had one face," Julia says, "I'd spit in it"). Only their husbands, if they've had one — Anna has not — are exempt, possibly because they are not Englishmen. About them they are vague, faintly guilty and chronically confused. "In the end I grew fond of him," Jean Rhys said of the Dutch poet, "but by that time he wasn't any longer fond of me. I think that happens quite often, don't you?"

She has been married three times, once divorced (the poet) and twice widowed. When I murmured something about courage she said "It's not courage, but an obstinate decision to be happy. I had the stupid idea that I wanted to be happy and I went on and on with the idea despite all discouragements. I just wanted to be happy and peaceful." (". . . I want to be happy. Oh, I want it so badly. You don't know how badly. I don't want to be hurt. I don't want anything black or miserable or complicated anymore. I want to be happy." — *Quartet*.

"Were you happy and peaceful in Cornwall?" I asked, remembering that she had lived there for years with her third husband.

"Not always happy, but peaceful."

"Marrying three times. You must have equated happiness with men."

"Oh, no, no. But. . . I'm not sure whether men need women, but I'm perfectly sure women need men."

When her husband got sick, someone gave them the cottage in Devon and there they lived until he died. After his death, she could not endure being there alone and went to London, had a heart attack and entered a convalescent home. She came back to Devon where, she says, "No one ever wrote to me. I suppose they thought that after being sick I'd never work again." She was obsessed, however, with Mrs. Rochester but every time she tried to put her on paper wrote the same words over and over again. "I'd go up and down the kitchen corridor," she said, pointing to a short hallway furnished by a bookcase choked with old Penguin paperbacks, "reading ancient books like *King Solomon's Mines*." Then a man, the friend of a friend, heard about Jean Rhys and started to call. He encouraged her — "it was funny, he doesn't even like my books, says they're ephemeral" — and she finished *Wide Sargasso Sea*.

I can't think it was altogether coincidence. I feel more and more as if we're fated. It seems as if I was fated to write, which is a horrible fate. . . I never meant to be a writer. Something had happened which made me sad so I started writing about it. . . I'm passive, I suppose. I drift. . . And I'm a coward."

"Your women never kill themselves, do they?" I interrupted. "They're always standing by the river but they never jump."

"As I've never managed it, I wouldn't know exactly how it felt. I tried it once

— but was I really trying? No, I've never had the pluck. It's like that poem by Dorothy Parker, the one that ends "You might as well live'. . .

"I can only do the one thing. I think I'm rather useless, but not as useless as everyone thinks. I tried to be an actress and I tried to be a chorus girl and I tried to start a shop. I was interested in beauty . . . cosmetics, but once when I was trying to make a face cream it blew up. I think I can cook, but everyone else thinks I can't." She held up her glass towards her daughter and indicated a refill with a large, ludicrous wink. "Jean," her daughter said, "your winks are *not* subtle." "Well I just told you," she said smiling, "I could only do the one thing. . . . But I'm rather astonished that I could have done that many words, done all those mix-ups."

It is tempting, easy, to say that all those words, all those mix-ups add up to the most precise portrait yet painted of woman as nigger. But it puts a gross limitation on Jean Rhys' achievement. She is a woman and she has written about herself, but in doing so she has written about all the people who know how to survive but not to fight. Who are dependent on others for money and for a sense of their own value. Who have no self image without a kindly mirror, a lover, to reflect them. They cry and they rage; they are not cool or shrewd. Their sins, when they commit them, are of omission. And they struggle with life the way a sleeper struggles with a tangled blanket.

"I used to feel alone in thinking these things," Jean Rhys told me, "Until I wrote the books and people started writing in and saying 'I've had a life exactly like yours.' So I no longer think that I'm unique.

"I rode a swing — swing high, swing low. That's been my life."

# THE HOLE IN THE CURTAIN

*Jan van Houts*

The village was one street: a few houses, two overhanging shop signs and a child playing on the pavement.

'I'll drive you home,' he sang, new words to a new tune. He couldn't sing, unlike her. 'You'll drive me home, you'll drive. . .' For a moment she broke off. The child had run into the road. He'd been expecting it and swerved to the right. A near thing he thought: you never knew with a strange car. 'Did you see that?' 'Of course, but I knew you'd seen it too.' He turned to look straight into her eyes. 'Sing another one.' Each time she spoke while he was driving she had turned her head towards him. 'Reach for that star again.'

He sang the song from 'The Man of La Mancha' and she hummed along.

As they drove into Exeter she said it had been wonderful to see the sea again. She had missed the sea so much and it had been a beautiful day. And she had always loved restaurants in cellars, something to do with agoraphobia, probably. He stopped at his hotel to pick up the bottles of wine. She mustn't drink anymore gin.

The doctor had been and had seen the waiting glasses and the bottles. He hadn't said anything. She would have told him that she was expecting a friend. No, she'd better cut out the gin. She'd switch to wine.

They drove through rolling countryside, red soil and three tall trees in the distance. She said that it generally rained — she'd said that in her letter — and that there was so little she could do now, old crock that she was.

She wore a blue hat. She shook her head, and looked out of the window and sang, 'You'll drive me home.'

She hadn't wanted to go out at all. Let's stay in, she'd said. But the sun had come out early that morning and when he knocked she already had her chic blue coat on.First he had to read something — such an odd letter from France. She wanted to know what he thought of it, but he was not to tell anyone. The post was on a wooden table in the kitchen. Reviews (Mercure de France) — 'In the letter it says they're good but I haven't read them yet — newspapers still rolled up in address labels, books in corrugated cardboard. And the letter from Lyon, written by a man under sentence of death. He begged her for help. He had read *Good Morning, Midnight* and thought she'd understand him and might be able to do something for him. He read the letter while she looked for a big vase in a cupboard. She found one that had had paraffin in it. Would that matter? She

28

arranged the flowers and he carried the vase into the living room. The book-case would be the best, don't you think? 'Put them by the photo of my daughter.' She sat down in the rocking-chair with her back to the light. 'It's a nice photo,' he said.

'It's an old one, taken in Holland, but it's my favourite. Do you think it's because of the light that they take such good photos there? It was the light that attracted all those painters to Holland.'

He looked at her daughter. She must have been about 17 then. 'That's right. It was taken just before the war.' She stood up to smell the lilies. They were lovely. Where had he got them? He said it was a long story. He had passed a woman beside the road with boxes of flowers. She'd asked if he'd like to look in the garden of the estate. Her husband was there and would show him the biggest and finest rhododendron bushes.

She nodded and said that the local people were very friendly. 'And was her husband there?'

'Yes, he was, but he couldn't speak. He'd had a stroke.' Tremendously proud, the man had walked round the enormous bushes with him. He had filmed it: the pinkish red clusters amid high banks of green and the man, who stood beside his creation, smiling and unable to form words.

Still standing, she rearranged the lilies slightly and looked at the girl in the photo. 'That must have been just before the war. After the divorce — I divorced him, me! — she spent half the year with me and half the year with him. Every year. But early in May, 1940, he phoned to say that the Germans were about to invade England and that she'd be better off with him in Holland. So she went. She wanted to be with him. Caught the last plane and I didn't see her again for five years. Heard nothing at all for five years.'

'Does she come often?' he asked, getting up.

'No, she doesn't like England.' But she had come when she was ill. That had been at Christmas. She'd taken care of everything, very capably and efficiently. It had been so nice to have her there. She glanced at the photo and pointed outside, at the small field with narcissi and beyond it the cows in the sunshine. 'It gets terribly cold here. It's nearly always cold.'

She hadn't asked about the letter again, and they had driven to the sea.

Now when they got back, the strange girl was there again, leaning against the hedge, as she had been that morning and the first time he came, looking for the right number. A terrace of six workmen's cottages, now called bungalows, with a hedge in front that seemed as high as the roofs. That girl was always there, she said. She saw everything and understood nothing.

He opened a bottle in the kitchen. She dried the glasses and pointed to the letter. Did he think that man had committed the murder? She got such strange letters, you never could tell. He shrugged and said that it sounded genuine enough, and he could understand why a man in jail would write to her.

'My books have done well in France,' she said. That was most unusual, because the French didn't much care for English or books about Paris by foreigners.

In the living room she proposed a toast, 'To Paris,' and said she would like to speak French again. Shall we? She had lived in Paris for ten years, but didn't dare go back, afraid of ending up in the wrong hotel. They said Paris had changed, but she wouldn't believe that.

'Have you got the hardback edition of *Voyage in the Dark*? I'd like you to have one. I think it's my best — other people don't but I think so.' She took a book from the shelf, Joyce's Paris. He was a nice man, very friendly. He leafed through the book, looking for her. Didn't he think that Sylvia Beach had fine features? As she stood in the doorway he asked if many men had loved her. 'That's a long, long time ago.'

She was a long time in the bedroom. She emerged wearing a jersey and skirt — a different woman. She was holding the hardcover edition and wanted to write something in it.

It had all started with that prize. She had been completely, utterly forgotten. But when she won that prize, in '66 or '67 for *Wide Sargasso Sea*, the place had been like bedlam. The village hidden away and the tiny cottage — which she'd bought unseen and wanted to sell the minute she'd set foot in it — and suddenly there they all were, flown over from America: *Time* and *Life* and reporters and TV crews with cameras and equipment. 'I was in the bath, and they were banging on the door and tapping at the window. The din they made! I kept shouting that I was in the bath and couldn't see them. But I wasn't going to let them in anyway — with all those lights and paraphernalia. They went away in the end. That's how the story started that I was living as a recluse, that I was shy of people and hiding.'

She gave him the book: 'To Jan from Jean Rhys —

Outside the machine.'

'Because you're outside the machine too,' she said. He nodded and got up to refill the glasses. He said he knew the story: 'Fifteen beds in a small room, a big English clinic near Versailles. The newcomer is at the far end of the room. The matron asks if she would mind doing without the rouge and powder and lipstick.'

'And do you remember what she replied, the patient?'

He nodded and pretended he was searching for the words, her words. He wanted her to say it.

'She didn't want to look too awful, because that always made her feel much worse,' she said flatly.

It had always been like that, he thought without saying so. He looked at her face and the large, knowing eyes, and only now saw what had taken so long when she was fetching the book.

'Those nurses were like machines,' she said. 'Like parts of a machine. They performed flawlessly.'

'A good title for that story. Your titles are always good.'

She said she had trouble with titles. They were very difficult. It was the same with this autobiography they wanted. They kept pressing her and it was going very slowly. 'I can remember everything except years and dates. I never know whether I was 6 or 8 or 12.'

It was hard going, but she had the beginning: 'Smile please, can't you smile?

Stop looking so serious.' She could still hear the photographer in Dominica saying it. 'It's so hard to bring the sun back into those memories, with the weather here . . . just look at those clouds. . .' she fell silent, stubbed out her cigarette, sought for another. Then she said, 'Would you . . . would you like to think of a title? That would really be a step forward. The title makes a book. The titles of my first books came to me in dreams. I dreamed them! I think you're good at titles. I like the titles of your poems. Please find a title for me. The 'flu took so much out of me.'

He frowned, wanting to succeed for her.

She seemed shy all at once. She drank her glass in one gulp and went into the kitchen.

He thought of the clinic in that story, the self-assured nurses who knew nothing of life and did everything according to the proper procedure, even when the machine ran amok. And the girl lying there, outside the machine and due to be dumped. 'Useless, this one.'

Wasn't that what it said? That she would be thrown on the rubbish heap?

He realized that she was opening another bottle in the kitchen. 'Let me do it,' he called. 'That's a man's job.'

They sat at the kitchen table and she set down fresh glasses. 'I work here,' she said. 'When I work. . .' She looked a little sad and shivered. 'Smile, please,' he said.

'That's the title!' She stood up and clinked her glass against his. 'See, you are good at titles.'

She had a radio, but she couldn't stand all that pop music. It was unbearable. For years she'd been searching for one of Chopin's études, with the sound of rain. Did he know it? No, she hadn't got a record player, but if she had that record perhaps she could play her own music.

She would have a record player, and that record. And she would stick to wine. He was sure of that. 'You're on your own too much,' he said.

She shrugged, spread her hands out on the yellow wood of the table, looked at them. 'Outside the machine,' she said. But she had a phone, and her meals were brought to the house, and there was a nice old man who drove her into town to do shopping. Yes, the man who said, 'Look after her — that's my girl,' when they drove off the day before.

And now and again there would be a really hectic day, like when the French television came. At first she'd refused to let them in — there were so many of them — but her daughter was there and she'd said, 'But you're so fond of Paris.' The interviewer didn't speak a word of English, but it had all gone very well. He knew what he was talking about.

It had been quite a commotion. And then there were the cows to watch while she waited for the morning post — it was marvellous to get letters in the morning. That was the start of her day, when the post arrived.

She couldn't understand the Americans, or their copyright laws. 'After thirty years a book has no protection. Over there anyone is free to reissue everything I published before 1940. The other day I got a cheque for $35 from the Bank of China: one of my stories had been dramatised for Hungarian television.'

They heard a voice outside. She was startled and looked up. 'That girl,' she said. 'She watches all the time. She won't leave till you do — just stand staring at the strange car or counting the empties in my dustbin.'

'Couldn't you move to somewhere in the sun? There are still lovely little places in France.'

'I'm an old crock, as I said in my letter. I can hardly do anything. It's very lonely at times.'

'But you came out with me today. . .'

'Today — today was glorious. The dogs splashing in the water, the deck chair in the sun, scampi in the cellar, Jacques Brel in the car. . . I did enjoy today. Will you come again?'

He remembered first arriving.

An unexpected week off. The plane to London. No planes to Devon. A night in a hotel in London with loud German voices. Paddington Station. A hotel in Exeter.

That was four days ago. He'd just put his suitcase on the bed when the phone rang. It was the man from Hertz: would he like the car now? Then the man could stay in bed on Sunday morning.

Practically next to the hotel was a sign: Crediton 10 miles. He got straight into the car to try driving on the left again and perhaps, with luck, find the way. He found Cheriton-Fitzpaine and the 'Bungalows'. He parked the car in front of the high hedge and just behind the watching girl. He went through the gateway, knocked carefully at no. 6, and waited. The door opened a little and she asked what he wanted. She was very shy and wary. He said that he was Jan, that he'd come from Holland and that he had an appointment with her for the next day.

Then she opened the door and he followed her down the narrow hall into the living room. He put the litre of duty-free whisky on the table, and was welcomed with a glass from it. She said the three words of Dutch she knew including 'verdomme' — 'damn' — he couldn't remember the other two. That had been the beginning, and on Sunday afternoon she decided to come for a drive after all and they had gone to Tiverton because Salinger had been one of the American troops stationed there just before D-day, and they both admired 'The Catcher in the Rye'. She pointed out how the trees belonged in the landscape, named them and complained about them being pulled down or replaced by 'these pines that shut you in.'

The sun shone and the roads were quiet.

They had a drink together and she had shown him the house where she'd been living for heaven knows how long now — years and years. She had liked Budapest, with its bars and girls dressed in white, and Vienna, but she'd been happiest of all in Paris. It had been the best of her cities in spite of everything.

'It's having a day out that makes me talk so much. It's so lonely here, so quiet, that sometimes I'm afraid I'll forget how to talk.' She'd been having unpleasant dreams recently. She dreamed of London and all the tall, large houses she remembered, but she couldn't find them. 'I'm left standing in front of holes in the ground and cellars, again and again, just standing there until someone says very loudly, 'This is going to be a fish-and-chip shop.' Then I wake up feeling upset.'

'I'm tired,' she said, 'but pleasantly tired. I won't have dreams like that.'

By now it was Friday, and they stood on a hill looking out over the rolling fields. The sun reddened the newly ploughed furrows.

She was wearing her sunglasses. When they were on the way back from Tiverton that Sunday afternoon, the light had been dazzling. She had rubbed her eyes and he had lowered the visor in the car, but it hadn't helped. 'Try my sunglasses,' he said and they fitted. They were very good. She would get a pair and wear them at home. As she got out of the car she handed them back, but he told her to keep them. She accepted and tried them out indoors.

'Hang onto them.'

'Alright, I will, to make sure you'll come back to collect them.' Later she stood at the door to the living room wearing a red suit, looking both shy and assured, an elderly, reserved lady in dark glasses. She told him he would see her entire wardrobe in the course of the week and asked whether he'd poured the drinks.

He said he was going to film her, but she didn't want that. If there was one thing she objected to, it was that. After the prize, after *Sargasso Sea*, they had wanted to take photos. They kept popping up all over the place. One silly pose after another, all done in a terrible rush, and then it was never her in the photo. . . 'No, I'm not willing!'

A few days later she consented after all. She wore a twin-set (he thought that was what it was) in a pale shade of pink. The next time he came she would be wearing a red wig. She knew she was too old, that it was unfair to inflict that on the village, but she'd always wanted red hair. He filmed her at the door and from outside while she pulled back the curtain and looked at the cows. She was holding a cigarette which burnt a bright red hole in the lace curtain. She noticed and looked at him without moving to see if he'd spotted it.

He filmed her by the sea, wearing her best hat, with a shine of happiness in her eyes. She went on talking naturally to him, completely at ease, and said that she liked to see him at work and that next time, when she had the red wig, it would be even better.

As he was leaving the first day, when she was tired, she asked if he'd ever taken drugs. She had smoked opium once. They'd said she was too shallow for it, and that it would have no effect. That stung her so much that she tried it: no reaction. She felt nothing. So she'd had a few drinks at home, and then she did feel something: she dreamed in balloons and colours. He saw her face from far away and close by then, as later when she burnt the hole in the curtain. 'You took my panorama as well,' she said when he finished filming. She was holding the daisy that she had shown him as he stood in the tall grass. It dropped from her hand and she picked it up and stared at it in wonder.

'I wish I could hear the sea here,' she had said suddenly, and the next day he had driven to the coast to reconnoitre. He had taken a ferry across to a village with pastel-coloured houses and a dilapidated quay, found the cellar 'Buttery and Bar,' and seen the rows of deck chairs propped against a wall.

'We know what we think of each other,' she had said as they sat by the sea. Which sea? Fortunately, he'd looked at a map in the evening at the hotel. Not the British Channel. He had found Teignmouth, and Torquay, where he had stretched out in the sun on a park bench on a hillside. At the edge of the beach there was a man in a white shirt and braces. He was feeding the gulls that circled him with high white wing-beats. He tried to see it through her eyes, and dozed off. The dogs chased and splashed after each other and suddenly stood still, two silhouettes in emptiness.

He stood behind her chair. The car was parked by the steps on the promenade. Her head turned. She knew he was there, her eyes large and grey under the brim of her hat.

'It's as if I've known you a long time,' she had said then.

Now it was over. The hours spent with her and the kilometres. They stood in the hall. A girl, an old-fashioned ice-skater, danced in a poster. 'It gets so cold here,' she said. 'I like posters and paintings.' It was in Lautrec style. At the bottom it said 'Palais de Glace'.

Are you happier talking to men rather than women?' he asked.

'Oh . . . there are nice women, too.'

He said he would have to go and that she shouldn't wait at the door. 'The hedge blocks the view anyway.' She offered her hand and he kissed it. As he closed the door he heard her say, 'And the girl. . .'

Jan van Houts
Translated from the Dutch by John Rudge
© J. van Houts, 1981

# MAKING BRICKS WITHOUT STRAW

*Jean Rhys*

I am sorry for any journalist landed with the job of interviewing me. To begin with, I am not at all lucky on these occasions; it so often happens that the last thing I want on that particular day is a stranger's questions. If I lived in London, it would be easy to cancel or postpone the interview. In Devon, by the time that I have decided that I really can't go through with it, it's too late, he or she is already on the way.

As usual several things have gone wrong. Perhaps somebody has turned my luck horseshoe upside down. Blue eye shadow. Too much? Too little? There is no one to tell me. But after all, this is something I have always insisted on deciding for myself. It will have to do.

Is the sitting room all right? Fairly, I think; shift a vase and try to decide which chair I ought to sit in. Some say back to the light on back-to-the-light days, others no, sunlight, unlike glare, is very becoming: face the light on sunny days. Just as I have decided, there is a knock, the interviewer has arrived.

"Please sit down," I say when I have opened the door and we have reached the sitting room and the interviewer plonks down in the chair I've chosen. I sit in the other, already feeling exhausted. There's not a thought in my head, not a word. I can only wonder if she (or he) will describe this place as a cottage, a semi-detached, or a horrid little bungalow with creepers and things all over it. I know already, it jumps to the eyes, as the French say. I wait to be questioned.

What are you to say when they ask you, "Were you glamorous in those days?" that all depends doesn't it. Should it be "Oh yes, I was very. People used to push little notes into my hand 'I love you.'" Fun! Or "Good heavens, no, not at all!"

The question-and-answer game goes on. I realize that I am being gently pushed into my predestined role, the role of victim. I have never had any good times, never laughed, never got my own back, never dared, never worn pretty clothes, never been happy, never known wild hopes or wilder despairs. In short, I have never been young or if I was I've forgotten all about it. Waiting, I have gone from tyrant to tyrant: each letdown worse than the last. All this, of course, leads to Women's Lib.

"It's all so different now," she says (this one's a woman).

"Don't you think it still depends a bit on the individual? But I suppose it's all different now," I add and suggest a drink. Sometimes I drink alone, sometimes not.

35

I pour myself out a large whiskey, for suddenly I am completely exhausted. Longing to have a cigarette and sit quietly by myself thinking it over.

> *Go without returning*
> *Go without remembering*
> *Just go. . .*

(old song)

I empty my glass, pour another, and this is where I begin to talk wildly, the real reason for the inaccuracies that have been written about me.

"I didn't like the suffragettes much," I say.

"Didn't you," she says, shocked.

"Not much, when you posted a letter you never knew whether it would get there. They used to set fire to post boxes, thinks like that. Such a nuisance."

Silence.

"You know the one who threw herself in front of the horse?" I say. "Well, I felt so sorry for the horse."

"But the woman was a martyr," the interviewer says.

"Perhaps she wanted to be a martyr, but the horse didn't. He had to be shot."

"But surely you realize the desperate heroism in what she did?"

"Yes, of course I know that, but I was still very sorry for the horse. She was wonderful, of course. They were all wonderful but as I left England at that period I really don't know much about it. Then I've been living down here for such a long time."

"How long have you been living here alone?"

"Oh, years and years, really I don't remember."

"You must be very brave," she says, looking around.

"Oh, I'm not brave at all," I say. "I'm afraid of almost everything, but I am faithful."

"I beg your pardon, you're what?"

"I'm faithful," I say again.

"Miss Rhys, I find that very interesting. Please do explain what or who you are faithful to."

"Oh, that would take far too long; besides I am a little tired now" (a hint).

"I'm afraid that's my fault. Thank you for giving me all this time." (Quite kind after that.)

When I read the article it is something like this:

> *Miss Rhys was very old and frail, has been living alone in a small remote bungalow for years and years, she says. She insists that she is not brave but faithful and rather coyly refuses to explain what she means by that! . . .*

I am left to remember other interviews, the time when I forgot to put the whiskey out. The time I mistook the interviewer for the lift boy. The time when a local reporter followed me into the hairdresser's and wanted to take my picture with my hair wet.

The time I was soaking in the bath when there was a succession of loud knocks on the door. The knocking went on and became louder and louder. At last I got out of the bath, opened the window, and called:

"I can't see anybody now, please go away." He went away and wrote that I was a confirmed recluse and refused to see or speak to anyone. This became a local legend, and it was not only local. Of course, I tell myself the poor interviewer had to produce a smooth article of so many words and I hadn't helped him much. Inaccuracies occur, for people must be entertained. So now I can read calmly of my dark dreadful life, extraordinary versions of my first marriage, that I worked on the stage for ten bob a week (this last annoys me), but as a rule I don't turn a hair.

# II. PERSPECTIVES ON JEAN RHYS

# PERSPECTIVES ON JEAN RHYS

As with the interviews of Jean Rhys, much of the criticism of Rhys is repetitive. However, the recent surge of interest in her fiction is responsible for an increasing number of studies contributing new ideas on Rhys the writer and her works. Although some of the selections appearing in this section were chosen from earlier material because of their import to the understanding of Rhys, many of the articles come from this new wave of criticism. All offer interesting and valuable perspectives on some of the most controversial issues about Rhys and her writings. Unlike the following section, which is devoted to the analysis of specific works, this part addresses broader issues affecting Rhys's literary output.

Martien Kappers-den Hollander is the first to compare Jean Lenglet's (Rhys's husband's), *Sous les Verrous*, a version of *Quartet*; Rhys's translation of it, *Barred*; the Dutch version of the book, and *Quartet*. Her study casts a new light on the much debated involvement of Rhys with Ford by introducing the voice of Jean Lenglet, the interested third party, whose own version of the affair had been ignored. More importantly, the work reveals Rhys's talent as a writer and editor.

Following Louis James's article on the influence of Rhys's West Indian background on her entire fiction are three pieces illuminating the controversy surrounding Rhys's stand on blacks and her view of the West Indies from the vantage point of exile. For Lucy Wilson, Rhys's "legacy to an unjust world" is her knowledge of that world and its expression in what Rhys calls "her dangerous books" (446). V.S. Naipaul, on the other hand, places Rhys "outside that tradition of imperial-expatriate writing in which the metropolitan outsider is thrown into relief against an alien background." He shows that Rhys does not try to explain herself or any particular society but rather the condition of not having a society to write about (Naipaul). And in an essay on the effect of Rhys's Dominican childhood on Rhys's works, Elaine Campbell demonstrates how Rhys used her fiction to bridge the gap between blacks and whites, achieving the kind of freedom and mutual acceptance between the races unattainable in Rhys's life.

Todd Bender's and Colette Lindroth's essays complete this collection of articles with unique perspectives on Rhys's writing technique. Bender explains Rhys's use of impressionism to let the reader question his own standard of judgment in assessing the Rhysian heroine while Lindroth analyses the power of implication in Rhys's fiction.

# A GLOOMY CHILD AND ITS DEVOTED GODMOTHER: JEAN RHYS, *BARRED, SOUS LES VERROUS* AND *IN DE STRIK*

*Martien Kappers-den Hollander*

In 1928 Jean Rhys published her novel *Postures* (*Quartet* in later editions)[1] which centred on a troubled year in her marriage to Jean Lenglet, a Dutch writer and journalist, who wrote under the pen-name of Edouard (Edward) de Nève. The events of that year in Paris, thinly disguised in *Quartet*, have become public knowledge. While Lenglet was arrested in 1924, convicted for embezzlement, and extradited from France in the following year, Rhys was given shelter in the home of her literary patron, the English writer Ford Madox Ford (pseudonym of F. M. Hueffer). Her subsequent entanglement with Ford and his common-law wife, the Australian painter Stella Bowen, was to prove fatal to Ford's union with Bowen as well as to Rhys' marriage with Lenglet.[2]

Beside *Quartet*, whose characters Marya and Stephan Zelli, Lois and Hugh Heidler, are based on the real-life enactors of this domestic drama, there are a number of other texts that have some bearing on the affair. Among these are de Nève's counterpart to *Quartet*, the novel *Barred* (1932), described as a 'true story" in its authorial preface; Ford's novel *When the Wicked Man* (1931) and Bowen's autobiography, *Drawn from Life* (1940).[3] These accounts, with their varying blends of fact and fiction, are now commonly agreed to represent a kind of fictional 'debate,' such as might take place between four witnesses of the same event, each of whom claims to be in possession of the "truth". Critical discussions of this debate, however, have tended to concentrate on the points of view of three members of the quartet only.[4] The voice of Edward de Nève is rarely heard, no doubt due to the difficulty in obtaining one of the few extant copies of *Barred*, or its Dutch and French versions, *In de Strik* and *Sous les Verrous*.[5]

For those who know Jean Rhys' work intimately, *Barred* provides a veritable "shock of recognition". Jan van Leeuwen's description of Stania, his wife, makes her so like a composite Jean Rhys heroine, that it creates a sensation of *déjà vu;*

> She believes in an inevitable fate. . . But when she wishes to do a foolish thing she sees quite clearly in front of her what is going to happen. Not that that stops her from doing it. . . No, she lets herself go. She disdains consequences. She sacrifices everybody who may suffer, starting with

herself. . . That, and her indolence and passivity, have sometimes made me
almost hate her (p. 85).

The difference with *Quartet* is that Jan van Leeuwen's (first-person) account
of Stania contains severe criticism of her. He is much harder on his spouse than
Marya Zelli is on hers: in Rhys' novel, narrated in the third person, she is
presented to us as judging Stephan rather more mildly than herself. Jan pictures
his wife as weak and selfish, and without proper regard for him, and he minimizes
his own share in the muddle she gets herself into. He blames her for more than
indolence. Where Marya Zelli only reluctantly accepts the Heidlers' offer to stay
with them, partly to keep Stephan from worrying about her, Jan van Leeuwen
presents Stania as disregarding his warning not to get mixed up with Hübner, her
Fordian protector. Furthermore, he hints that if it wasn't Hübner it would have
been someone else; "so many dogs after an easy prey" (p.102). He even charges
her with having been too lazy to fetch some papers from his office which he
needed to plead extenuating circumstances. And he suggests that after his
discharge from prison Stania presses him to rejoin the Foreign Legion, in order
to have free play with her lover. When he refuses, she betrays him to the Foreign
Police and he is expelled from France without a passport. Though at the end of
his story Jan van Leeuwen is still obsessed by his wife, the moral of *Barred* is
clear: Stania is a bad lot. She is not like other prisoners' wives, who somehow
manage to look after themselves while waiting for their husbands' release:
"Stania's nothing but a doll" (p.141).

As Edward de Nève informs us in his preface to *Barred*, it was Jean Rhys who
encouraged him to publish the French manuscript he showed her on a visit to
Amsterdam, and who translated it for him and found an English publisher for it.
However, a comparison of the original text with Rhys' adaptation reveals that she
not only translated but also rewrote her husband's novel, and that the picture of
Stania in *Barred*, harsh though it may be, is a watered-down version of an even
more merciless portrait in *Sous les Verrous*. Both Lenglet and Rhys went to some
lengths to gloss over the exact nature of her share in the English edition.[6] In his
dedication of *Barred* "to Jean," de Nève did thank her for taking "much trouble"
over "this gloomy child of mine," but apart from stating that "like a good guardian
and a devoted godmother you took care of its baptism," he did not go into further
particulars. *In de Strik*, the Dutch edition, did not mention Rhys at all, and it was
only in the preface to *Sous les Verrous* that de Nève hinted at a *difference* between
the three novels; "pour certaines raisons . . . il m'a fallu changer un peu
l'intrigue dans la version anglaise, changement que j'ai repris dans la version
hollandaise. La différence est minime". He did not mention the reasons for this
change. Jean Rhys, too, kept silent about the matter, except in a famous statement,
repeated by Diana Athill, that in translating "her husband's fictionalised version
of events . . . , she had given way to the temptation to cut a few — a very few
— sentences about herself which struck her as "too unfair."[7]

Such scanty information does not prepare the reader of *Barred* and *Sous les*

*Verrous* for the real extent of Jean Rhys' editing. The difference between the two novels is far from minimal. The change in "intrigue" de Nève referred to has important consequences for the development of character and plot while the passages omitted by Jean Rhys amount to rather more than "a few sentences". All in all, Rhys scrapped between six-and-a half and seven thousand words from her husband's narrative; about twenty-five pages of text, or one tenth of the entire manuscript.[8] The nature of Rhys' modifications soon becomes evident from a comparison of practically any page taken at random from the English and the French editions. Hardly a paragraph has remained unchanged. Where she did not cut or rephrase, Rhys changed the order of words within sentences, of sentences within paragraphs, and of paragraphs within chapters. She altered the arrangement of tenses and of de Nève's shifts between quoted direct speech, indirect speech, monologue and "pure" narration. The result is a text that strikes us as more economical and consistent than its rather ponderous and over-explicit predecessor. Lenglet must have recognized in Rhys *il miglior fabbro*, for with few exceptions he translated the Dutch version of his novel straight from the English, rather than from the original French manuscript.[9] It is indeed obvious that, as far as her stylistic emendations of *Sous les Verrous* are concerned, Jean Rhys must have been primarily motivated by artistic rather than 'personal' considerations. In many of the changes she introduced we sense her infallible writer's instinct, her perfectionism and perhaps also her desire (inseparable from these) to make her husband's work a little more like her own.

It is not difficult to perceive Rhys' method. She consistently eliminated passages that she thought superfluous or simply irrelevant.[10] Although Lenglet occasionally restored a phrase or two for emotional emphasis (pp.22, 21,18), he generally took over such alterations in the Dutch edition. Rhys especially condensed de Nève's longish passages of indictment against the French penitentiary system, presumably for dramatic purposes, since they detracted from the story's main interest.[11] She speeded up or slowed down Jan van Leeuwen's account, as the case might be, by changing from pure narration or (free) indirect speech to direct quoted speech, dialogue or (interior) monologue — and vice versa. This way Rhys avoided both narrative monotony, and the disturbingly frequent disruptions of the narrative voice so characteristic of Lenglet's text. Her use of tenses, too, especially in the transition from narrated past to historical present, and from historical present to interior monologue, is smoother than in *Sous les Verrous*.[12] Rhys turned many of the protagonist's frequent rhetorical questions into affirmative statements (pp.48,43,50). A meticulous editor, she inverted the order of many words, lines and paragraphs for the sake of narrative logic, sometimes even moving phrases from one chapter to another.[13] Lenglet's long-winded sentences and paragraphs were broken up, and his chapters subdivided. Of some pages, rewritten in their entirety, few traces of the original remain (pp.247-48, 247-48, 211), a time-consuming task, even without the numerous additions Jean Rhys made to her husband's work, often for the sake of clarity or emphasis (pp.246, 246, 210). She patiently inserted transitional sentences to clear up inconsistencies (pp.120,122,105), some of which were created by her own pruning and cutting. Other additions, like a bit of Rhys pathos at the end of Chapter IV, are more difficult to defend and these were not always taken over by Lenglet. Puzzling, however, is that he agreed to change the names of various Paris locations, with "l'Hôtel Trianon" becoming "Hôtel du Nord," "La Rotonde" "Le Panthéon": mistake, correction of faulty topography, or Rhys' deliberate attempt to prevent identification of place and event? Inevitably, the English version also contains a few genuine mistakes. Of errors like "twice a week" for "deux fois par mois," a slip surprisingly retained in the Dutch version,[14] the most intriguing is Rhys' repeated translation of "bureau of anthropology" for "à l'anthropométrie". The mistake does not recur in the Dutch edition (pp.45, 46 ,40). We can only surmise Jean Rhys had never heard of the humiliating "measurement" the hero is subjected to after his arrest.

However, the literary biographer's main interest is not in the manifold formal alterations Jean Rhys made in her husband's novel. It is, rather, in the implications of what Diana Athill wrote about Rhys in her preface to *Smile Please*. When Jean Rhys confessed to her editor that she had scrapped from Lenglet's portrait of Stania what she felt to be "too unfair," she was really saying that she had cut out those "sentences about herself" that clashed with her own view of the role she had played in the events, fictionalized in his novel. And if Rhys erased or altered bits of what she felt to be an ungenerous picture of herself, the changes she made in the portrayal of the other characters must have been motivated by the same desire: to reshape de Nève's view of them; to bring it closer to her own view. "Pour la version française j'ai préferé conserver le manuscrit intact pour lui garder son originalité incontestable," Lenglet wrote in his foreword to *Sous les Verrous*. It is, indeed, only in that edition that we can hear his authentic voice, see what he saw, feel what he felt. In the English translation the focus has been re-adjusted; "slightly pulled from the straight," as Virginia Woolf put it, in a different context.[15] The translator corrected not only the author's language but also his point of view.

Rhys' first move in a series of changes necessary to complete this process of adjustment was to eliminate one of the characters, Mme Hübner, from Lenglet's story. The omission cannot be defended on artistic grounds, for Hübner's wife has a specific role to play in the events of *Sous Les Verrous*, and her disappearance creates various awkward narrative hitches, which neither Rhys, nor de Nève in his Dutch translation, managed completely to overcome. With the quartet turned into a somewhat less unusual 'eternal triangle,' the relationship between Hübner, Stania and Jan van Leeuwen is placed in a different light. Stania, though still the unfaithful wife, is no longer in Jan's eyes quite so spineless, so deficient in self-respect as when , in the French edition, she lets herself be manipulated into an affair with a married couple. Since the focus of narration resides with Jan van Leeuwen, his change of opinion also affects the reader's view of Stania's and Hübner's culpability[16].

Rhys' removal of Mme Hübner from the scene involved numerous alterations, ranging from nominal and pronominal references to statements about the Hübners having a daughter (pp. 202-03, 199, 172). Vanished are Jan's jeers at Mrs Hübner's complicity, his attacks on her "complaisance horrible" (pp. 113-116, 99) regarding her husband's escapades (pp. 94, 95-96, 82), his insinuations about her plotting and scheming (pp. 192, 189, 163), to the point of eliminating even incidental references to the frequency of *ménages à trois* among foreigners in Paris (pp. 161, 161, 139).

But it is in Jan's conversations with Stania that we find the most significant omissions. In *Sous les Verrous*, the Hübners' bad moral reputation is the cause of Jan's immediate suspicions when Stania moves in with them. Among the passages Rhys did not translate are his efforts to make her see that she is being manipulated: "sa femme a laissé faire, t'a encouragée pour que le caprice de son grand homme soit plus vite passé "(pp. 213, 210, 180). Stella Bowen's autobiography confirms that in such scenes, where Jan van Leeuwen tries to confront his wife with an unwelcome truth, Lenglet's fictional version of the role Bowen played as Ford's permissive partner is factually correct[17]. By removing Hübner's wife, Rhys certainly spared her fictional self such a confrontation. At the same time she took away much ground for Jan's feeling that Stania is being victimized, by rewriting various episodes in which his wife unwittingly encumbers him with incriminating evidence (pp. 113, 116, 99). Other changes concern the nature of the Hübner's financial assistance to Stania. In *Sous les Verrous*, she tells Jan not to worry about her because the Hübners have asked her to stay with them and have collected a little money from friends. In *Barred*, Stania claims her friend Mathilde Dubar is helping her and has introduced her to Hübner, who will give her a "a sort of job" and find her a better room (pp. 123-24, 126, 108).

The change in *Barred* of Stania's residence, at an hotel instead of at the Hübners' flat, is the cause of a slightly jarring effect in some of the conversations she has with her husband. In the French version, Stania says at one point that she has put up at a hotel because the Hübner's infant daughter needs her room (p. 203). Since on moving into their apartment she had told Jan "Je dormirai avec Mme Hübner" (p. 124), he suspects the whole manoeuvre to be a cover-up for an estrangement between the lovers, engineered by Mrs Hübner. When Jan asks Stania why it is that she has also stopped working for Hübner at his flat, she answers, quite plausibly: "Parce que nous y sommes dérangés tout le temps" (p. 211). In *Barred* Stania moves to a different hotel "because the other place gave me the blues," which makes Jan's subsequent question illogical ("Have you stopped working for him?"), and her answer cryptic ("Yes. Because we're interrupted all the time". (p. 208). Lenglet must have noticed the inconsistency because he rewrote the sequence in Dutch, with slightly better results: "werk je niet meer voor him? Zeker . . . maar we worden voortdurend gestoord" (p. 179).

However, Stania finally admits that Mme Hübner is being difficult and always has been: "Lorsque cela a commencé, j'ai voulu les quitter . . . elle me refusait l'argent pour partir". This explodes the myth of "friends" helping her, as her husband is quick to point out: "L'argent? Mais c'était à toi. . . Pourquoi n'es-tu pas allée voir Mlle Dubar et tous les autres?"(p. 212-13). The English and Dutch versions of this conversation are again illogical: instead of putting it on to Hübner's wife, Stania, at this late point in the story, suddenly blames his relatives, whose existence had never been mentioned before (pp. 210, 180).

In the English translation the plausibility of other scenes suffers from the occasional replacement of Mme Hübner by Stania's friend, Mathilde Dubar. Since she is a minor character, and not particularly intimate with either Stania or Hübner, the question arises what she is doing at his side all the time, for instance in the painful confrontation scene between the hero and his wife's lover (pp. 192, 188-89, 163). It is difficult to see, too, why Stania should be as upset as she is by Mathilde's unexpected return to Paris (pp. 186, 184, 158), or why she takes such pains to hide from her friend a few kissing-marks her lover has left on her upper arms (pp. 185, 185, 158-59). But exchange Mathilde for Mme Hübner in the English and the Dutch edition, and all becomes clear.

Beside effacing Lenglet's attacks on Stella Bowen, Rhys also toned down his hero's bitter criticism of Hübner, the Ford character. With Miss Dubar replacing Hübner's wife as chaperone, Jan has less reason to object to Hübner's contacts with Stania (pp. 98, 100, 85). While the more notorious side of Hübner's sexual reputation simply vanished alongside with his condoning partner, a page-full of stories about women protégées ruined by the painter-critic was cut out altogether (pp. 94, 95, 82). In *Sous les Verrous* the hero is especially incensed at Mme Hübner's excuses that her husband needs his affairs for his artistic development ("elle prétend que sans cela son art n'existerait pas")[18], but such insinuations about Hübner abusing his artistic reputation are absent from *Barred*. Rhys also carefully removed the most merciless of Jan's comments on Hübner's obesity, his false teeth, his "gencives anémiques," and toned down or scrapped the invective directed at him: "goujat hypocrite," "pantin," "canaille"[19]

*Barred* notably weakens Hübner's hold over Stania, who in *Sous les Verrous* rarely takes a decision without consulting him first. To her husband's question whether she will come abroad with him after his release from prison, she answers: "Je ne sais pas; ça dépendra de ce que Hübner dira". In the English translation, Stania's answer has become a question, put by Jan: "I suppose you'll ask Hübner to advise you?," the sarcasm of which is emphasized in Dutch: "Ik zou het aan Hübner vragen als ik jou was,"[20]. On the whole the protagonist of *Barred* (and *In de Strik*), though no less mistrustful of his rival than his counterpart in *Sous les Verrous*, has less ground for suspicion; "quelque chose se prépare contre moi' is watered down to 'these plans!" (pp. 124, 126, 108).

This also applies to the grudges he holds against his wife. Omitted in the English translation are some bitter remarks by van Leeuwen about Stania's habit of getting about with men "rencontrés au hasard," regardless of the risks. Rhys cut out some of Jan's sexual complaints as well: ". . . Stania n'a jamais compris était-ce mes élans. Etait'ce pudeur, raisons de santé, crainte? Je ne sais. Toujours est-il que là nous ne nous sommes pas compris comme il le fallait" (pp. 85, 86,

74). Remarks about his wife's irritability and her bad moods were likewise scrapped or rewritten, although *In de Strik* retains a few instances[21]. Stania's sneering comment "tu es un mesquin" was omitted in both translations (pp. 242, 241, 206).

Rhys definitely made Stania appear less dishonourable. In *Sous les Verrous*, her words and actions convince her husband (and the reader) that she must have been an easy conquest for Hübner. In the English version, the reader no longer shares Jan's feelings to quite the same extent, for Stania gives him less food for distrust; the effect is that the hero is made to look over-suspicious, his wife somewhat less culpable. Precisely how Stania is involved with Hübner remains largely a matter of speculation until the end of the story, and their affair is pictured as developing gradually rather than "en si peu de jours" (p. 98, 100, 86). Jean Rhys cut out those passages in which Stania mentions to her husband various facts he considers compromising, like Mme Hübner leaving her alone with Hübner on a holiday. Some of the things she tells him in *Sous les Verrous* strike her husband (and the reader) as premeditated cruelty; for instance her explanation of some bruise-marks on her shoulders: "Hübner m'a pincée" (translated as "Somebody must have pinched me")[22]. Because of such alterations, Jan's strongest grievance against Stania: her indifference to his feelings, could be cut. What she tells him gives him less cause for sarcasm: "gentille attention . . . de la part de Stania, de me le faire savoir"[23].

A significant modification takes place in connection with Stania's remissness about the papers that her husband needs to prove his innocence. In *Sous les Verrous* she tells him that she has not written to his office for them because both Hübner and Miss Dubar advised against it. In the English version, Stania's near-criminal negligence is softened: there has been no reply to her letters; she is reluctant to go since she is afraid she will be humiliated; Miss Dubar has convinced her that there is no point in going (pp. 115, 118, 101). Such excuses, which make Stania's actions more understandable, and perhaps also more acceptable, recur several times[24]. Can we hear in them Jean Rhys pleading her case, defending herself against her husband's charges, long after the dust has settled on the unhappy entanglement with her literary patron? Whatever the answer, van Leeuwen's accusations about Stania's duplicity and lack of support are considerably toned down[25], to the extent that he is even made to function as his wife's mouthpiece: "I began to make excuses for her. Once she had told me that because life had always been hard for her something in her was frozen and afraid" (pp. 116, 118, 101-02). ) Of such thoughts there is no trace in the original. Rhys also painted Stania as more loving, more concerned about her husband, adding sentences like "I worry about you all the time" (pp. 140, 140, 120), and transforming what was in *Sous les Verrous* a wishful thought into reality: "(Stania) kissed me more affectionately than she had done earlier in the day" (pp. 184, 183, 158).

In her translation of her husband's novel Rhys omitted all categorical statements made by Stania about her infidelity, except in the climactic final scene[26], and she "censured" Jan's report of the lovers together. "Je vois Stania sourire à ce gros homme gras, de son sourire plein de soumission et d'admiration" is translated as "I saw how Stania looked at him" (the Dutch stays closer to the original: "ik zag hoe verliefd Stania tot hem opkeek. . ."). An identical phrase is scrapped altogether[27]. Interestingly, *Barred* turns the heroine into a less helpless creature than de Nève's "mouche sans défense" (translated as "silly little fly"), and it cuts out Jan's plans for rescuing the creature from Hübner's web[28]. However, one remarkable addition seems to point in the opposite direction. "If I were a man, and in your place, that's what I would do," Stania declares when Jan discusses with her whether to rejoin the Foreign Legion (pp. 244, 244, 208-09); it makes him wonder whether she is trying to get rid of him. But the remark also raises another question: was Jean Rhys suggesting something here about Stania's greater handicap, as a woman, in taking her fate in her own hands?

Such, then are the "very few sentences about herself" Jean Rhys omitted, changed or added to Lenglet's portrait of Stania, with the purpose of making it less 'unfair' to (her view of) herself. That Edward de Nève took over the great majority of these modifications in the Dutch version of his novel is intriguing. But not quite so intriguing as his move, surely unprecedented in literary history, to allow the intrusion of his wife's point of view in his fictional self-portrait as Jan van Leeuwen, both in the English and in the Dutch edition. What Rhys seems to have aimed at in rewriting Lenglet's version of himself, was to prevent the expression of certain thoughts and feelings he had once had about her. She altered or eliminated passages concerning the hero's suffering, especially his bitterness against his wife: "Que j'ai grimacé de fois derrière ce masque joy du rire depuis que je connais Stania!"[29]. She cut out many of his sentiments of loving sorrow (pp. 219, 215, 185), pity and concern (pp. 212, 209, 180), his sense of loss (pp. 51, 53, 46) and of his strong physical desire for her (pp. 197-98, 194, 167). Of the line "Je cache ma tête dans le coussin que je mords à pleines dents en l'étreignant, pour que ne retentisse pas le cri de désir que je pousse vers Stania," the last seven words were not translated[30].

Rhys also removed introspective passages full of self-pity, smugness, and self-righteousness[31]. The pathos of "Ah! si j'avais un ami, un seul, un vrai," scrapped in *Barred*, returns in the Dutch translation, as does a detailed account of the help Jan van Leeuwen receives from his own true *copain*, an Apache (pp. 154, 154, 132). Presumably, Rhys curtailed this story because she wanted to speed up the narrative, though she surprisingly retained the hero's moralistic discourse about the contrast between the solidarity found among criminal males and the fickleness of women in general (his wife in particular, pp. 251, 253, 215). She also carefully rewrote many passages centering on his feelings of humiliation and self-contempt; the tone of mortification is not as strong in *Barred* as it is in *Sous les Verrous*. Self-indictment and rationalizations about the hero's "apathie déshonorante," "résignation coupable et honteuse," and "lâche complaisance," have disappeared[32]. De-emphasized, too, is Jan van Leeuwen's growing conviction that, in trying to spare Stania, he has killed in her all feelings for him: "S'il n'en était pas ainsi à ma sortie de la prison, ma résignation devant le fait accompli, et ma soumission à ses exigences et à celles des Hübner l'ont éloignée pour toujours de moi"[33].

The hero that emerges from *Barred* and *In de Strik* is a man who feels less for his wife and suffers less because of her than the protagonist of *Sous les Verrous*. Also a man who is a somewhat less reliable narrator. Perhaps the most remarkable omission in Jean Rhys' translation is a two-page entry in which Jan van Leeuwen is given a "good character". After his release from prison, his lawyer tells him that he has put his hands on the letters Jan had sorely needed during his trial, and that he is willing to reopen the case if Jan can pay for them (pp. 187-88, 186, 160). The episode strengthens Jan van Leeuwen's stature as a dependable informant about the facts of his arrest; it also speaks loudly against his wife. By removing it from *Barred* altogether, Rhys eliminated a conspicuous reminder of Stania's marital negligence, symbolized in the lost letters.

When Jean Lenglet took over Jean Rhys' adaptation of *Sous les Verrous*, he put his seal of approval on her view of the events that had generated his novel. Rhys did not try to put "the real facts" in the place of his fictions; she proposed another fiction, which he accepted as "fairer" than his own "true story". The intrusion of the focus of the unfaithful wife into the narrative perspective of the betrayed husband substantially alters our picture of the betrayal. Though *Barred* is very different from *Quartet* in outlook and perception, the distance between the latter novel and *Sous les Verrous* is greater still, indeed almost unbridgeable. *Barred* may be seen as an effort to bridge the gap, an effort which was successful because of the cooperation that took place on both sides. De Nève thanked Rhys for having been a "good guardian" to the "gloomy child" he created out of the ruins of their marriage. Rhys took "much trouble" over his text, which she turned into a more effective, and also a less bitter narrative. Reading the three versions of Edward de Nève's counterpart to *Quartet*, one hears Jean Rhys and Jean Lenglet engaged in a long conversation about events still painful to them both, with *Barred* answering the charges made by *Sous les Verrous*, and *In de Strik*, offering the final gesture of reconciliation.

Footnotes:

[1] *Postures*, London, Chatto and Windus, 1928; *Quartet* in American and subsequent English editions. For the relationship between Rhys' life and her novels see Diana Athill's foreword to Jean Rhys' unfinished autobiography, *Smile Please*, London, Andre Deutsch, 1979, pp. 9-10. 'All her writing, she used to say, started out from something that had happened . . . truth to its essence was vital to the therapeutic function of the work as well as to its value to other people. . .'.

[2] Rhys and Lenglet separated in 1925 and were divorced in 1933. Ford and Bowen parted company in 1927.

[3] Edward de Nève, *Barred*, London, Desmond Harmsworth, 1932; Ford Madox Ford, *When the Wicked Man*, New York, 1931 and Stella Bowen, *Drawn from Life*, London, Collins, 1941 (revised ed. Maidstone, George Mann, 1974). Of these texts only

Bowen's claims to be strictly factual. In his preface to *Barred*, de Nève characterized his novel as 'here and there . . . a photograph, not a work of the imagination'.

Paul Delany, in "Jean Rhys and Ford Madox Ford: What 'Really' Happened?", *Mosaic*, XVI, 4 1983, pp. 15-24, makes a case for reading Ford's *The Good Soldier* (1915) as a 'prospective' text about the affair, 'an emotional program that Ford was driven to act out many times in his own life' (p. 16).

[4] See, however, Martien Kappers "Jean Rhys and the Dutch Connection", *Journal of Modern Literature*, 11, 1, 1984. p. 159-173; and Delany, op. cit.

[5] *In de Strik*, Amsterdam, Andries Blitz, 1932, and *Sous les Verrous*, Paris, Librairie Stock, 1933. Lenglet published various other Dutch-language novels, two of which form a sequel to *In de Strik*. In *Kerels* (1932) Jan van Leeuwen lives in The Hague and begs Stania, in Paris, to come and see him. In *Schuwe Vogels* (1937) the hero's wife, deserted by her lover in Paris, lives in England. He pays her a disastrous visit which ends with her death. See "Jean Rhys and the Dutch Connection", op. cit.

[6] Even their daughter, in recent years, would go no further than postulate that her mother 'corrected and perhaps somewhat rewrote the English version' (see 'Jean Rhys and the Dutch Connection,' op.cit.).

[7] Foreword to *Smile Please*, op.cit., p.15.

[8] This is a rough estimate, which does not take into account the words and phrases Rhys eliminated in the process of rewriting numerous passages from *Sous les Verrous*; a process which also necessitated the addition of other words and phrases.

[9] In de Nève's English preface he expresses his admiration for Rhys' "beautiful work". Interesting in this connection is a remark made in 1933 by Victor van Vriesland, a Dutch writer who helped Rhys and Lenglet in their literary careers, that of the three versions, the English was stylistically far superior (see "Jean Rhys and the Dutch Connection", op.cit.).

[10] See, for instance, *Sous les Verrous*, pp.136-137 and 149, *Barred*, pp.135-36 and 148-49; *In de Strik*, pp.115-17 and 128. Unless otherwise indicated, the first of all subsequent page-references will refer to the French, the second to the English, and the third to the Dutch edition of de Nève's novel. It may be tacitly assumed that the Dutch version follows Rhys' translation: exceptions will be explicitly stated. The examples given are to be considered as representative and in no way exhaustive.

[11] Cf. *Sous les Verrous*, p. 51, *Barred*, pp. 53 and *In de Strik*, p. 46. As we learn from Lenglet's preface to the French edition it was passages like these that caused the long delay of his novel's publication in France.

[12] Cf. *Sous les Verrous*, pp. 22-26, 37 and 41, *Barred*, pp. 21-25, 37 and 42, and *In de Strik*, pp.18-22, 33 and 37.

[13] Compare, for instance, the ending of Chapter I and the beginning of Chapter II in the three editions. See also pp.55, 57, 49; 199, 202, 171-72; and 221, 217, 187.

[14] Pp.59, 62, 53. The context shows the original version to be correct. The same applies to pp.107,108, 93, where 'soupe froide', rendered as 'soup', is correctly rendered in Dutch. In *Barred*, p. 51, Rhys appears to have missed de Nève's irony, by omitting his quotation-marks in "salle de danse" (for place of third-degree police-interrogation, p.49). The quotation-marks reappear in Dutch (p.44) Or are all these printers' errors?

[15] Woolf's phrase applies to the interference of a male point of view in the works of nineteenth-century women novelists. See *A Room of One's Own*, London, The Hogarth Press, 1929, p.111.

[16] It is, of course, intriguing that Rhys, some ten years after the events fictionalized by de

Nève, removed all traces of Stella Bowen's role in them. Her portrait of Lois Heidler in the earlier *Quartet* is almost as merciless as de Nève's picture of Mme Hübner in *Sous les Verrous*. It is tempting to speculate that Rhys may have had second thoughts about Bowen, especially after Ford had discarded her (See Delany, op. cit., p. 21).

[17] See Stella Bowen, op. cit., pp. 165-167: "In order to keep his (Ford's) machinery running, he requires to exercise his sentimental talents from time to time upon a new object . . . female devotion is always a drug on the market." She adds: "I simply hated my rôle!"

Conversations like the following are scrapped in the English version:

'— . . . tu comptes sans sa femme.
— Il l'aurait quittée, il me l'a dit souvent.
— Il te l'a dit, il te l'a dit! Et tu as cru cela?
—Oui, il le voulait. C'est moi qui m'y suis opposé.
—Tu es la première femme qui n'en veut pas à une autre de partager l'amour d'un homme.'
(pp. 242, 241, 206).

[18] Pp. 94, 95, 82. The passage includes similar remarks, also cut, about Hübner abusing "[le] prestige que sa situation d'artiste-peintre et critique d'art connu lui confère. Il en profite pour cultiver les caprices spéciaux." Rhys also eliminated all such innuendo about the Hübner's social circle; "c'est pour l'art que tous ces gens prétendent vivre, c'est en son nom qu'ils se permettent les pires débauches" (pp. 162, 162, 139).

[19] See pp. 196, 193, 166; 192, 189, 163; 124, 127, 109; and 190, 187, 161. 'Canaille' (pp. 141, 140, 121) was watered down to 'beautiful fellow'.

[20] Pp. 141, 140, 120. See also pp. 157, 156, 135; and pp. 174, 173, 149.

[21] Pp. 141, 140, 120. See also pp. 245, 245, 209. the adjective "ennuyée", when applied to Stania, is consistently translated as "worried", or scrapped altogether. *In de Strik* retains the note of annoyance, with Dutch "verveeld" or "bits".

[22] Pp. 173, 172, 149. Cf. also pp. 186, 185, 159.

[23] Pp. 113, 116, 99. For complaints about her cruel indifference to his feelings, see also pp. 157, 156, 135; 184, 183, 158; and 190, 187, 161.

[24] Pp. 98, 100, 85. For explanations of why she cannot visit her husband in prison more often, cf. pp. 100, 102, 87.

[25] Cf., for instance, pp. 121, 124, 106.

[26] Pp. 248, 248, 221.

[27] Pp. 196, 193, 166 and pp. 192, 189, 163; cf. also pp. 192, 189, 161.

[28] Pp. 179, 178, 154 and pp. 203, 200, 172.

[29] Pp. 86, 87, 75. Cf. also pp. 197, 194, 167, 176, 175, 151.

[30] Pp. 151, 150-51, 130. The Dutch version sticks to the original French.

[31] Pp. 134, 133, 115; 71, 74, 63; 119, 121, 104; and 138-39, 137-38, 118-19.

[32] Pp. 180, 179, 154; see also pp. 175, 174, 150 and pp. 116, 119, 102.

[33] Pp. 198, 195, 167-68.

# WITHOUT A DOG'S CHANCE:
## AFTER LEAVING MR. MACKENZIE

*by V.S. Naipaul*

Jean Rhys was born in the small Caribbean island of Dominica and went to England when she was sixteen, not many years before the 1914 war. Two hundred or even 150 years ago, when the sugar colonies of the Caribbean were valuable and important, the white West Indian in Europe was better known. Smollet satirized jumped-up Jamaican slave overseers taking the waters in Bath; Captain Marryat's father owned plantations and Negroes in Trinidad; Leigh Hunt was a Barbadian. But by the 1920s, when Jean Rhys began to write, the Caribbean and the Spanish Main belonged to antique romance; and the West Indian needed to explain himself.

Jean Rhys didn't explain herself. She might have been a riddle to others, but she never sought to make her experience more accessible by making it what it was not. It would have been easy for someone of her gifts to have become a novelist of manners; but she never pretended she had a society to write about. Even in her early stories, of Left Bank life in Paris, she avoided geographical explicitness. She never "set" her scene, English, European, or West Indian; she had, as it were, no home audience to play to; she was outside that tradition of imperial-expatriate writing in which the metropolitan outsider is thrown into relief against an alien background. She was an expatriate, but her journey had been the other way round, from a background; of nothing to an organized world with which her heroines could never come to terms.

This journey, this break in a life, is the essential theme of her five novels, *Quartet* (1928) *After Leaving Mr. Mackenzie* (1930), both recently reissued, *Voyage in the Dark* (1934), *Good Morning, Midnight* (1939),* and though it is "historical," set in the 1830s, and stands apart from the others, *Wide Sargasso Sea* (1967). The Jean Rhys heroine of the first four books is a woman of mystery, inexplicably bohemian, in the toughest sense of that word, appearing to come from no society, having roots in no society, having memories only of places, a woman who has "lost the way to England" and is adrift in the metropolis.

The women she meets are outsiders like herself, thrown off by organized society. They are, inevitably, cruder and less gifted; but they have been schooled by their society in the arts of survival. They have the saws and the supporting philosophy, the folk wisdom about men and money. "It might have been much

54

worse." "When you start thinking about things the answer's a lemon. . . But it's no use worrying." "Even if I have to do without, I still bank half of everything I get, and there's no friend like that." Men and money are connected: in this half-world men are the only people with money, and they are at once predators and prey, sexual partners, arbitrary providers of dinners, rooms, clothes. Their jobs remain vague, their larger, legitimate lives unknown. No homes are entered; the metropolis is reduced to a few cafés, boardinghouses, and hotels.

The great events of the world are far away: Jean Rhys's world is as without dates as Jane Austen's. In the four last novels there is only one explicit and startling-date: 1914. Cinemas, when they do appear, are places that provoke private thoughts; there isn't even the spurious community of radio and television. The society is closed; the isolation of the expatriate, the woman, the outsider, is complete; she exists in a void. "And I felt as if all my life and all myself were floating away from me like smoke and there was nothing to lay hold of."

The mysterious journey from an unknown island, the break in a life: concrete experience turns into the purest of symbols, and the themes which in the 1930s must have seemed obscure and perverse, deriving from too particular an experience, are today more accessible. But writing exorcises nothing for the writer. The concrete experience remains; what is damaging is damaging.

> It was as if a curtain had fallen, hiding everything I had every known.
> It was almost like being born again. . . . Sometimes it was as if I were
> back there and as if England were a dream. At other times England was
> the real thing and out there was the dream, but I could never fit them
> together.

This is how *Voyage in the Dark*, published in 1934, begins; and the words might serve as an epigraph for *Wide Sargasso Sea*, published thirty-three years later.

*Wide Sargasso Sea* is historical. It is the story of the first Mrs. Rochester, the mad West Indian wife in *Jane Eyre*, and it is set in the 1830s, not long after slavery has been abolished in the British colonies. An order has collapsed and some people are "marooned." The whites who are weak become "white cockroaches," preyed on by Negroes and half-castes. Africa shadows the mind, the servile turn vicious ("I knew that the ones who laughed would be the *worst*"); a world that appeared simple is now seen to be diseased, and is no longer habitable. Across the sea there is England, no longer home: an attic, imprisonment, flames. *Wide Sargasso Sea* remains in the mind as a brilliant idea for a nightmare; and it completes Jean Rhys's world. It fills in the West Indian scene and makes more explicit the background to that journey, which turns out not to have been from innocence to darkness, but from one void to another. There is no innocence in Jean Rhys's world; there has always been loss.

There is passion. "I wanted to go away with just the same feeling a boy has when he wants to run away to sea at least, that I imagine a boy has. Only, in my adventure, men were mixed up, because of course they had to be. You understand, don't you? Do you understand that a girl might have that feeling?" The thirty-six-year-old heroine of *After Leaving Mr. Mackenzie* speaks for all Jean Rhys's

heroines. It is easy to run away, but passion is the complication; and passion, as
dissected by Jean Rhys, is an ambiguous thing. It is an aspect of loss, of being
adrift, of being without money; it is an aspect of dependence.

Anna, the eighteen-year-old heroine of *Voyage in the Dark*, is a chorus girl
without prospects in a provincial touring company in pre-1914 England. When
she was a child in the West Indies Anna wanted to be black. "Being black is warm
and happy, being white is cold and sad." Now the journey has been made, and
England is indeed cold and sad. On the sea front at Southsea one day Anna is
picked up by a man. He does "something in the City." The full apparatus of
Edwardian seduction follows: dinners, private rooms, champagne. From being an
observer Anna becomes involved. Her lover is remote but kindly; Anna leans on
him more and more; she is learning the habit of dependence. Her perceptions of
her lover — totally banal, as he presents himself to her, no more than a discreet
sketch for a man — and of her own exclusion from the world do not alter. But she
is caught. When she is abandoned she will be damaged. Again and again — like
the middle-aged heroine of *Good Morning, Midnight*; looking only for disen-
gagement and calm — Anna will be a victim.

Passion is not a romance with the self. The Jean Rhys heroine knows sensu-
ousness, a delight in the body, in clothes, in remembered tropical landscapes. But
there is no real relishing of the world; at the center there is always something like
withdrawal. "It doesn't matter, there I am, like one of those straws which floats
round the edge of a whirlpool and is gradually sucked into the centre, the dead
centre, where everything is stagnant, everything is calm." Passion is dependence,
a further diminution of the capacity to survive. And dependence is, curiously, like
a drama in the head, something worked up and willful, yet in the end real and
necessary: it is the woman's half-world. *Demi-monde*: exile and dependence give
the words an exact meaning.

Jean Rhys's novels, written over a period of thirty-seven years, modify one
another and make a whole. They record a total experience, with varying emphasis.
*Wide Sargasso Sea* is the vision of nightmare at the end, with the historical setting
giving distance, as in a nightmare. *Voyage in the Dark* and *Good Morning,
Midnight*, the most subtle and complete of the novels, and the most humane, are
the most immediate. *After Leaving Mr. Mackenzie* is the most brutal. It doesn't
dissect a passion. It examines solitude and the void.

"Nowadays something had happened to her. She hardly ever thought of men,
or love." Julie is thirty-six. She has been pensioned off by a former lover, Mr.
Mackenzie, and for six months or so has been living as a solitary in a cheap Paris
hotel, deadened by a "sore and cringing feeling, which was the legacy of Mr.
Mackenzie." Abruptly one day she is informed that Mr. Mackenzie's weekly
allowance to her will be discontinued. Humiliated, hysterical, Julia seeks Mr.
Mackenzie out. He isn't mysterious or very far away. Absurdly, he lives just
around the corner; and when he is encountered in a nearby restaurant— the whole
scene is marvelously done — he turns out to be a man of fifty, middle class,
correct, "of medium height and colouring," with "enough nose to look important,

enough stomach to look benevolent." Almost Dickensian in that description, hardly an object of passion, a nobody, and perhaps for Julia always a nobody . . . it is the absurdity of her dependence. Julia's energy leaves her; the scene that seems to be preparing fades on a feeble climax. She strikes Mr. Mackenzie with her glove, but lightly; and it is she who looks beaten.

This little crisis is at the heart of the novel. All that follows is background. Acting on an impulse, Julia goes to London and puts up at a Bloomsbury hotel, chosen at random. There are people to be looked up: an old lover from whom she will get money: an uncle (shipwrecked himself, living in a Bayswater boarding-house) with whom she will quarrel; an embittered unmarried sister, imprisoned in suburban Acton by poverty and a family responsibility: an invalid mother who, when Julia arrives, is in a coma and dying. This shred of a family life emphasizes the emptiness and threat outside, and the sisters are uneasy with one another. Pity and concern are submerged by jealousy, brutality, and hysteria. The mother dies: the sisters separate. An embarrassing half-affair — always developing, never consummated — that Julia has been running with a romantic and kindly but self-regarding and timid man finally aborts. So the ten London days pass, "a disconnected episode to be placed with all the other disconnected episodes which made up her life"; and Julia goes back to Paris.

After *Leaving Mr. Mackenzie* is lucid, exact, and swift; the writing is exceptionally clean. But unlike the other novels it is written in the third person, with the novelist roaming at will among all her characters, so that the material is at once more "loaded." The West Indian background is excised. Julia therefore has no past and is without the "hall-marks" of nationality and social background; and her bohemianism, set against the hollow lives of lovers and family, is made to appear as both more defensible and more awful, part of a comprehensive damnation. Julia's would-be lover returns at the end to his familiar "world of lowered voices, and of passions, like Japanese dwarf trees, suppressed for many generations." There is a hint that Julia's unmarried sister, passions unspent, her life all but wasted, is about to pass into the greater aridity of a liaison with a mannish woman nurse. Within and without "the social system" people are trapped.

It is a depressing conclusion, not easy to take; but the attitude will be modified in the novels that follow. For Julia Mr. Mackenzie and his lawyer "perfectly represented organised society, in which she had no place and against which she had not a dog's chance." Nine years later, in *Good Morning, Midnight*, the middle-aged narrator will say something like this, but with a different emphasis:

> Well, let's argue this out, Mr. Blank. You, who represent Society, have
> the right to pay me 400 francs a month. That's my market value, for
> I am an inefficient member of Society, slow in the uptake, uncertain,
> slightly damaged in the fray, there's no denying it. So you have the
> right to pay me 400 francs a month, to lodge me in a small, dark room,
> to clothe me shabbily, to harass me with worry and monotony and
> unsatisfied longings till you get me to the point when I blush at a look,

cry at a word. . . . But I wish you a lot of trouble, Mr. Blank, and just
to start off with, your damned shop's going bust.

This is the Jean Rhys tone: the drama, of dependence and defeat, lies all in the head. What is formulated by the narrator is less of a "statement," more balanced and effective, lighter and truer.

But *After Leaving Mr. Mackenzie* is the writer's first extended attempt at coming to terms with a chaotic experience; and brutality of the novel, like the nightmare of *Wide Sargasso Sea*, is an essential part of the record. The four novels stand together. Out of her fidelity to her experience, and her purity as a novelist, Jean Rhys thirty to forty years ago identified many of the themes that engage us today: isolation, an absence of society or community, the sense of things falling apart, dependence, loss. Her achievement is very grand. Her books may serve current causes, but she is above causes. What she has written about she has endured, over a long life; and what a stoic thing she makes the act of writing appear.

# REFLECTIONS OF OBEAH IN JEAN RHYS' FICTION

## by *Elaine Campbell*

It was only during the last years of Jean Rhys' life that she became recognized as a West Indian writer. Kenneth Ramchand was one of the first West Indian critics to identify her fiction, along with that of Geoffrey Drayton and Phyllis Shand Allfrey, as belonging to the work of the white West Indian minority. In 1978, the year before Rhys' death, Louis James published a critical study of all her fiction in which he asserted:

> Even in her books written wholly about Europe, the sensibility is not wholly European. Her sensitivity to heat and to cold, to bright colour or the absence of colour, her sense of another life behind the mask of society conventions, were formed in the Antilles.[1]

And Thomas F. Staley expressed a similar judgment a year later:

> Leaving aside the problematic relationship between life and art, it became clear to me from the first reading of her work that her background and culture not only set Rhys apart from her contemporary novelists, but also shaped a widely different sensibility and radical consciousness.[2]

True, Ford Madox Ford had sensed some special connection between Jean Rhys' birthplace and the subject matter of her first collected short stories when he stated in his long, diffuse Preface to *The Left Bank* (1927):

> And coming from the Antilles, with a . . . terrific . . . passion for stating the case of the underdog, she has let her pen loose on the Left Banks of the Old World. . .[3]

But Ford failed to take his observation beyond the simple suggestion that there was some connection between 'coming from the Antilles' and 'stating the case of the underdog'.

One other commentator, Alec Waugh, noted (in 1949) that 'Dominica has coloured her temperament and outlook. It was a clue to her, just as she was a clue to it'.[4] However, neither Ford nor Waugh explored the literary effects of Jean Rhys' West Indian-ness, and now some attempt should be made to go beyond the identification of Rhys as a West Indian writer to an effort at understanding *how* Rhys' fiction reflects the special qualities of her cultural background. The purpose of this essay is to demonstrate how a specific cultural aspect of Rhys'

Dominican childhood affected her imagination and her literature. The specific cultural feature to which I refer is the Dominican practice of Obeah.

The version of Obeah practiced on Rhys' home island of Dominica has been described by Rhys herself as a milder version of Voodoo such as is practiced on Haiti, like Dominica a formerly French island where a French patois is spoken. In Rhys' unfinished autobiography, *Smile Please*, she says about Obeah, '. . . even in my time nobody was supposed to take it very seriously' but she confirms the existence of Obeah with an example of a practitioner in her own family household: "I was told about her [Ann Tewitt, the obeah woman] in a respectful, almost awed tone."⁵ In fact, Obeah was taken seriously on Dominica at the turn of the century and it was taken seriously by the child Gwen Williams (Jean Rhys). Obeah was a pervasive feature of Dominican life during Rhys' childhood and adolescence; her immediate household included a respected practitioner of Obi ritual; and, there were other additional vestiges of Obi observance closely surrounding her — all of which influenced her thinking during her formative years.

I cannot claim to be the first Rhys critic to point to the importance of Obeah in her writing. In his critical study on Jean Rhys, Louis James states that 'her imaginative awareness of *obeah* was to enable her to create the most hallucinatory scenes of Wide Sargasso Sea'. James in turn cites Thomas Atwood's *The History of the Island of Dominica* to indicate how deeply the Dominicans were committed to what Atwood called 'witchcraft and idolatry' at the time of Atwood's visit in the late seventeen hundreds. Thus, witchcraft and Obeah were documented on Dominica at least a hundred years before Rhys' birth, and they undoubtedly extend back to the arrival of African slaves in Dominica which Dominican historian Lennox Honychurch dates to the mid-eighteenth century. It is Rhys' awareness of an imaginative participation in this heritage of what Atwood calls 'witchcraft' that I shall detail today.

Before doing so, however, I wish to make one last obeisance to a critic and writer of West Indian literature who perhaps best understands Rhys' imaginative participation in Dominican Obeah. Wilson Harris' sensitivity to Rhys' art is demonstrated in his *Kunapipi* article on Rhys, 'Carnival of Psyche'. Harris points out Rhys' dual ancestry (Welsh and Creole), and identifies her imaginative insights as both 'white' and 'black', a combination Harris exemplifies by Christianity and Obeah. Harris states the 'Obeah is a pejorative term' and continues to say that 'it reflects significantly a state of mind or embarrassment in both black and white West Indians, a conviction of necessary magic, necessary hell-fire or purgatory through which to re-enter 'lost' origins, 'lost' heavens, 'lost' divinity'.⁶

Harris' statement that "Obeah is a pejorative term' is problematic because he does not clarify for whom he believes it exists in a pejorative sense: himself, Londoners, expatriate British in the West Indies, North Americans, West Indians. All such possible candidates aside, Jean Rhys did not consider Obeah as a pejorative term or even as a word conveying a negative value. In fact, she so internalized the cultural values of Dominican Obeah that she eventually came to view herself as the white witch, the West Indian Obeah woman among the alien inhabitants of England.

The initial literary manifestation of Rhys' psychic involvement with the phenomenon of witchcraft appears in her first published material, the collected short stories of *The Left Bank*. Rhys had been away from Dominica for twenty years when the stories were written. However, despite two decades of absence from the West Indies, the memory of Rhys' Dominican homeland remained strong, working its way in various manners into the collection. *The Left Bank* admirably exemplifies what Harris calls the combination of black and white tones, containing as it does pieces such as 'Trio', 'Mixing Cocktails', and 'Again the Antilles' which are distinct West Indian counterparts to the Montparnassian pieces. The Montparnassian pieces themselves contain frequent repudiations of Anglo-Saxon behaviour and attitudes while there are also some strange extrusions of heterodox material which do not seem to fit into the mainly anecdotal matter set in a European context. For example, heterodoxy is illustrated in the piece entitled 'In the Rue de L'arrivée' wherein Dorothy Dufreyne, pointedly cited as an Anglo-Saxon lady, dreams of dying and being conducted willingly to hell. Her concern, expressed in the final line of the story, is that hell might turn out to be heaven. This unusual point-of-view for an Anglo-Saxon lady bears out Harris' observation that Obeah 'reflects , . . a state of mind . . . in both black and white West Indians . . . [of] a conviction of . . . necessary hell-fire or purgatory through which to re-enter 'lost' origins'. That the actuality of Obeah had not faded from Rhys' consciousness even after twenty years away from Dominica is demonstrated in 'Mixing Cocktails', where she evokes a figure who turns up again and again in her writing, that of 'our cook, the old Obeah woman', here named 'Ann Twist'.

In "Mixing Cocktails' the Rhysian character receives her first lessons from the Obeah woman. She 'mustn't look too much at de moon'. The narrative voice explains,   'If you fall asleep in the moonlight you are bewitched.' The little Creole girl who is prone to falling asleep in the verandah hammock is thus warned against the danger of moon madness. As a child, then, the Rhysian heroine connects Obeah, witchery, and madness — a congeries that peaks in *Wide Sargasso Sea*. "Ann Twist's white counterpart emerges in the last piece of the collection, the lengthy approximation of Rhys' flight through continental Europe. In 'Vienne' the heroine Francine and her husband escape arrest in Vienna by fleeing to Budapest and from Budapest to Prague.

> It was an odd place, that hotel, full of stone passages and things. I lay
> vaguely wondering why Prague reminded me of witches. . . I read a
> book when I was a kid — *The Witch of Prague*. No. It reminded me
> of witches anyhow. Something dark, secret and grim.[7]

The story 'Vienne' and the collection *The Left Bank* end in Prague, leaving Francine to adopt the style of the city that reminds her of witches: 'I noticed at lunch that the grand chic at Prague seemed to be to wear dead black. I groped in the trunk for something similar, powdered carefully, rouged my mouth, painted a beauty spot under my left eye.' Making up her face as if for carnival, Francine assumes the dark dress of the city of witches. At this point in Rhys' fiction, the black and white tones are still separate: Ann Twist, the black Obeah woman, and Francine, the white witch of Prague.

The Obeah woman Ann Twist becomes Anne Chewett in Rhys' self-declared favourite novel, *Voyage in the Dark*. The eighteen-year-old heroine sinks into reverie tinged with delirium shortly before the abortion with which the novel concludes. The heroine, Anne Morgan,[8] recalls the extraordinary mountainscape of her home island, conjuring up its image by mentally listing the mountains' patois names. Morne Diablotin, by free association, releases the memory of Anne Chewett who 'used to say it's haunted and obeah'. Anne Chewett's authority for identifying a spot consecrated to Obi is attested by the fact that she has been failed for practicing Obeah. These repeated literary references to the Williams Family's resident Obeah woman may seem to indicate little more than the indelibility with which Ann Tewitt's presence was etched on Jean Rhys' childhood. However, *Voyage in the Dark* includes that important new piece of information which helps provide insight into Rhys' evaluation of the Obeah woman's social position: Anne Chewett has spent time in jail for practicing Obeah. This information reflects Wilson Harris' observation that Obeah carries a pejorative value, and, more central to Rhys' canon, it reflects the demonstrated social fact that women who practice either African or European witchcraft are routinely punished by the dominant society to which they belong as non-typical members.

The almost casually offered information that Anne Chewett had been incarcerated for Obeah practice takes on a new dimension in the uncollected short story 'I Spy A Stranger'. Here there is no reference to the West Indies or to Obeah practice. But there is a reappearance of the Witch of Prague motif. Such a reappearance is not entirely surprising, even though 'I Spy A Stranger' was published in 1966, thirty-nine years after 'Vienne'. As the Obeah woman motif is inapplicable to a thoroughly English protagonist in a totally British setting, it is simply replaced by the more appropriate allusion to a European conjure woman: the Witch of Prague.

Jean Rhys told Marcelle Bernstein in a 1969 *Observer* interview that the villagers of Cheriton Fitzpaine had accused her of being a witch after she had settled there. One of her neighbours 'told the whole village I practiced black magic'.[9] This sort of hostility, which Rhys encountered in England even after decades of British residency, informs 'I Spy A Stranger'. The 'I' of the title is the collective village mentality and the 'Stranger' is Laura, the middle-aged heroine who visits a female cousin in England during the second world war. Mutual antagonism is displayed in 'I Spy A Stranger' and it is the 'stranger' who is eventually punished. Laura's punishment is similar to that of Anne Chewett, the West Indian woman jailed for practicing Obeah. After an unsuccessful attempt to bring civil charges against Laura for violating blackout regulations, the villagers, headed by Ricky, adopt the time-honoured mode of removing an objectionable woman from society: incarceration for madness. The sanatorium to which Laura is shanghaied equates the attic to which Antoinette Rochester is incarcerated as a madwoman in *Wide Sargasso Sea*: 'There was a photograph on the cover of a prospectus showing a large, ugly house with small windows, those on the two top floors barred. The grounds were as forbidding as the house and surrounded by a high wall.'[10] Laura, early in her visit dubbed as the Witch of Prague, is jailed as a madwoman because the disposal of witches by burning lacks social approval in World War II England. It is reserved for Antoinette, the white witch of *Wide Sargasso Sea*, to suffer both incarceration, the established punishment for Obeah practice, and burning, the traditional punishment for witchcraft.

What Wilson Harris calls Rhys' 'mythic' treatment of West Indian Obeah enabled Rhys to transcend the social barriers imposed by her skin colour. Anna Morgan exclaims: "I wanted to be black, I always wanted to be black,' and Jean Rhys attests in her autobiography that she prayed ardently as a child to be black. The frustration of belonging to a minority race is illustrated in Anna Morgan's description of her social relationship with her childhood companion Francine:

> The thing about Francine was that when I was with her I was happy. She was small and plump and blacker than most of the people out there, and she had a pretty face. . . But I knew that of course she disliked me . . . because I was white; and that I would never be able to explain to her that I hated being white.[11]

What racial barriers prevented Rhys from achieving in actual life, literature enabled her to accomplish through art: an erasure of racial barriers with a resultant free flow between black and white identities. The first indication of this free flow is Rhys' naming of her white witch of Prague (in 'Vienne') after her black childhood friend Francine.

In her autobiography, Rhys verifies Francine's real life role described in *Voyage in the Dark*.

> I made great friends with a negro girl called Francine. . . Francine's stories were . . . full of jokes and laughter, descriptions of beautiful dresses and good things to eat. But the start was always a ceremony. Francine would say, 'Tim-tim.' I had to answer 'Bois sêche,' then she'd say, 'Tablier Madame est derriere dos'. . . She always insisted on this ceremony before starting a story and it wasn't until much later, when I was reading a book about obeah, that I discovered that 'Bois sêche' is one of the gods. I grew very fond of Francine and admired her; when she disappeared without a word to me I was hurt. People did disappear, they went to one of the other islands, but not without saying goodbye.[12]

Rhys' young friend was in her own way a minor practitioner of Obeah, invoking one of the ceremonial forms and one of the ceremonial figures. She required young Gwen Williams' participation in a fragment of Obeah ritual, and she helped establish the general atmosphere over which Ann Tewitt presided with greater authority. Francine was Gwen Williams' own age and it was easier for the young girl to identify herself with her companion than with the older woman. The extent to which the young white Creole did identify with the young black Creole is displayed in *Wide Sargasso Sea* when the players of the Dominican drama are transformed into the characters of the novel: Antoinette Cosway and Tia, Antoinette's childhood friend.

Tia and Antoinette share many childhood hours, swimming together, cooking and eating treats, sleeping together. And Tia deserts Antoinette. When Antoinette runs to Tia for solace during the firing of Coulibri, Tia betrays Antoinette by throwing a rock at her. 'As I ran, I thought, I will live with Tia and I will be like her. . . When I was close I saw the jagged stone in her hand but I did not see her throw it. I did not feel it either, only something wet, running down my face.' Antoinette's affection for Tia blocks out the treasonous rock. Tia's ambivalence, engendered by racial politics, expresses itself after she throws the stone that wounds Antoinette. 'I looked at her and I saw her face crumple up as she began to cry. We stared at each other, blood on my face, tears on hers. It was as if I saw myself. Like in a looking-glass.'[13] Tia disappears from Antoinette's life in the novel but readers of the novel know that in its final scene Antoinette returns to an apparition of Tia as she flings herself from the parapet of Thornfield Hall. Never forgotten, Tia, like Francine, remains a lifelong influence. And when she disappears from the novel she is replaced by Christophine as the child Antoinette matures into adulthood and needs an adult companion.

While Tia only recited isolated incantations to an Obeah god, Christophine delves more deeply into Obeah practice, consummating as it were, the initiation over which Tia officiated. Christophine is the Obeah woman from Martinique of whom the local folk are afraid. She inspires the same respect and fear that Ann Tewitt inspired in Gwen Williams' childhood home. Of Christophine, young Antoinette recounts:

> The girls from the bayside who sometimes helped with the washing
> and cleaning were terrified of her. That, I soon discovered, was why
> they came at all — for she never paid them. Yet they brought presents
> of fruit and vegetables and after dark I often heard low voices from the
> kitchen. (p. 21)

The fealty to an Obeah woman implied in this quotation; the presents brought in possible payment for services rendered 'after dark' are most subtly suggested. A more graphic imaginative construction of Christophine's association with Obeah is created by the child Antoinette who superimposes the paraphernalia of Obeah over the austerity of Christophine's bedroom at Coulibri:

> I knew her room so well — the pictures of the Holy Family and the
> prayer for a happy death. She had a bright, patchwork counterpane, a
> broken-down press for her clothes, and my mother had given her an old
> rockingchair.
>
> Yet one day when I was waiting there I was suddenly very much

> afraid. The door was open to the sunlight, someone was whistling near
> the stables, but I was afraid. I was certain that hidden in the room . . .
> there was dead man's dried hand, white chicken feathers, a cock with
> its throat cut, dying slowly, slowly. . . No one had spoken to me about
> obeah — but I knew what I would find if I dared to look. (pp. 31-2)

The question of whether or not Christophine actually practices witchcraft is resolved later in the novel when she is importuned by Antoinette to prepare a love potion. She complies, all the while warning Antoinette that her magic does not work well for békés.

That Christophine is the literary descendant of Ann Twist, 'our cook, the old Obeah woman' of 'Mixing Cocktails' is illustrated by a story Antoinette tells her new husband Rochester. Awakening during the night and finding herself watched by two rats, the child Antoinette ran onto the verandah to sleep in a hammock.

> There was a full moon that night — and I watched it for a long time.
> There were no clouds chasing it, so it seemed to be standing still and
> it shone on me. Next morning Christophine was angry. She said it was
> very bad to sleep in the moonlight when the moon was full. (p. 83)

Linked with Obeah and witchcraft, with earlier Obeah women in the Rhys canon, Christophine is threatened with jail when she suggests to Rochester that he return to Antoinette a portion of her dowry. Rochester sends Christophine away and she disappears as Tia disappeared before her.

Christophine's replacement by Antoinette is infinitely more subtle than the earlier replacement of Tia by Christophine, just as the doubling of Tia and the child Antoinette is more explicit than the doubling of Christophine and Antoinette. Both Creole women share an empathy for and understanding of their surroundings that Rochester can never approximate. Their understanding of West Indian experiences crashes, however, against Rochester's English behaviour and values. Christophine's magic potion fails and Antoinette's witchery of beauty and fortune crumble before the severity of Rochester's self-service. Seeking to escape from Rochester with Antoinette, Christophine's power to incite fear and respect in those she encounters fades before his alien point-of-view; similarly, Antoinette's spirit is quenched when Rochester withdraws his love.

After the dismissal of Christophine, Rochester needs only pressure Antoinette into some semblance of madness in order to dispose of her also. Lacking Christophine's sorcery to help her in dealing with Rochester, Antoinette develops the moon madness that enables her to liberate herself from Rochester — something she could not do while sane or through Christophine's intervention. Tall, dark, and fierce, mad Antoinette now incites in those around her the terror which Christophine once commanded. She escapes her jailer and sets fire to her jail. She then unites herself with Tia whom she sees call to her from beneath the parapet of Thornfield Hall. At last Antoinette is able to emulate Tia whom sharp stones did not hurt and for whom fires always lit.

Written in Jean Rhys' seventies, after fifty years away from her Dominican home, *Wide Sargasso Sea* is Rhys' contribution to the dissolution of social barriers grounded in racial differences. It is a *tour de force* of imaginative art by which she resolved for herself her childhood friendship with Francine, and through which she painted for her readers an extraordinary facet of West Indian experience.

Footnotes:

[1] Louis James, *Jean Rhys* (London: Longman, 1978), p. 33.

[2] Thomas F. Staley, *Jean Rhys* (Austin: University of Texas Press, 1979), p. 1.

[3] Ford Madox Ford, Preface, *The Left Bank*, by Jean Rhys (Freeport, New York: Books for Libraries Press. 1970), p. 24.

[4] Alec Waugh, *The Sugar Islands* (New York: Farrar, Straus and Company, 1949), pp. 95-6.

[5] Jean Rhys, *Smile Please* (London: André Deutsch, 1979), p. 22.

[6] Wilson Harris, 'Carnival of Psyche', *Kunapipi*, II, No. 2, p. 146.

[7] Jean Rhys *The Left Bank*, p. 252.

[8] Anne Morgan, the heroine who bears such an historically significant West Indian surname, shares with Anne Chewett a close variant of the Obeah woman's given name.

[9] Marcelle Bernstein, 'The Inscrutable Miss Jean Rhys', *London Observer*, 1 June 1969, p. 42.

[10] Jean Rhys, 'I Spy A Stranger', *Art and Literature*, 8 (Spring 1966), p. 52.

[11] Jean Rhys, *Voyage in the Dark* (New York: Popular Library, n.d.), p. 60.

[12] Jean Rhys, *Smile Please*, p. 31.

[13] Jean Rhys, *Wide Sargasso Sea* (New York: Popular Library, 1066), p. 46. All further references are to this edition and are included in the text.

# "WOMEN MUST HAVE SPUNKS": JEAN RHYS'S WEST INDIAN OUTCASTS

*Lucy Wilson*

Since Wally Look Lai described *Wide Sargasso Sea* as "one of the genuine masterpieces of West Indian fiction" (17), quite a number of critics have focused on the Caribbean aspects of that novel, as well as *Voyage in the Dark* and several of Rhys's short stories. Louis James (111) and Mary Lou Emery (421), for example, have shown that Rhys's Caribbean concerns situate the intensely personal vision of her fiction within a much larger historical context. More specifically, Nancy Fulton has pointed to the parallels between black and white characters in *Wide Sargasso Sea* (344). Similarly, Helen Tiffin explains that Antoinette's suffering and enslavement by Edward Rochester reinforce her identification with the black Creole community (339), and Antoinette's ambiguous relationship with blacks has been explored by Charlotte Bruner as well (237).

Despite considerable critical attention to Jean Rhys's West Indian themes and characters, however, there has been relatively little focus on the black characters themselves. This is a significant oversight because two black West Indian characters — Selina Davis in "Let Them Call It Jazz" and Christophine Dubois, Antoinette's former nanny and only friend in *Wide Sargasso Sea* — are unique among Rhys's female characters. The "typical" Rhys protagonist, such as Anna Morgan or Antoinette Rochester, is a social outcast cut off from meaningful contact with other human beings. Abandoned but not free, she is powerless to alter her condition. Powerlessness, in fact, intensifies the misery of the social outcast for it cuts her off from the sources of pleasure, knowledge, and discourse that, according to Michel Foucault, are induced by the productive nature of power in society ("Truth and Power" 61).

But unlike Rhys's white protagonists, Selina and Christophine seem to thrive on adversity and to draw strength from their opposition to the prevailing power structures. Although no more a part of mainstream society than Anna or Antoinette, Selina and Christophine draw upon inner resources and possess a kind of resiliency that their white West Indian counterparts lack. Furthermore, their insights into the uses and abuses of power in their respective societies reveal the full scope of Rhys's social vision as well as her commitment to truth, which places her at odds with centuries of erroneous beliefs and practices initiated and perpetuated in the interests of successive power groups.

Anna Morgan, the actress-turned-prostitute in *Voyage in the Dark*, and Anto-
inette-Bertha Rochester, the Creole heiress of *Wide Sargasso Sea* who becomes
the mad prisoner of Thornfield Hall, are both West Indian by birth and victims
of nature. Living in and near London in the 1930s and touring with a third-rate
theatrical group, Anna falls prey to the machinations of a debonair insurance man,
Walter Jeffries. Anna justifies her acceptance of money in exchange for sex on
the grounds that she will "do anything for good clothes. Anything — anything for
clothes" (22). This may seem callous, but the conditions of Anna's life — her
youth and the fact that she is orphaned, exiled, alone in a foreign land without
financial or emotional support — alleviate the crassness of her materialistic aims.
"In effect," explains Arnold Davidson, "Rhys uses her protagonist's naiveté as
a lever to move the reader to unlikely judgments — judgments that do not simply
reiterate the dictates of the society" (56). The structural device that reinforces
Anna's naiveté and the reader's predisposition to be sympathetic is the juxtaposition of Anna's bleak, cold, English present with flashbacks to her sunny, warm,
West Indian girlhood. It is in these memories that Anna comes closest to her
nineteenth-century counterpart, Antoinette (nee Cosway) Mason Rochester.

For both Anna and Antoinette, the warmth and vibrant energy of the West
Indies is epitomized in the lives of the black inhabitants of the islands. As a child,
Anna spent many hours listening to Francine, the black cook, tell stories. Anna
claims:

> I wanted to be black. I always wanted to be black. I was happy because
> Francine was there, and I watched her hand waving the fan backwards
> and forwards and the beads of sweat that rolled from underneath her
> handkerchief. Being black is warm and gay, being white is cold and
> sad. (27).

On the other hand, Antoinette, living in Jamaica just after the Emancipation
Act was passed in 1838, is not as forthright in her identification with the black
islanders, for she is very much aware that, as a member of the former slave-
owning class, she is disdained by both the blacks and the newly rich whites who
call her kind "white cockroach" and "white nigger." Despite the contempt and
even physical harm that she and her family experience at the hands of the former
slaves, the child Antoinette sees her own image in the face of Tia, a young black
girl who had been her friend until racial tension came between them. As
Antoinette's family estate is burned to the ground by an angry mob of former
slaves, she turns to Tia for refuge:

> As I ran, I thought, I will live with Tia and I will be like her. Not to
> leave Coulibri. Not to go. Not. When I was close I saw the jagged stone
> in her hand but I did not see her throw it. I did not feel it either, only
> something wet, running down my face. I looked at her and saw her face
> crumple as she began to cry. We stared at each other, blood on my face,
> tears on hers. It was as if I saw myself. Like in a looking glass. (38)

The desire to be black, expressed by both Anna and Antoinette, is reiterated
by Rhys herself in her unfinished autobiography, *Smile Please*:

> I have watched carnivals on television. They are doubtless very
> colourful but it seems to me that it is all planned and made up
> compared to the carnival I remember, when I used to long so fiercely
> to be black and to dance, too, in a sun, to that music. The carnival I
> knew has vanished. (43)

Rhys, like her protagonists, envies the black Creoles because they have 'more
freedom, particularly sexual, than the white islander who must conform to the
constraints of the colonist' (Bruner 247). But the identification of white with
black West Indian goes even deeper. Anna's desire to be black reveals her longing
for 'a racial heritage which seemed in natural harmony with life' (Staley 62) and
a rejection of "European materialism in favor of the vitality of the black folk
culture' (James 112).

Antoinette's ambiguous identification with Tia takes its final form at the
conclusion of *Wide Sargasso Sea* when Tia appears to Antoinette in a dream and
entices her to jump from the battlements of Thornfield Hall, now nearly engulfed
by flames. Antoinette interprets this dream as a sign, and her ensuing destruction
of Thornfield Hall has been compared to the "typical slave retaliation in the firing
of the great house" (Tiffin 339). However, to see Antoinette's suicide as a
triumphant assertion is to detract from the tragic implications of her life and
violent death. Despite her imprisonment, Antoinette is not a slave: her own
passivity brings her to England and leaves her with no options except death.

Nevertheless, critical response to Antoinette's suicide is consistently positive,
even when qualified. Her death is seen as "her most decisive action and her final
escape from domination" (Davidson 39), as a from of rebellion and assertion
(James 124), as "a leap into the life she was never permitted to live" (Fulton 348),
and even as a triumph over her surroundings (Wolf 152, Emery 428). I would
argue, however, that Antoinette Rochester's suicide is no more a triumph than
Anna Morgan's nearly fatal abortion at the end of *Voyage in the Dark*. These
attempts to call Antoinette's desperate leap by any other name reveal a reluctance
on the critics' part to accept her defeat, as if to do so would somehow diminish
Rhys's remarkable achievement.

But this is not the case. Rhys has created the syntax and vocabulary needed to
bridge the gap between the outcast and society, and her novels — especially *Wide
Sargasso Sea* — give voice to the inarticulate anguish of solitude and rejection.
Antoinette's demise is a tragedy, not a victory. It is the final act in a complex
historical drama that pits those with power against those without. Both Anna
Morgan and Antoinette Rochester are casualties of social and political conflicts
that transcend the personal or sexual battles that each character is forced to wage.
Although they identify with the black West Indians, their destinies more closely
parallel the fate of the Caribs who, Anna recalls, "are now practically exterminated" (*Voyage* 91). Antoinette *is* exterminated, and Anna's abortion symbolizes
the end of her line of descent. Kenneth Ramchand maintains that the original
inhabitants of the West Indies "were virtually eliminated" and today "are
regarded as marginal to society" (164). The same could be said of Antoinette and

Anna, one doomed to death by her own hand, the other to life in rented bed-sitting-rooms on the fringes of a hostile city.

However, Anna and Antoinette are not Rhys's final word on the subject of survival in a hostile environment. Significantly, it is two black characters who provide an alternative. An exile like Anna, Selina Davis, in "Let Them Call It Jazz," is a West Indian woman living in London. If anything, her situation is more tenuous than Anna's, for Selina is harassed by racists who despise not only her lilting foreign-sounding speech patterns but the color of her skin as well. She has been robbed of her life savings and evicted from her home, yet she still finds reason to sing and dance: "After I drink a glass or two I can sing and when I sing all the misery goes from my heart" (46). Selina is not one to suffer quietly or passively to acquiesce to her own oppression. After she throws a rock through the window of an antagonistic neighbor, she asks herself: "Why I do that? It's not like me. But if they treat you wrong over and over again the hour strike when you burst out that's what" (55). The Holloway prison song, which Selina hears from the courtyard below the punishment cells, epitomizes the spirit of the oppressed: "She was singing from the punishment cells, and she tell the girls cheerio and never say die. . . Some day I hear that song on trumpets and these walls will fall and rest" (60-61).

Selina Davis stands bravely at the intersection of individual human freedom and the power of institutional authority, yet frequently critical response to this story has focused on the negative side of her situation: a "woeful portrait" one critic calls it (Staley 126), while another aligns himself with Selina's neighbors when he disparages her "foul talk" and "obscene dancing" (Wolfe 46). Louis James is correct, though, when he observes that the white composer who steals Selina's song cannot "take away what the song means to her, just as the exploitation of black music cannot remove the black sense of jazz" (115). "Never say die" is the message of Selina's song, and its rhythm gives her the courage and strength to go on living. Rhythm, claims West Indian novelist Wilson Harris, provides the energy for civilization. He writes:

> Life, it would appear, realizes itself in potentiality and peril with the
> appearance of rhythm. . .When the toy-man, the exploited man, be-
> comes aware of original rhythms within the oppression of his world,
> contradictions are bared in a manner terrifying and yet containing the
> secret of change. (18-19)

For Selina, the secret of change is her discovery that she is "not frightened of them any more — after all what else can they do?" (62)

How unlike her white West Indian counterparts is this high-spirited black woman. Anna Morgan, for example, seems to drift through life in a semistupor. Her friend Lauri warns her: "You always look half-asleep and people don't like that" (*Voyage* 110). On another occasion, the masseuse Ethel Matthews exclaims: "You're not all there; you're a half-potty bastard. You're not all there; that's what's the matter with you" (124). Anna's will has not been "crushed" (Staley 67), for there is no evidence that she ever possessed an assertive nature.

And this is true as well of Antoinette, who accedes to her own exploitation and debasement as the wife of Edward Rochester long before she even meets the man. As a child Antoinette has a recurring and prophetic dream that she is walking in a forest with a man who hates her, yet she does not offer any resistance: "I follow him, sick with fear but I make no effort to save myself; if anyone were to try and save me, I would refuse. This must happen" (*Wide Sargasso Sea* 50). In fact, years later two persons do try to save her, and Antoinette is good to her word.

Antoinette's marriage having completely deteriorated, she turns for advice to Christophine, who urges her to leave Edward. But when Antoinette argues that she must stay because she will be laughed at and because she has no money, Christophine cannot contain her indignation: "Why you ask me, if when I answer you say no? Why you come up here if when I tell you the truth, you say no?" (90). At this critical moment, with Antoinette's happiness and ultimately her life in the balance, this free-thinking Creole girl, whose charm is in direct proportion to her identification with the mysteries of her West Indian homeland, suddenly adopts the racist, imperialist language of her husband and stepfather: "I stared at her, thinking, 'but how can she know the best thing for me to do, this ignorant, obstinate old negro woman, who is not certain if there is such a place as England'" (93). the ultimate betrayal in *Wide Sargasso Sea* is not Edward Rochester's agreeing to a loveless marriage for monetary gain, or even his infidelity with the servant girl Amelie; it is Antoinette's betrayal of her own heritage, the submersion of her West Indian identity in the rhetoric and attitudes of imperialism.

The second time Antoinette refuses the help of another who attempts to free her from the bonds of "English law" occurs when Sandi, her beloved black cousin, asks: "Will you come with me?" and Antoinette responds, "I cannot" (151). Why can she not? English law may have placed her inheritance in the hands of her husband, but marriage is not slavery: no one could stop her from walking away. Antoinette begins to resemble her predecessors in Rhys's earlier novels — Anna Morgan, Marya Zelli, Julia Martin, and Sasha Jansen — in her inability to choose personal integrity over financial dependency.

The most perceptive analysis of Antoinette's position is provided by Christophine, herself an outcast, a Martinican obeah woman who has spent the the better part of her adult life living among Jamaicans who fear and envy her. Christophine has spent time in jail because of her obeah practice. Hers has not been an easy life, but she has the strength and resiliency that are so clearly lacking in her white mistresses, Antoinette and her mother, Annette. Christophine defies the powers that be and lives a full life on the fringes of respectable society:

> [Christophine] spat over her shoulder. "All women, all colours, nothing but fools. Three children I have. One living in the world, each one a different father, but no husband, I thank my God. I keep my money. I don't give it to no worthless man." (91)

Christophine has no patience for Antoinette's passivity. When Antoinette is immobilized by despair, Christophine admonishes her: "Get up, girl, and dress yourself. Woman must have spunks to live in this wicked world" (84). Like Selina

Davis and her "never say die" song, Christophine embodies the life force. When Antoinette was a child, it was Christophine who kept her family alive — despite Annette Cosway's death wish: "I dare say we would have died if she'd turned against us and that would have been a better fate. To die and be forgotten and at peace. Not to know that one is abandoned, lied about, helpless" (19).

The shift in power, as a result of the Emancipation Act, from the former slave owners to the newly rich whites is the cause of Annette's despair and the Cosway family's social descent. But to Christophine, the abolishment of slavery is a source of contemptuous amusement:

> No more slavery! She had to laugh! These new ones have Letter of the Law. Same thing. They got magistrate. They got fine. The got jail house and chain gang. They got tread machine to mash up people's feet. New ones worse than old ones — more cunning, that's all." (22-23)

Christophine is nobody's fool. She has an intuitive grasp of the subtle ebb and flow of power in Jamaican society. In a few short sentences she captures the essence of what Michel Foucault describes as "the endlessly repeated play of dominations":

> Humanity does not gradually progress from combat to combat until it arrives at universal reciprocity, where the rule of law finally replaces warfare; humanity installs each of its violences in a system of rules and thus proceeds from domination to domination. . . . The successes of history belong to those who are capable of seizing these rules, to replace those who had used them, to disguise themselves so as to pervert them, invert their meaning, and redirect them against those who had initially imposed them; controlling this complex mechanism, they will make it function so as to overcome the rulers through their own rules ("Nietzsche" 85-86)

Rhys's former slave owners have, in fact, been overcome through their own rules: "Old time white people nothing but white nigger now, and black nigger better than white nigger," Tia proclaims to Antoinette the last time they play together as friends (21). Christophine is not impressed by talk of the Emancipation for she recognizes a new form of tyranny in the "Letter of the Law" and a new breed of tyrant in the professional classes and the police: "That doctor an old-time doctor. These new ones I don't like them. First word in their mouth is police. Police — that's something I don't like" (125).

To appreciate fully Christophine's incisive analysis of Jamaican society after the abolition of slavery, it is helpful to compare it with that of Douglas Hall, taken from a paper he read at the Royal Institute for International Affairs in London two years *after* the first publication of *Wide Sargasso Sea*. According to Hall,

> The abolition of slavery ostensibly removed the legal supports of these [class] divisions. After August 1, 1838, all were equal citizens — in the eyes of the law. But all were not equal in the eyes of society or in the eyes of those who were the makers and administrators of the

> law. . . . Slavery as a legal institution had gone; but the society
> shaped by slavery remained with its criteria of whiteness, wealth, and
> education (8).

Because she is black, poor, and wanted by the police, Christophine is as powerless to alter the tragic course of Antoinette's life as she is to redress social and political injustice in nineteenth-century Jamaica. But as a narrative device, Christophine represents Jean Rhys's unequivocal assertion of defiance in the face of injustice and coersion. This defiant stance places Jean Rhys in the ranks of other socially committed writers, like Michel Foucault, whose insight into power and its abuses closely parallels Rhys's own, less systematic social theorizing.

Not long before she died, Rhys told novelist David Plante that as a child, living in the small West Indian island of Dominica, she had been called "socialist Gwen" because she had taken the side of the blacks and the workers against the white ruling class. She pleaded with Plante to "tell the truth" in the face of all the lies: "You must tell the truth about them. . . . You must tell the truth against their lies" (50). Rhys's white protagonists are passive victims of society's injustice. But Rhys herself, like Selina Davis and Christophine Dubois, could not be coerced into self-betrayal. In a dialogue with herself, Rhys describes her writing as "dangerous" because of the madness that others perceive in her. "But if everything is in me," she reasons, "good, evil and so on, so must strength be in me if I know how to get at it" (*Smile Please* 133). Strength through knowledge: this is Rhys's legacy to an unjust world.

Rhys intuited that her thought and writing were "dangerous" to the establishment. Foucault, echoing Nietzsche and Artaud, articulates a similar insight when he gives the lie to the myth that "historical consciousness is neutral, devoid of passions, and committed solely to truth." Rather, as a manifestation of "the will to knowledge," historical consciousness "discovers the violence of a position that encourages the dangers of research and delights in disturbing discoveries" ("Nietzsche" 95). Whereas Rhys was implicitly political, Foucault was overtly so. He saw political responsibility as the highest duty of the intellectual, whose task "is to criticize the working of institutions . . . to criticize them in such a manner that the political violence which has always exercised itself obscurely through them will be unmasked, so that one can fight them" (qtd. in Rabinow 6).

Power and powerlessness, discourse and silence, prisoners, patients, and the machinery that keeps society functioning: these are the dominant concerns addressed by Jean Rhys. These are Foucault's concerns as well, and the similarity is significant. Rhys would agree with Foucault that the "battle for truth" is "not a matter of a battle 'on behalf' of truth, but a battle about the status of truth and the economic role it plays" ("Truth and Power" 132). Rhys reveals her own awareness of the arbitrary relationship between truth and power through Christophine's insight into history's succession of dominations, each touting its version of "Truth" and "Letter of the Law."

But the courage and strength exhibited by Christophine and Selina merely emphasize the weakness of Rhys's white protagonists who, though sympathetically portrayed, leave the reader feeling oddly unmoved precisely *because* of their passivity and detachment. Detachment from history is simply the converse of passive submission to it; neither is an adequate response to the social, economic, and cultural challenges that face mankind. Rhys accepted the challenge by writing "dangerous" books. Had she shirked her responsibility; Rhys felt that she would "not have earned death" (*Smile Please* 133). Moreover, she would not have earned a place next to Nietzsche, Artaud, Foucault, and other radical thinkers who dared to challenge the comforting lies, passing as articles of faith, that throughout history have drawn the line between those who dominate and those who are dominated.

Bruner, Charlotte H. "A Caribbean Madness: Half Slave and Half Free." *Canadian Review of Comparative Literature* 11 (1984): 236-248.

Davidson, Arnold E. *Jean Rhys*. New York: Ungar, 1985.

Emery, Mary Lou. "The Politics of Form: Jean Rhys's Social Vision in *Voyage in the Dark* and *Wide Sargasso Sea*." *Twentieth Century Literature* 28 (1982): 418-430.

Foucault, Michel. "Nietzsche, Genealogy, History." Rabinow 76-100.

_____. "Truth and Power." Rabinow 51-75.

Fulton, Nancy J. Casey. "Jean Rhys's *Wide Sargasso Sea*: Exterminating the White Cockroach." *Revista Interamericana* 4 (1974): 340-349.

Hall, Douglas. "The Colonial Legacy in Jamaica." *New World Quarterly* 4.3 (1968): 7-22.

Harris, Wilson. "The Question of Form and Realism in the West Indian Artist." *Tradition, the Writer and Society*. London: New Beacon, 1967. 13-20.

James, Louis. "Sun Fire — Painted Fire: Jean Rhys as a Caribbean Novelist." *ARIEL* 8 (1977): 111-127.

Lai, Wally Look. "The Road to Thornfield Hall." Rev. of *Wide Sargasso Sea*. *New world Quarterly* 4.2 (1968): 17-27.

Plante, David. *Difficult Women. A Memoir of Three*. New York: Atheneum, 1983.

Rabinow, Paul, ed. *The Foucault Reader*. New York: Pantheon, 1984.

_____. Introduction. Rabinow 3-29.

Ramchand, Kenneth. *The West Indian Novel and Its Background*. 2nd ed. London: Heinemann, 1983.

Rhys, Jean. "Let Them Call it Jazz." 1960. *Tigers are Better-Looking*. New York: Penguin, 1981.

_____. *Smile Please: An Unfinished Autobiography*. Berkeley: Creative Arts/Ellis, 1979.

_____. *Voyage in the Dark*. 1934. New York: Penguin, 1980.

_____. *Wide Sargasso Sea*. 1966. New York: Penguin, 1980.

Staley, Thomas F. *Jean Rhys: A Critical Study*. Austin: U. of Texas P. 1979.

Tiffin, Helen, "Mirror and Mask: Colonial Motif in the Novels of Jean Rhys." *World Literature Written in English* 17 (1978): 328-341.

Wolfe, Peter. *Jean Rhys*. Boston: Twayne, 1980.

# JEAN RHYS AND THE GENIUS OF IMPRESSIONISM

*Todd K. Bender*

Although Ford Madox Ford was deeply troubled in 1924 by the financial collapse of his international literary magazine *Transatlantic* and by Conrad's death, followed by the attack of Jessie Conrad on Ford's memoir of his friend, he was at the height of his creative power, engaged in writing the Tietjens Tetralogy. Living rather extravagantly with Stella Bowen in Paris, he met the beautiful young actress and author Jean Rhys. Jean Rhys had grown up in the West Indies, daughter of a Creole mother and Welsh doctor. Ford and Stella asked Jean to live with them, so that Ford could help her with her literary work. The relationship between Jean Rhys and Ford soon became intimate, "entangling" in his eyes, and Stella and Ford arranged for Jean to leave Paris to work as a translator in the south of France.

What was a casual episode in Ford's generally untidy life was far more painful for the impoverished young woman. If we can take her fiction as a reasonable representation of the affair, Jean Rhys records in *Postures* and *After Leaving Mr. Mackenzie* a very unsavory picture of her former friends, Ford and Stella. If after all these years she still feels wounded, it must have been some gratification for her to be hailed by *The New York Times* as the greatest living novelist on the occasion of the publication of *Wide Sargasso Sea* (1966), an evaluation that could not have been made of Ford himself, except perhaps in an autobiographical vein. And yet, *Wide Sargasso Sea* owes much to Ford and his fellow impressionists and deserves to stand with impressionist masterpieces like *Heart of Darkness, Lord Jim,* and *The Good Soldier.*

*Wide Sargasso Sea* originates in Charlotte Brontë's *Jane Eyre* (1847). Jane is prevented from marrying Rochester because he has hidden away a mad West Indian wife, called Antoinette or Bertha, who finally perishes in the fire which she sets, burning down Rochester's ancestral home and blinding him. Only after the conflagration can Jane and Rochester be united. It is easy to see why Jean Rhys, a poor alien, feeling betrayed by the English and apparently wealthy (or at least middle class) Stella and Ford, might find her personal anxieties embedded in Charlotte Brontë's work, so that she casts herself vaguely in the role of the alien West Indian woman deprived of her man's love. The contemporary reader may smile at the idea of Ford Madox Ford playing the role of Rochester, but for Jean Rhys it was no joke. In *Jane Eyre* the West Indian wife is shown entirely from the

75

exterior, and she lurks as a fearsome dark presence in Rochester's house. Seen mainly through his eyes or those of the English rival, she naturally takes on a hideousness altogether unbearable. In these words Rochester reveals her existence (in Chapter XVI): "Bertha Mason is mad; and she came of a mad family; — idiots and maniacs through three generations! — as I found out after I had wed the daughter: for they were silent on family secrets before. Bertha, like a dutiful child, copied her parent in both points." When Jane looks on the madwoman she sees: "In the deep shade, at the further end of the room, a figure ran backwards and forwards. What it was, whether beast or human being, one could not, at first sight, tell; it grovelled, seemingly, on all fours; it snatched and growled like some strange wild animal; but it was covered with clothing; and a quantity of dark, grizzled hair, wild as a mane, hid its head and face." The "hyena" with "bloated features" attacks Rochester in this scene, biting his cheek before being subdued.

*Wide Sargasso Sea* is the sympathetic history of this madwoman from her youth in the West Indies until the moment when she takes her candle to fire Rochester's home. Much of the tale is told in the stream of consciousness technique, looking through the eyes of Antoinette. On the simplest level, we can imagine *Wide Sargasso Sea* as an attempt to render justice, to present the alien woman's point of view and plead her case, or to explain plausibly how she and her husband have got to the sorry state evident in *Jane Eyre*.

Part I of *Wide Sargasso Sea* is narrated by Antoinette, who was growing up in Jamaica shortly after the Emancipation Act was passed. Rejected by both the black community and the white in a state where civil disorder and violence are common, she lives in isolation and constant fear, impoverished on the crumbling estate of her widowed mother. Her companion is Christophine, a Martinique obeah woman, a voodoo witch. Her mother remarries, to a Mr. Mason, and their fortunes improve temporarily until the blacks revolt, burning her beloved home, Coulibri, and killing her half-witted brother. In town, she goes to a convent school, and a colored "cousin" Sandi protects her from more hostile blacks.

Part II of the tale shifts to young Rochester as narrator on the honeymoon trip to their country estate. Following the details of the fictive "reality" outlined by Charlotte Brontë, he reveals how his marriage to Antoinette was arranged for financial reasons. After a period of uneasy passion, Rochester receives a denunciation of Antoinette from another half-caste colored "cousin," Daniel Cosway, who accuses her of incipient madness and unchaste behavior with Sandi. As Rochester's doubts grow, Antoinette gets a love potion from Christophine. True to its nature, the charm works for one night only. Antoinette, her future now in Rochester's control and surrounded by hostility, is torn away from her native land, transported to England, to confinement, and to her suicidal act.

Clearly, Jean Rhys saw that Brontë's presentation of the evil madwoman and the completely dead love of Rochester demanded a more fully fleshed, more rounded treatment. Reading her work, we "see round" Antoinette in a new way. Our sympathy comes in to play and we are much more aware of the limitations of Brontë's Rochester. Those shortcomings in Jane Eyre's future husband are cu-

riously ignored in Brontë's novel. Bringing Jean Rhys' characterizations to bear
on Brontë's not only develops the blank character Antoinette, but converts
Rochester into a much more interesting, equivocal figure. It counteracts his
flatness in Brontë's version and questions the nature of Jane's judgment. "Why
is Jane so uncritical of Rochester?" we ask as we turn from *Wide Sargasso Sea*
to *Jane Eyre*.

It is not unusual for a novelist to base his story on another writer's fiction.
George Macdonald Fraser's *Flashman* (1970), for instance purports to follow the
career of the the villain of *Tom Brown's Schooldays* (1856), showing that he is
the veritable hero of Victorian Imperialism. T. H. White's *Mistress Masham's
Repose* (1946) treats Swift's Lilliputians rediscovered by an English schoolgirl
as a paradigm for colonial paternalism in England.Jean Rhys similarly raises
issues latent in Brontë's work: the English suspicion and fear of foreigners and
the male domination of English society and wealth. But her work has a much more
intimate connection with its prototype than does Fraser's or White's. *Mistress
Masham's Repose*, altogether a charming story, does not alter our reading of
*Gulliver's Travels* (1726). But once we have read *Wide Sargasso Sea*, we can
never again read *Jane Eyre* in quite the same way. This power to read into the past
and *transform* the nature of previous text is the mark of high critical power which
*Wide Sargasso Sea* derives from the theory of literary impressionism as practiced
by Ford and Conrad in their best work.

Ford's memoir *Joseph Conrad: A Personal Remembrance*, completed in some
sixty days in late 1924, is bound to be misunderstood if the reader expects
"historical accuracy." Like Ford's Fifth Queen Trilogy, *Joseph Conrad* is better
seen as fiction with a historical setting. The reality of Henry VIII does not suffer
in these novels although Ford made up for him speeches which are clearly
fictions. So, too, Conrad's real existence is independent of the obvious fictions
in the memoir constructed by his devoted friend. The author who uses fiction to
"bring to life" a character does homage to that figure whether it be Henry VIII,
Joseph Conrad, or Charlotte Brontë's Bertha Mason. When Ford claims that he
and Conrad were the vanguard of literary impressionism in England, it does not
entirely discredit his claim to show that much of *Joseph Conrad* is invented. In
any case, Ford's explanation of the nature of their art may illuminate our
knowledge of their work. *Joseph Conrad* shows us how a character can be
vitalized and at the same time tells us the nature of that creative process.

In *Joseph Conrad*, Ford depicts the act of creating impressionist fiction.
Impressionist writers aim to record the way impressions impinge on consciousness to make that "shimmering haze" which is life, and they try to control and
manipulate the constructive activity of their audience as it registers an impression
of their work, much like a pointillist canvas by Seurat. The pointillist canvas
actually is covered with separate dots of color; only the fusion on the retina of the
observer's eye creates the color and shape of the picture. To accomplish such
aims, impressionist fictions typically utilize an "affair" as plot, limited "unreliable" narration, and "psychological" structures of time and space, so as to require

a constructive activity from each reader. This is the formula to which *Wide Sargasso Sea* is written.

The "affair" at the center of *Wide Sargasso Sea* is Antoinette's insane, suicidal conflagration, an event which has already "happened," like Jim's abandonment of the Patna in *Lord Jim*, the disintegration of the foursome in *The Good Soldier*, or the death of Kurtz in *Heart of Darkness*. The story progresses in widening circles of understanding as the reader sees the scene through the eyes of one or more witnesses and tries to judge what the "facts" of the case may be. In such stories the reader struggles with multiple, limited, unreliable narrations in order to deduce and judge the true state of affairs. The plot is open to multiple, contradictory interpretations. Was Antoinette guilty of unchaste acts with Sandi? Or is she mad and only imagining such scenes? Is the voodoo charm of Christophine "really" magic? Or is it, as Rochester thinks, just poison? When Rochester confronts Christophine and says, "I would give my eyes never to have seen this abominable place," is Christophine "really" a witch when she replies, "And that's the first damn word of truth you speak."[2] Is all of *Jane Eyre* nothing but the working out of voodoo curse? A curse pronounced in another book?

Since the story is told in limited narration, it follows psychological processes of the speaker — in Antoinette's case, the mental processes of an incipient madwoman. What is fictive reality, what demented vision? The story shifts freely from fictive reality to fantasy. For example, at the end of *Wide Sargasso Sea*, the madwoman Antoinette describes, in detail which corresponds point for point to Brontë's description, her setting fire to the house and perishing in the flames despite Rochester's efforts to save her. The reader has no reason to suspect that these paragraphs are not fictive reality until she says she "woke" to find her nurse, Grace Poole, watching her. She says, "I must have been dreaming" (p.190). But now she knows what she must do and within a few lines she takes up the candle to enact, presumably, the vision she has just "dreamed." As in the fiction of Robert Coover, the unwary reader is soon entangled in a hopelessly confused web of shifting levels of "reality" in the tale.

The audience is forced into a constructive role in impressionism and becomes intensely involved in the work of art when the limited unreliable narrators give the audience such suggestive, tangled glimpses of the affair. This structure gives the author a tool for creating a very strong emotional response in his readers. The artist cannot represent all possible impressions and associations of the mind. He must choose to present some and to suppress others from his writing. Ford insists that the whole of art consists of this selection. The principles of selection are therefore what distinguishes art from chaos. The author must, of course, choose to render only those impressions which carry the story forward or interest the reader, but the most important principle for selection is to seek what Ford in *The March of Literature* calls the "unearned increment":

> Impressionism began with the — perhaps instinctive — discovery . . . that the juxtaposition of the composed renderings of two or more unexaggerated actions or situations may be used to estab-

lish, like the juxtaposition of vital word to vital word, a sort of frictional current of electric life that will extraordinarily galvanize the work of art in which the device is employed. . . . Let us put it more concretely by citing the algebraic truth that $(a + b)^2$ equals not merely $a^2 + b^2$ plus an apparently unearned increment called $2ab$ plus the expected $b^2$. . . . The point cannot be sufficiently labored, since the whole fabric of modern art depends on it.[3]

Through the structure of a past affair reported in the fictive present by limited unreliable dramatic speakers, the impressionist writer forces his audience into a constructive role, like a jury, building up the story in its own mind. But merely to use the word "unreliable" shows how the impressionist writer tricks us. In a courtroom a witness is called unreliable when his report does not match the event he describes, perhaps because he is dishonest or does not know the facts. But a fiction is different; there is no real event reported by its speakers. We could compare a reader of fiction to a jury in a schematic way and see that where a jury tries to find "reality," the reader of fiction is forced to construct a second, unstated fiction:

### Schematic Representation

| *Real Event* | *Real Reporter* | *Real Jury* |
|---|---|---|
| 1. Real Accident | 2. Witness | 3. Decides whether witness' report matches event |
| *Unstated Fiction* | *Stated Fiction* | *Constructed Fiction* |
| 1. Unstated fictional event, the affair | 2. "unreliable" narrator's report | 3. Audience constructs what it imagines unstated fiction to be |

In reality the jury's judgment that a report is unreliable means that it does not correspond to the real event. In fiction the "unreliable" report means a story so constructed as to force the reader into a constructive activity, perhaps because the fiction as stated has internal contradictions or seems incomplete. Some "unreliable" narrations can be "solved." Mystery stories often have a single, clear-cut answer. But many fiction defy solutions, and platoons of clever literary scholars feel called upon the construct conflicting versions of the basic meaning of the work.

*Wide Sargasso Sea* supplies the second term of a collage creating what Ford calls an "unearned increment." Brontë's version of Antoinette and Rochester is A, Rhys's is B, but the two in conjunction are more significant than either separately. *Jane Eyre* is a "closed" fiction. The reader does not read it a second time with the same interest as at the first reading. Like a mediocre mystery or detective story, it is solved, "used up," in a single reading. We discover "who done it." The dark shape in Rochester's house is revealed and purged. Jane and Rochester are to live happily ever after. Contrast such a "closed" plot to that of an "open" fiction like *Villette*. In this instance, the second reading is of the same quality as the first, for the same questions remain. In *Wide Sargasso Sea* Jean Rhys has "opened" *Jane Eyre* by altering the reader's relationship to the text. *Wide Sargasso Sea* may be a misreading of *Jane Eyre*, but it creatively shifts the reader's activity in an important way and this alteration is accomplished through the techniques of literary impressionism.

The general situation of Rochester's alien wife recurs frequently in Jean Rhys's works. For example in *Good Morning, Midnight* one of Sasha Jansen's gentlemen friends tells her of an incident that happened when he was living in a room near Notting Hill Gate in London. Hearing an eerie cry in the passage outside his room, he finds a half-Negro woman lying weeping on the floor. She tells him she is from Martinique. She was living with an Englishman on the top floor of the house, but for two years she had not gone out of her room except after dark. She finally ventures forth and meets a little English girl on the stairs who says she is dirty, smells bad, and has no right to be in the house. The child says, "I hate you and I wish you were dead." The mulatto woman drinks a whole bottle of whiskey and falls drunk in the hallway. The hatred of the women in the house after that is unbearable. Another example: in the short story "Let Them Call It Jazz," the West Indian Selina lives at Notting Hill Gate until her money is stolen. Temporarily given shelter by a man in an ancient decaying house, she lives in isolation, until through the hostility of her English neighbors she is sent to prison for disorderly conduct. While in Holloway prison, she hears a woman confined to the punishment cells, high in a turret, sing the "Holloway Song" letting her fellow prisoners know that she is equal to the ordeal. When Selina is released, she sings the song for a musician who turns it into a trivial jazz tune. In such stories, an alien, half-white, West Indian woman is emotionally and financially dependent on an Englishman, who abandons her to the prejudice and hostility of English society. She is confined to a room in a Gothic structure, misunderstood, drinks heavily, and is goaded to self-destructive activity.

Once we have defined a general pattern for works overtly similar to *Wide Sargasso Sea*, we can see that there is a basic similarity in *all* the fiction by Jean Rhys. She tells the same tale over and over, a powerful feminist plea. All of her stories are about the indignity, the personal damage, which flows from a woman's financial and emotional dependence on men in an alien world. In a society where she is systematically denied the right of self-sufficing employment, what can a woman do to maintain her freedom? Perhaps only symbolic gestures are possible. In *Good Morning, Midnight*, for example, Sasha Jansen refuses to be brought by men and refuses to buy herself a gigolo. In the concluding scene, in order to avoid rape, she tells a man to take whatever money she has from her dresser drawer and get out. When he has left, she finds that he has not, in fact taken all her money. As she lies alone in the darkness, in a collage of hallucination and fictive reality, she imagines him returning to her bed, and opens the door for him, only to receive the truly slimy man in a dressing gown who lurks in the hotel corridor. It is a bitter ending for an incredibly bitter book. It perhaps could be argued that the area of female freedom is so narrow, so limited, that only such a choice seems to Jean Rhys free from the taint of the marketplace in European society.

The main theme of her later fiction is stated in her first book, a collection of impressionist sketches, *The Left Bank* (1927). Ford Madox Ford wrote in the preface for this work that he wanted to be associated with it because "hundreds of years hence" when "her ashes are translated to the Panthéon, in the voluminous pall . . . a grain or so of my scattered and forgotten dust may go in too, in the folds."[4] Ironically, his prophecy may turn out to be more nearly true than he expected in 1927. In these early stories, especially in such pieces as "Mannequin," the central idea of Rhys's later fiction is virtually complete. The female is given by society a limited number of roles to play. She is paid or rewarded only when she plays these roles to perfection: each of the twelve mannequins in the dress shop knows her type and keeps to it, "Babbette, the gamine, the traditional blonde enfant: Mona, tall and darkly beautiful, the femme fatale, the wearer of sumptuous evening gowns. Georgette was the garçonne. . ." (p. 163). At the conclusion of the story there is a surrealistic tinge to the evening as all the mannequins come out of their shops and make the pavements gay as beds of flowers before the girls are swallowed up in the night of Paris. But if a story like "Mannequin" looks ahead to the theme of her later fiction, it also looks back to the great dramatic poems of the Victorian period, like Browning's *Men and Women*.

The formula that Browning exploits in his dramatic monologues is to create a tension between the reader's sympathy and his judgment of a character. Typically, Browning does so by taking a strongly stereotyped character and giving us a view of inner feelings and motives which contradict the stereotype. For this reason he is particularly fond of depicting churchmen who have natural impulses at odds with their public roles, like the Bishop at St. Praxed's, Fra Lippo Lippi, and Bishop Blougram. Bishop Blougram explains Browning's characterization when he asserts that he will always be interesting because he is an enigma, a man who knows about skepticism yet believes with the faith of a true bishop. How can he exist within the confines of his public role? He says such characters will eternally hold our interest:

> The honest thief, the tender murderer
> The superstitious atheist, demirep
> That loves and saves her soul in New French book—
> We watch while these in equilibrium keep
> The giddy line midway; one step aside,
> They're classed and done with. I, then, keep the line
> Before your sages, — just the men to shrink
> From gross weights, coarse scales and labels broad
> You offer their refinement. Fool or knave,
> Why needs a bishop be a fool or knave

When there's a thousand diamond weights between?

All of Jean Rhys's fiction has as its central figure a strong female stereotype, a mannequin of one kind or another, cast in some role thrust on woman by society. Then, like Browning's monologues, her work lets us into the interior of the character and sets up a contradictory, crossed purpose, showing us that the stereotype is painful to play. For example, the short story "Illusion" depicts Miss Bruce, tall, thin, a shining example of what "British character and training" (p. 151) can do for a woman. In Paris, surrounded by the cult of the beauty and love, she is always severe, sensibly dressed in "neat tweed costume in winter, brown shoes with low heels and cotton stockings" (p. 152). Miss Bruce suddenly falls ill, and the narrator of the tale enters her flat to get some necessities for her in hospital. When she opens Miss Bruce's wardrobe she finds a "glow of colour, a riot of soft silks . . . everything that one did not expect" (p. 153). Evidently the clothes are never worn, but indicate that the sensible Miss Bruce is afflicted "with the perpetual hunger to be beautiful and that thirst to be loved which is the real curse of Eve" (p. 154). Miss Bruce is shown acutely embarrassed that her friend knows she collects clothes, and she asserts at the conclusion of the story that she never would make such a fool of herself as actually to wear them. The reader finds such characters fascinating for the same reasons as he does Browning's church-men. How can the Bishop at St. Praxed's, with all his love of luxury and the pleasures of the senses, play the role of ascetic? How can Miss Bruce, with her streak of feminine longing for soft, bright fabrics, play the role of the sensible British woman? The core of such characters is repression. At what cost must Miss Bruce's love of clothes be repressed? At what cost must Bishop Blougram combat his skeptical thoughts or St. Praxed's Bishop his sensuality?

This is, of course, the pattern of Conrad's *Lord Jim* as well. Such characteri-zation produces split figures. *doppelgänger*. As in a morality play, the good or socially approved type struggles with a bad or disapproved tendency. One pole is the repressed type, the other is the freedom of personal inclination. Failure to repress the personality results in social ostracism, loss of affection, incarceration, madness. All of Jean Rhys's heroines are trying to be "good girls," but find it impossible to fit into the stereotype. They are forced to "misbehave" socially and sexually, to drink excessively, to commit all sorts of excesses," until they are disgraced. Many readers will see in *Jane Eyre* a similar split in the central character. Jane herself is the heroine of repression, control, decency. Her dark twin lurking in Rochester's home is the mad, unrepressed, licentious West Indian. Only when the dark woman is burned out, can Jane unite with Rochester. Jane effects purgation through intense suffering and British schooling, elements which Jean Rhys shows as unacceptable to Antoinette. Rather than killing the dark, sensual, loose shadow in order to become the prim governess and wife, Antoinette overpowers the stereotype and rages destructively against the re-straints of British customs. No reader doubts that Antoinette must be judged to fail in fitting into British expectations, but the real sympathy for her lies in her questioning the cultural assumptions on which the stereotypes of British female decency are built. In the light of Jean Rhys's fiction, the madwoman is the true heroine, not the submissive Jane Eyre.

Many of Jean Rhys's stories involve deviations from normal perception, such as hallucinations induced by extreme pain or suffering, drunkenness, or madness. Such scenes raise questions about what is normal, what is normative in the fiction. What are the bases for the reader's formation of judgments? For instance, in *Voyage in the Dark*, the heroine is a young West Indian who hates England and is forced to tour as a chorus girl to earn a pittance. An older, wealthy Englishman, Walter, keeps her as his mistress. A climax of the novel occurs when the heroine and Walter spend a weekend in the country with his friend Vincent, a sneering young man, and Vincent's girlfriend, Germaine. They reveal that Walter is about to leave for America for several months; then they ask how old the heroine is and where Walter met her. She replies that she was in a show in Southsea. Vincent jokingly asks Walter what he was doing on a pier in Southsea, and the three English people begin to laugh. The heroine does not understand what they are laughing at. The others ignore her when she asks them to explain the joke. Suddenly, she grinds her lighted cigarette into the back of Walter's hand. The act is as mad and destructive as Antoinette's blinding Rochester by fire. It is self-destructive as well; because, from that episode on, Walter is set on deserting her. But the act of burning Walter's hand seems crazy or antisocial only if we do not question the assumptions of the society, if we assume that the laughter of Walter, Vincent, and Germaine is acceptable aggression; whereas, burning his hand is beyond the limits of reasonable action. The thrust of the story, however, is to question that normative framework. It is not so crazy to burn Walter's hand, it is not really incomprehensible that Antoinette burns Rochester's house, provided we are willing to see things from their side.

Many critics feel that a major value of literature lies in the exploration of human values embodied in social behavior. When the traditional roles and patterns of behavior available to individuals in a society seem unacceptable, fictions allow us to examine possible ways to fit our desires to traditional expectations. Many fictions present characters with a possible choice, such as marriage. We can ask three questions about the character's possible behavior: is it approved by society? is it profitable? is it desired by the individual? If the answer to all three questions is "yes," there is no need to write a novel. On the other hand, if the answer to one of the questions is "no," we have the formula for literally thousands of fictional works analysing how to reconcile approved and profitable behavior with the desired. Both Jean Rhys and Charlotte Brontë personally lived through this kind of conflict between social roles available to them and their contrary desires. Both can claim to be more than ephemeral writers, because they give serious exploration in fiction to such conflict.

A frequent question about *Wide Sargasso Sea* is: does this novel work independently of *Jane Eyre* or does it perhaps simply cannibalize the work of Brontë? It would appear that no novel can be read entirely "independently" of a literary tradition. It is perhaps better to rephrase the question: can *Wide Sargasso Sea* be read profitably with reference to the general tradition of the nineteenth-century novel, rather than specifically with reference to *Jane Eyre*? The answer to this question is "yes," both on practical and theoretical grounds. Practically, I have worked with many young readers who respond favorably to Rhys's work without suspecting that it refers to Brontë's. Theoretically, we can see that such responses are possible because her work is in the general tradition of the novel of serious social criticism exploring the limitations of available social roles, especially of young women, in Western culture.

Footnotes:

[1] By the imperial parliament in 1833. Slaves became actually free in 1838, after a time of "apprenticeship." —Ed.

[2] *Wide Sargasso Sea* (New York: Norton, 1966), p. 161.

[3] Ford Madox Ford, *The March of Literature*, from *Confucius to Modern Times* (London: George Allen and Unwin, 1947), p. 734.

[4] Ford Madox Ford, "Preface to Stories from *The Left Bank*," rpt. in Jean Rhys, *Tigers are Better-Looking with a selection from the Left Bank* (New York: Harper and Row, 1968), p. 150. Subsequent references to stories by Jean Rhys appear parenthetically to this edition.

# WHISPERS OUTSIDE THE ROOM:
# THE HAUNTED FICTION OF JEAN RHYS

## by Colette Lindroth

An artist whose prose is loaded with political, even revolutionary, implication, Jean Rhys nevertheless eschews direct political statement; a woman whose entire subject is the mistreatment and exploitation of women, she also eschews direct feminist statement. In fact, Rhys avoids any direct statement at all. Hers is the art of hint and indirection, of symbol and suggestion. Her narrative voice speaks to the reader in whispers overhead from just outside the room; her metaphors present glimpses seen at the edges of mirrors, fragments of images that whisk out of sight the instant they are addressed directly. Rhys's fiction is a haunted world.

This lack of direct comment, while it might help to account for the long eclipse of Rhys's reputation, is entirely appropriate to her vision of reality. For the Rhys world is one of pointless, purposeless activity. Going nowhere (and often going there in the dark) and finding nothing when she gets there, the Rhys heroine feels no inclination to make statements. The reader, like the heroine herself, must proceed with no clear destination, making such discoveries as are to be made as she goes along. Nor do these discoveries do the heroine much good. From the maelstrom-lives of Julia Martin (*After Leaving Mr. Mackenzie*) and Anna Morgan (*Voyage in the Dark*) to the becalmed impotence of Bertha Mason (*Wide Sargasso Sea*), the Rhys woman has already given up the fight before the fight begins. Modern, rootless, alienated, rudderless, and valueless, she nevertheless has a core of hard-won identity, a sense of self and privacy that remains unchanged and uncompromised. Refusing to make political statements for the downtrodden or feminist statements for the exploited, Rhys still convinces her reader of the ugliness of social injustice and the validity of feminism.

Much of the unique richness of the Rhys world stems from the hazy ambiguity, the "not-quite-there" quality of her description. Colored by the aimless lives of the characters, the settings blur into sameness. Julia's Parisian lodgings are unforgettably vivid; she lives in a "cheap hotel on the Quai des Grands Augustins, . . . a lowdown sort of place [where] the staircase smelt of the landlady's cats, but the rooms were cleaner than you would have expected." Poverty is poverty, however, whether in Paris or London, and Julia's room in London is indistinguishable from the other: "There were an iron bedstead, an old-fashioned washstand with a tin slop-pail standing by the side of it, and a dressing-table with a wad of newspaper stuck into the frame to keep the glass at the required angle" (*Mackenzie*, 65). One city or another, it makes no difference; neither has any identity, any distinguishing characteristics. In fact, Julia seems to keep any national identity consciously blurred; she frequents "a German restaurant in the Rue Huchette" in Paris and suggests "an Italian" in London (*Mackenzie*, 16, 144). Citizenship in a country, England or France, means nothing. The Rhys woman is a citizen of poverty and the dank, dark, cheerless dwellings to which the poor must always return.

Anna Morgan's circular voyage underlines this fact. As a touring chorus girl forever on the road, she dislikes England, where "the towns . . . always look so exactly alike. you were perpetually moving to another place which was perpetually the same. There was always a little grey street leading to the stage-door of the theatre and another little grey street where your lodgings were . . . [and] a Corporation Street or High Street or Duke Street or Lord Street where you walked about and looked at the shops." Her first bedroom is decorated with a "picture of a little girl in a white dress with a blue sash fondling a woolly dog" (*Voyage*, 8); at the end of the novel, after her voyage has been completed, her new bedroom affirms the same false middle-class cheer: ". . . over the bed the picture of the dog sitting up begging — *Loyal heart*" (*Voyage*, 127). Nothing has changed; Anna has gone through several friendships and several lovers, has traveled from the South Seas to London, from hysteria to despair, but her life is still one of perpetual motion and perpetual sameness. The relentless, dishonest coziness of the prints on her bedroom walls underscores this fact.

That this recurrent setting is meant to reflect the character's spiritual condition is made clear at the end when, desperately ill from a botched abortion, still remembering "the dog in the picture *Loyal Heart*, Anna hears the doctor's reproach of her behavior: "'She'll be all right. . . . Ready to start all over again in no time, I've no doubt'" (*Voyage*, 156, 159).

The correctness of the doctor's conclusion is affirmed by Julia Martin, who has in fact lost her child but who can feel nothing: "'It was just my luck, wasn't it. . . . When you've just had a baby, and it dies for the simple reason that you haven't enough money to keep it alive, it leaves you with a sort of hunger. . . . And then, of course, you've indifferent — because the whole damned thing is too stupid to be anything but indifferent about'" (*Mackenzie*, 111-12). Indifference is the only defense against a pointless, impoverished, exploited existence, Rhys suggests. Since one is voyaging in the dark anyway, what reason is there to struggle?

If the characters are indifferent, however, they are not ignorant of their situation or its meaning. Julia, for example, exists in a kind of limbo at the beginning of *After Leaving Mr. Mackenzie*, subsisting on the largess of a former lover who can hardly be expected to maintain her forever. When she is coldly told, by letter, that "from this date, the weekly allowance will be discontinued," she is frightened but not surprised: "She had always expected that one day they [Mackenzie and his lawyer] would do something like this" (*Mackenzie*, 19). Her foreknowledge does not lead to wisdom, however. Left with a substantial sum of money, she is as purposeless as she was before. She repeatedly tells herself she must "do something" but, losing "all sense of the exact value of the money" (*Mackenzie*, 19), she can only think excitedly of buying extravagant new clothes. Although she contends that "'if you have any money, you can go one way,'" when in fact she does have money she continues to drift, as she has before, "from man to man" (*Mackenzie*, 26). Knowing her behavior is self-destructive does not motivate her to change it; it only gives her the opportunity to comment ironically on herself.

Faced with an imperative need to do something, Julia, predictably, ignores the significance of that need; she turns life into an absurd joke. Urged by her new lover to join him in London, to "take a chance" (*Mackenzie*, 55), Julia decides to leave even that chance up to chance. Waking up in her dreary lodgings, thinking she must get away, she decides, "'If a taxi hoots before I count three, I'll go to London. If not, I won't'" (*Mackenzie*, 57) And off she goes when indeed the taxi does hoot, into a London indistinguishable from Paris, a Mr. Horsfield indistinguishable from Mr. Mackenzie, a life without meaning or future. The novel ends as it began; back in Paris she receives money and a good-bye from Mr. Horsfield — money which, again, she plans to spend on "'a black dress and hat and very dark grey stockings.' . . . A ring with a green stone for the forefinger of her right hand' (*Mackenzie*, 182). Her life is exactly as it was. Her mother's death, her quarrel with her uncle, and her reconciliation with her sister are all matters of indifference. She wants nothing but "to walk somewhere straight ahead" (*Mackenzie*, 187), but even this is impossible. Following that course brings her right back to Mr. Mackenzie — from whom, predictably, she borrows another hundred francs. Like the debris on the Seine she walks beside, her life will move sluggishly one moment, strongly the next; but whatever its pace, it will always be directed by forces outside Julia herself.

Nor is there any doubt in Julia's mind where these directing forces come from. However rarely she speaks of it, Julia always knows that she is a social outcast, a worthless and powerless woman for whom the fight was over before it began. She reflects on Mr. Mackenzie and his lawyer, men whom she finds capable of doing infinite damage to people like her: "Together, the two perfectly represented organized society, in which she had no place and against which she had not a dog's chance" (*Mackenzie*, 22). This society, unlike Julia herself, is very clear about what is important; it "tells you all the time, Get money, get money, get money, or be for ever damned'" (*Mackenzie*, 90). Given that narrow choice, Julia, like Rhys's other women, refuses either to fight or scrabble for money. Forever damned she may be, but it will be by her own choice and on her own terms. What money she gets will be spent on herself, not to make herself presentable to society.

If the idea of life as a maelstrom of aimless movement pervades Rhys's early novels, even that has disappeared by the time of *Wide Sargasso Sea*. Here there is no movement at all, even in response to outside stimuli; here there is only stasis, stagnation, alienation, and madness. Even the point of view, aimless perhaps but still clearly defined as Julia Martin or Anna Morgan, has disappeared, and the reader flounders like the characters themselves with a first-person narrator who is at one moment Antoinette, at another her husband. Even the line between male and female is blurred. The floating point of view plunges the reader into the midst of trouble in the novel's first paragraphs, forcing him to figure out the background as the narrative progesses:

> They say when trouble comes close ranks, and so the white people did. But we were not in their ranks. The Jamaican ladies had never approved of my mother, "because she pretty like pretty self," Christophine said.
>
> She was my father's second wife, far too young for him they thought, and, worse still, a Martinique girl. When I asked her why so few people came to see us, she told me that the road from Spanish Town to Coulibri Estate where we lived was very bad and that road repairing was now a thing of the past. (My father, visitors, horses, feeling safe in bed — all belonged to the past.)[3]

As if piecing together bits of gossip, the reader must puzzle alone for the information behind these statements and attitudes. Why did the white people close ranks against them? Who is Christophine? What is wrong with Martinique girls? Why are road repairs, fathers, safety and comfort all things of the past? What is the reality behind this pervasive anxiety? The questions are never dealt with directly; the reader learns, eventually, that the family's isolation is a result of political action (the emancipation which has freed Jamaican slaves but left Jamaican plantations to rot and ruin), that Christophine is a servant, that the world is cold, haunted, and hostile because there is no longer a place on these islands for the remnants of a savage, slaveholding past. The reader, like the child Antoinette herself, must decipher hints, overheard whispers, snatches of distant conversation, gossip, and speculation to determine the direction of the narrative. The only clear elements are the feelings of fear, threat, alienation, and foreignness, the conviction that whoever this "I" is, she does not belong in her world.

In part 2 the reader has the same task. Without warning, the point of view has shifted; we still listen to an "I" but it is no longer Antoinette. With the first sentence we are again confronted with problems, and again they are formless: "So it was all over, the advance and the retreat, the doubts and hesitations. Everything finished, for better or for worse" (*Sargasso Sea*, 66). Only by referring to his "wife Antoinette" does the new point of view reveal his relationship to what the reader already knows. The sense of impending disaster, of fatalistic paralysis, is clear; any sense of fixed identity is not.

This sense of being adrift is appropriate to the novel's meaning, for it accurately reflects the condition of its characters. Even more than Rhys's other women, Antoinette is a victim's victim. Isolated from her neighbors by her white skin, increasingly estranged from her mother, she moves from alienation to paranoia. Her very identity seems to slip away from her as her name is changed to suit others' needs. When her mother remarries to improve their social and financial situation, she becomes Antoinette Mason, not Cosway; later, Rochester rejects the mother's name of Antoinette to call her by her second name, so that as the novel goes on Antoinette Cosway becomes Bertha Mason without so much as putting up a struggle.

As she loses her name in a meaningless muddle of other people's decisions, so does she first acquire, then lose, her husband and his love. Rochester, himself a victim of his family's greed rather than a free agent, marries her to improve his fortune just as her mother had done. Like everyone else in this Sargasso Sea, he is alienated and threatened; stared at by strange eyes, he loses "the feeling of security" (*Sargasso Sea*, 75) along with any sense of purpose or of fairness. Told with rumor and innuendo that his wife is immoral and an inheritor of madness, Rochester does not question for a moment; he rejects her as suddenly and pointlessly as he had chosen her in the first place. No questions are asked, none answered; caught in their stasis of hatred and suspicion, the characters are incapable of action. Antoinette is urged by Christophine to "pack up and go" when Rochester turns away from her. Paralyzed, she rejects the advice: "'going away to Martinique or England . . . is the lie,' " she insists. " 'Running away . . . is the lie'" (*Sargasso Sea*, 113). So she stays to confront what her passivity now makes inevitable, to sink into the despair and madness, not of an inherited fate but of her own isolation. When she finally does take action, it is the desperate action of annihilation. Holding her candle, she realizes at last " why [she] was brought here and what [she has] to do" (*Sargasso Sea*, 189): burn down the mansion which has become her prison instead of her home. It is appropriate that Bertha, the only Rhys woman to take real initiative, can achieve only death and destruction by her action.

Perhaps the most revealing aspect of *Wide Sargasso Sea* is the fact that in it Rhys chooses to develop characters presented very differently in Charlotte' Brontë's *Jane Eyre*. The difference in emphasis and significance in the two novels is dramatic. Both Brontë and Rhys deal with social injustice and the issues of feminism, but they present them in an entirely different ethical world. Clearly, Brontë sees a world in which, however gross the injustice, remedies exist and the individual has value. Good is good, evil is evil in *Jane Eyre*; Jane's sacrifices, her courage, her passionate espousal of virtue and justice win out in the end and Jane triumphs. She begins as a victim but moves purposefully, guided only by her own strong conscience, to success and reward. For Rhys's characters, good and evil are indistinguishable. Behavior is unmotivated and incomprehensible, humanity mysterious and opaque, misfortune inevitable. Struggle is useless since there is no place like Brontë's neat, orderly English countryside where justice can triumph. Jamaica is a lost Eden whose false perfection was based on social injustice to begin with, and England is a cold "cardboard house where I [Bertha] walk at night" (*Sargasso Sea*, 181). The struggle which gains so much for Jane would be useless here.

Yet Rhys's novels suggest more than stagnation and muddle. Despite the aimless lives her characters lead, despite the ambiguous world they live in, the women themselves — strong, clever, often witty, aware of their predicament but too shrewd to struggle against it. In the maelstrom of their lives, one constant remains: themselves. This sense of identity, of a self which can be relied on when nothing else can be, provides Rhys with some of her most powerful metaphors. Swept along by the maelstrom, her characters stop to look, not at the chaos around them, but into mirrors — at themselves. After her mother's death, Julia stands "under a lamp-post and powders her face" in her compact mirror, arranging a mask under which to hide her feelings. Later, after her life has come completely apart, she stands in the room from which she is being evicted, making "an involuntary little grimace" at her reflection in the glass while she straightens her hat (*Mackenzie*, 125, 171). Even Antoinette, in a nightmarish image in which she sees "'two enormous rats, as big as cats'" looking at her in her room, can stare them down when she sees herself "'in the looking-glass [on] the other side of the room'" (*Sargasso Sea*, 82).

The essential thing for the Rhys woman is not moral triumph but survival, in a day-to-day fight she cannot win but in which she means to conduct herself honorably: the carefully applied make-up, the carefully adjusted hat, and the reassurance of a self looking back from the glass provide her with a mask behind which she can protect the core of her own existence. Julia herself understands this. She praises a picture "'by a man called Modigliani'" of a woman whose face is "'like a mask. . . . The eyes were blank, like a mask but when you had looked at it a bit it was as if you were looking at a real woman, a live woman'" (*Mackenzie*, 52). With this image Rhys captures the genius of her own elusive prose style. Her characters at first seem blank, as if they are wearing masks; when you look at them a bit, however, you discover the real woman underneath. In the end, her enigmatic presentation is more memorable and powerful than any direct statement could be.

Footnotes:

[1] Jean Rhys, *After Leaving Mr. Mackenzie* (1931; reprint, New York: Harper & Row, 1982), 1. All further references to this work appear in the text.

[2] Jean Rhys, *Voyage in the Dark* (1934; reprint, New York: Penguin Books 1982), 8. All further references to this work appear in the text.

[3] Jean Rhys, *Wide Sargasso Sea* (1966; reprint, New York: W.W. Norton & Co., 1982), 1. All further references to this work appear in the text.

# III. THE WORKS OF JEAN RHYS

# THE WORKS OF JEAN RHYS

According to Roland Barthes, criticism can be regarded as a dialogue between two histories and two subjectivities (*Essais critiques* 255). In the case of Jean Rhys criticism, the histories and subjectivities are European (or American) and West Indian; the dialogue is between Jean Rhys, an author who straddles these two worlds, and critics who belong to either, or, like Rhys, to both. In analyzing her works these critics not only address the discipline of language and technique, but align themselves with either sensibility depending on their vantage point. This explains the polarity which, for the most part, characterizes the criticism of Rhys's fiction and the fact that the majority of critics from the Caribbean who wrote about Jean Rhys chose to address *Wide Sargasso Sea*, Rhys's novel entirely set in the West Indies. The essays in this section represent both points of view.

The sub-division of this section into genres allows for comprehensive coverage of Jean Rhys's fiction, giving the general reader and/or student of Rhys a convenient overview of it. The overwhelming majority of articles on Rhys centers on the same three areas, the plight of the under-dog, the alienation of the white creole, and the autobiographical aspect of her work at the expense of its artistic dimension. In order to be of more value to the reader, the essays chosen for this section present a variety of critical approaches, thematic, psychological, and structural. Finally, by complementing the preceding section, devoted to insights into the general literary canon of Rhys, the focus on individual works in this third and last part not only offers a comprehensive analysis of Rhys's oeuvres, but also suggests new areas of investigation and/or the expansion of traditional ones. It fulfills the purpose of this *Critical Perspectives on Jean Rhys*, which is to afford the general reader as well as scholars and serious readers a convenient way to have within reach a variety of insights and evaluations available only through the time-consuming process of combing through periodicals and books and searching for articles not readily available.

# THE WORLD OF JEAN RHYS'S SHORT STORIES

## by A. C. Morrell

Jean Rhys's world, as seen in her three volumes of short stories, is a unified one. In every story a central consciousness, whether narrator, implied narrator, or protagonist, perceives and responds to reality in essentially the same terms. Rhys has said of her work: "I start to write about something that has happened or is happening to me, but somehow or other things start changing."[1] One might argue that thus is all fiction forged. But in Rhys's work, the autobiographical beginnings are responsible for this central consciousness which we may take to be Rhys's own; the other things that "start changing" are her patternings of women's experiences into a coherent world-view. Rhys is not at all interested in creating individual characters. She does create again and again a society of types acting out the attitudes and assumptions which keep that society intact. Her stories have the strong cumulative effect of a sorrowful, scornful anatomy of essential evil.

I will examine the four stories "In a Café," "Goodbye Marcus, Goodbye Rose," "Till September Petronella," and "I Used to Live Here Once." These range from the beginning to the most recent part of Rhys's writing career; they are set variously in Paris, Dominica, London and the English countryside; they include her two modes, i.e., episode and complete story; the last three show stages in the development of Rhys's typical female character from childhood to adulthood to late middle age; and these four together outline the ideas and themes which comprise Rhys's work. With the exception of the first, "In a Café," in which the narrator is a cynical observer of what Rhys later explores in depth, each portrays a central consciousness struggling to fulfill her desires or reaching out for understanding from others. She fails and is failed by them. She subsides into the only attitude or role she is allowed as others reject or merely use her. By the end of each story, the social order, in which outcasts are necessary to carry the burden of guilt for the rest, has been perpetuated.

Stories like "In a Café" make up the bulk of the 1927 *The Left Bank* volume and were not chosen for republication in the 1968 *Tigers are Better-Looking* or the 1976 *Sleep It Off, Lady*. Stories in the later volumes are less scornful, more detailed and sympathetic analyses. However, "In a Café" is a good early example of Rhys's central consciousness as observer rather than participant, it fully prefigures her later arrangements of ideas, and it is skillfully wrought.

In this café, the musicians are "middle-aged, staid," and go wonderfully well with the café itself.[2] They are capable of playing in "the serene classic heights of Beethoven and Massenet." The patrons are dignified whether they are business men with their "neat women in neat hats," or artistic types accompanied by "temperamental ladies . . . [wearing] turbans;" the atmosphere is peaceful and conduces to philosophic conversation. The alliance of respectable manners and religious certainty is made plain in this satiric comment:

> . . . The atmosphere of a place that always had been and always would be, the dark leather benches symbols of something perpetual and unchanging, the waiters, who were all old, ambling round with drinks or blotters, as if they had done nothing else since the beginnings of time and would be content so to do till the day of Judgement.

Into this eternity of calm steps a vulgar Hermes, ancient phallic pillar and artificer of music, to sing about the "grues" of Paris. His song is accompanied by the piano in a "banal, moving imitation of passion;" it tells the pathetic story of the making of a "grue", of her warm-heartedness, finally of the despicable, now decorously married, hero who passes her by in the street when she is reduced to utmost misery. The patrons are embarrassed: women look into their mirrors and rouge their lips; men drink their beers thirstily and look sideways. The song is applauded tumultuously. This jolting of the habitual world of the café is brief. A calm, self-assured, fair-haired American girl buys two copies of the song. The staid, respectable atmosphere is resumed with the request for the American song, "Mommer loves Popper. Popper loves Mommer," the title of which the pianist chalks up "for all the world to see."

This is Jean Rhys's world. The implied contrast between the two songs is ironic. The singer cares as little for the "grues" as do the café patrons. Like a pimp, he capitalizes upon the economic condition of certain unfortunate women, and upon the "necessities" of monied, respectable men. As prostitutes are not mentioned in polite circles, he has caused a tremor of guilty unease certain to sell his song. The idea of the "grues" has been again sentimentally indulged; the individual woman is still invisible. Conventional sentiment is restored with "Mommer loves Popper" — the world goes on.

"Goodbye Marcus, Goodbye Rose" is part of the latest, 1976, volume *Sleep It Off, Lady*. It relates an episode in twelve-year-old Phoebe's life. An elderly Englishman, Captain Cardew, intrudes himself into her peaceful childhood world of Dominica, shattering her secure illusions and providing her with new ones. Until his wife Edith objects to his friendship with the child, and they return to England, Captain Cardew rids himself of a temptation by giving in to it.[3] He first clamps his hand around "one very small breast," remarking, "Quite old enough." Subsequently while walking with Phoebe he restricts himself to:

> . . . ceaseless talk of love, various ways of making love, various sorts of love. He'd explain that love was not kind and gentle, as she had imagined, but violent. Violence, even cruelty, was an essential part of it. He would expand on this, it seemed to be his favourite subject.

During the narrative section of the story, Phoebe's response to all this is confused. She is pleased to be taken for walks by Captain Cardew because he treats her "as though she were a grown-up girl." She is perfectly passive under his onslaught. She remains still when the Captain grabs her breast, thinking only that he is making a great mistake, is being absentminded, and will take his hand away without really noticing what he's done. She says nothing about the incident. Nobody would believe her, or if they did, she'd be blamed. She knows he ought not to talk as he does to her, is shocked and fascinated, but cannot bring herself to speak, afraid that she will only manage "babyishly 'I want to go home.'" Phoebe is caught between two worlds, neither of which is secure: in the familiar world of childhood, she will be blamed for wrongdoing; in the "adult" world of Captain Cardew she fears not being "quite old enough." This paralysis lasts until the Cardews leave the island. Alone, Phoebe attempts to make sense of her experience.

The progression of Phoebe's thoughts, which form the conclusion of the story, is startling in its inexorable rejection of everything she has believed or been heretofore. The stars are no longer her "familiar jewels" but are "cold, infinitely far away, quite indifferent." Sure that Captain Cardew behaved as he did because he "knew" she was not a good girl, she examines ideas of wickedness. Wasn't it more difficult to be wicked than good? Didn't Mother Sacred Heart say "that Chastity in Thought Word and Deed was your most precious possession?" and that a chaste woman would have "a thousand liveried angels" to lackey her? Phoebe relinquishes the promised angels as she had the stars and experiences a sense of "some vague irreparable loss." She now understands the connection between chastity and economic security. Before, she had envied the girls who put up their hair, went to dances, and married "someone handsome (and rich)." Anxiety about whether one would be chosen in marriage is reflected in the child's rhyme:

> If no one ever marries me
> And I don't see why they should
> For nurse says I'm not pretty
> And I'm seldom very good . . .

That was it exactly.

Only a few weeks ago, like other girls, she made secret lists of her trousseau and named her future children. Now children, as well as heavenly jewels and angelic servants, are relinquished:

> Now goodbye Marcus. Goodbye Rose. The prospect before her might
> be difficult and uncertain but it was far more exciting.

The lewd chatter of an old man has introduced Phoebe to the whole world of loveless sex and she accepts it buoyantly.

In "Goodbye Marcus, Goodbye Rose" two possibilities for women are presented to Phoebe. One is the respectable, conventional life she has been taught to expect: in it, chastity is a woman's sole guarantee of marriage, jewels, ser-

vants, children, freedom and respectability. On the practical level, Phoebe is
mistaken to believe this way is not possible for her. In fact, her virginity is intact.
Intuitively, however, she is correct: her chastity is gone forever. Her great
mistake is to believe that the life reserved for wicked, unchaste women is her, or
anyone's alternative. The Cardews are "respectable" people; yet the brutality of
the Captain's sexual attitudes touches his wife intimately. The supposed two
worlds are one. In her turn Edith Cardew punishes Phoebe:

> 'Do you see how white my hair's becoming? It's all because of you.'
> And when Phoebe answered truthfully that she didn't notice any white
> hairs: 'What a really dreadful little liar you are!'

The social web of appearance ("For nurse says I'm not pretty"), respectability,
religion and economic necessity traps equally the chaste and the unchaste, the
respected and the outcast.

"Till September Petronella" is from Rhys's middle volume, *Tigers are Better-
Looking* of 1968. It features Petronella, who could well be Phoebe ten years later,
alone in London. The action of this story is more complex and extended than that
of the other three. Petronella receives a telegram from the painter Marston,
inviting her to spend a couple of weeks in the country. Also at the cottage are the
music critic Julian and his girlfriend Frankie, who is, like Petronella, an artist's
model; the two couples eat, drink, and make clever-cynical conversation. The
next day, Petronella and Marston are treated with suspicion by country people,
and the four drink a lot of wine and become rude and quarrelsome. Marston weeps
because Petronella won't sleep with him, Julian insults her, and she runs away.
A farmer gives her a lift in exchange for sex; he takes her to a pub, back to the
cottage for her suitcase, then to Cirencester where she catches the train back to
London. There, Petronella meets a stranger, a young man named Melville. They
go to Hyde Park then on to what seems to be a hotel suite for dinner and sex. He
drops her off at her bed-sitting room, where she sits alone waiting for the church
clock to strike. In this story, unexplained actions seem random and meaningless.
The significance of "Till September Petronella" is revealed in Petronella's vague
half-thought, in what is said, and in the gradual accumulation of symbolic detail.

The most important refrain in the story is Petronella's missing her French
friend Estelle, who has recently returned to Paris. Estelle "walked the tightrope
so beautifully,"[4] that is, managed a life similar to Petronella's with more ease.
Estelle's bed-sitting room was more like something out of a long romantic novel
than a Bloomsbury room. She brought brightness and friendship to Petronella's
life; it was after she left that Petronella "hit a bad patch." She remembers Estelle
at significant moments. Her sympathetic understanding was a contrast to
Marston's unfathomable demand that Petronella be "gay". Back in London, she
doesn't want to return to her house because: "'When I pass Estelle's door . . .
there'll be no smell of scent now.'" On her way to dinner with Melville she is
reminded of pleasant evenings with Estelle, who very practically insisted on the
necessity to eat one good meal a day. But the illusion that Estelle is walking

alongside her vanishes: "'I shall never see her again — I know it.'" Finally, back at the Bloomsbury house, Petronella passes the door of Estelle's room: "not feeling a thing as I passed it, because she had gone and I knew she would not ever come back."

As Petronella accepts the loss of her only friend she descends to the hole that is what people expect of her. An artist's model, dependent upon her looks (for as long as they might last) for a living, semi-suicidally depressed and very poor, Petronella has, in losing Estelle, lost the self-respect which might have kept her from part-time prostitution. She has successfully avoided the unattractive Marston for some time: Julian's and Frankie's opinion that she has been leading him on for his money drives her away from the cottage. But it is as if they have clarified reality for Petronella. In their loveless world, she might as well get what she can, however she can. Her response to Marston will be different in September.

After her sexual encounter with the farmer, which is implied rather than stated, Petronella's thoughts and words are mainly repetitions. She is started on this track when the farmer says of her what others have said: "'Well, you look as if you'd lost a shilling and found sixpence.'" On the train to London, she repeats Marston's words to herself: "'Never mind . . . never mind, never mind . . . Don't look so down in the mouth, my girl, *look gay.*'" She kisses herself, now, in the cool glass as she had before kissed a plaster cast of a Greek head. When Melville offers her the taxi, she associates him with the farmer: "'*You have it,*' *he said. The other one said, 'Want a lift?'*'" As she and Melville drive along, Petronella thinks of her landlord's reaction when she received Marston's invitation: "'There's a good time coming for the ladies. There's a good time coming for the girls.'" In Hyde Park, as he evaluates the poetic phrases she quotes to him, Petronella judges Melville and every man in the terms Julian had used about her: "'How do they know who's fifth-rate, who's first-rate and where the devouring spider lives?'" To describe her experience at the hotel with Melville she amends Marston's opinion of steak:

> 'I've been persuaded to taste it before, 'Marston said. 'It tasted exactly as I thought it would . . . But Marston should have said, 'it tastes of nothing, my dear, it tastes of nothing. . .'

To keep herself awake in the taxi, Petronella sings for Melville the same song she had sung for the farmer: "'Mr. Brown, Mr. Brown, Had a violin . . .'" She then tells him about her failure to be graduated from the chorus to a speaking part because she could not remember how to say the one line she had been taught: "Oh, Lottie, Lottie, don't be epigrammatic." At her house, Melville promises to write. Petronella quickly repeats what the farmer had said girls want: "'Do you know what I want? I want a gold bracelet with blue stones in it. Not too blue — the darker blue I prefer.'" As she quips, "'The pleasure was all mine,'" Melville repeats her lost line: "'Now Lottie, Lottie, don't be epigrammatic.'" Alone in her room, Petronella recalls the girls in the dressing room on the night she'd fluffed her line saying to her, "'What a waste of good tears!'" and says aloud to herself,

"'Oh, the waste, the waste, the waste!'" As she sits waiting for the church clock to strike, we realize that time has stopped for her. Having finally learned her lines, Petronella has stepped into a state of suspended animation; henceforth she will only be able to repeat, in words and actions, what she has been taught.

This is a fully-realized story unified by time, place and symbols. It begins in Petronella's room and ends there two days later. References to the arts provide the allusive backbone of meaning: the barrel organ plays *Destiny, La Paloma* and *Le Rêve Passe*; Petronella becomes immersed in long romantic novels; Julian whistles the second act duet from the opera *Tristan*; a reference is made to Samson and Delilah; the picture in Marston's studio is *The Apotheosis of Lust*; Petronella has kissed a plaster cast of a Greek head, then her own reflection, ironically recalling *Pygmalion*; a man named Peterson wrote a play about Northern gods and goddesses and Yggdrasil; Marston quotes poetry about unrequited love; in the pub there are three pictures of Lady Hamilton; and a club is called the Apple Tree, a reference to Adam and Eve, and perhaps a satiric allusion to Galsworthy's tale "The Apple Tree". These are like signposts in a foreign country in a language Petronella has begun to understand. By incorporating these references, Rhys is making a point about the mythical, religious, and artistic bases of behaviour in the culture to which Petronella must adapt.

"I Used to Live Here Once" is the last story in the latest volume, *Sleep It Off, Lady,* of 1976. It is a tiny story, less than two pages long, which, because of its location in Rhys's *oeuvre* gives the impression of a finale. It relates a brief, emotionally significant incident during Jean Rhys's return after many years of exile to her old home in Dominica.

The character in "I Used to Live Here Once" balances between memory and the present until the final sentence, which is like the fall of a tightrope-walker. "She" is "extraordinarily happy"[5] walking alone, recognizing the setting and noticing changes. When she approaches the boy and girl on the lawn of her old home she calls "Hello" several times to them, says "I used to live here once" and "her arms went out instinctively with the longing to touch them." The boy gazes expressionlessly at her, says to the girl "'Hasn't it gone cold all of a sudden. D'you notice? Let's go in . . .'" and she watches them running from her. The last sentence is: "That was the first time she knew."

What she knows is that she has brought on the cold. Her strangeness inspires mistrust if not fear in children; they cannot know they represent to her the long-ago relinquished Marcus and Rose. And there can be no return home to her warm and colourful West Indian world.

There is another, a symbolic, reading of this episode. The stepping stones across the river, variously safe and treacherous, represent a dangerous passage through life. It is as if the character has died in that life and is crossing the eternal river searching for her lost heaven. As she walks the broad road feeling "extraordinarily happy," dangers past, she looks up at the blue glassy sky, which is strange to her, unremembered, as if she has entered a new sphere. The description "glassy" is a warning hint: glass is man-made, hard. Still she goes on, and with great excitement looks at the house she has been wanting to see. It is white and "worn stone steps" lead up to it. At the top are two very fair children. But as she approaches them, asserting that she belongs here too, they flee from a draught of cold as if she were a ghost they cannot see. If this was the heaven she had struggled and travelled to reach again, she has just been cast out by the angels, doomed to remain in the limbo of death in life she has known. I accept this reading as Rhys's final comment on life and the life to come. It is all too likely that, heaven being man-made, painted white and peopled by angels in whom "white blood is asserting itself against all odds," there, as here, the orderly and respectable citizen will be preferred to the chaotic yearning consciousness of the exile. This is what "she" and Rhys know: to be an outcast in life is to be an outcast for eternity. This bleakly poetic final vision is the most fitting culmination of Rhys's world-view.

I have mentioned that Jean Rhys writes two types of stories, the episode and the completed experience. The effect on the reader of the first is like watching ripples radiate out from a stone thrown into still water. "Goodbye Marcus, Goodbye Rose" and "I Used to Live Here Once" are intensely observed, economically presented brief periods in a life, which expand in meaning after reading until we understand the whole of the characters' lives and the attitudes of the society which produced them. "In a Café" and "Till September Petronella" are complete stories which present the organization of a whole world: their effect on the reader is that of looking at a mandala. The circle image also applies to Rhys's stories as a whole and describes her world-view.

The central, organizing consciousness contributes much to the overall impression of oneness. This consciousness is Rhys's own; each female character represents a fragment of it. Each is alone, and learns, if she can, the same lesson about her relation to the world. One might almost say that Rhys has told the same story 46 times, only finding different characters, settings, and symbols to convey her meaning. I do not mean by this to slight the real range and diversity of Rhys's stories. Her compelling rendering of the exact spirit of each place and her haunting references to earlier literature deserve separate studies.

Her stories insistently expose the position of the lone woman in any society, whether West Indian, French, or English. Money, the need to have it, is very important. Most of Rhys's female characters have little or no training, no family, no secure position. As Marston says:

> 'What's going to become of you, Miss Petronella
> Grey, living in a bed-sitting room in Torrington
> Square, with no money, no background and no nous?
> Is Petronella your real name?[6]

Indeed, these women have no real name, no separate identity; money is only one aspect of that. Young Phoebe's coming from a secure family does not protect her.

It is not by chance that Phoebe, Petronella and all the others are exiles or outcasts. Especially in "In a Café," "Goodbye Marcus, Goodbye Rose," and "I Used to Live Here Once" is the alliance of religion and respectability emphasized. "In a Café," "Goodbye Marcus, Goodbye Rose," and "Till September Petronella" show staid middle-class men casually using vulnerable and unfortunate females and, incidentally, the disdain and cruelty of women who intend never to be in that position. Phoebe and Petronella and all their sisters are altered by men's treatment of them; in the future they will behave so as to fulfill the men's and society's original intention for them.

Rhys's world-view is uncompromising: the making of scapegoats is society's first and necessary evil. The so-called "respectable" men, the Captain Cardews, the Parisians in the café, Petronella's farmer, as well as her "unacceptable" but rich artistic friends, project their sexuality outside of their comfortable religious, family, and social establishments onto designated outcasts. These men are destroying an aspect of themselves inimical to society's smooth functioning: this is why Rhys's lone women are dismissed by polite society and ultimately destroyed. Stray, "wicked" women are shown to be necessary to the perpetuation of the "decent" world. "I Used to Live Here Once" flatly dismisses sanguine hopes for a more tolerant future, whether placed in a new generation or in a life hereafter and thus completes the circle of social relations which is Jean Rhys's central preoccupation.

Footnotes:

[1] Elgin W. Mellown, "Review of *Sleep It Off, Lady,*" *World Literature Written in English*, XVI, 2 (November 1977), 473-4.
[2] Jean Rhys, "In a Cafe," *The Left Bank and Other Stories* (Freeport: Books for Libraries Press, 1970), p. 49.
[3] Jean Rhys, "Goodbye Marcus, Goodbye Rose," *Sleep It Off, Lady* (New York: Harper & Row, 1976), p. 28
[4] Jean Rhys, "Till September Petronella," *Tigers are Better-Looking* (London: Andre Deutsch, 1968), p. 11.
[5] Jean Rhys, I Used to Live Here Once," *Sleep It Off, Lady,* p. 175.
[6] Jean Rhys, "Till September Petronella," p. 17.

# CHARACTER AND THEMES IN
# THE NOVELS OF JEAN RHYS

*by Elgin W. Mellown*

[Author's Note written for this edition:] the following essay was written in 1969-70, and since that time more accurate biographical information has become available. Jean Rhys was born in 1890 and came to England in 1907; she attended Sir Beerbohm Tree's Academy of Dramatic Arts (it later became the Royal Academy); she was twenty-eight years old when she married for the first time. The BBC broadcast of *Good Morning, Midnight* took place in 1957, not 1958; and Rhys began composing *Wide Sargasso Sea* even before this date. I give a full account of Rhys's books and the criticism devoted to them in my forthcoming Garland bibliography. Finally, the name of the heroine of *Good Morning, Midnight* is Sasha (*not* Sacha) Jansen — a proof-reading error for which I apologize.

Jean Rhys, born in the West Indies in 1894, published five books between 1927 and 1939. Her first collection of stories was sponsored by Ford Madox Ford, and her four succeeding novels were praised by reviewers in England and America. But because of the outbreak of war in 1939, her books were not reprinted, and she dropped out of public attention. Then, in 1958, the BBC broadcast a dramatized version of her novel, *Good Morning, Midnight*. Its critical reception encouraged Rhys to publish some short stories which she had written and to begin work on the novel which in 1966 gained the highest praise of any of her writings, *Wide Sargasso Sea*. In it she tells the story of the first Mrs. Rochester, the shadowy figure whom Charlotte Brontë only lightly sketched in *Jane Eyre*.

*Wide Sargasso Sea* is both an imaginative *tour de force* and a novel valuable in its own right. It places the earlier novels in a new perspective which shows that Jean Rhys is not one of the also-rans but a master of her genre. In her novels she depicts the character of one particular type of woman, while exploring certain human themes and constantly attempting to develop a close relationship between style and content. Her books are now again in print and are being read throughout the world, especially in Holland, Belgium, and France, where Pierre Leyris is translating her stories.[1] Yet Rhys remains a mysterious figure — so much so that when, in 1969, the London *Observer* published Marcelle Bernstein's interview with her it was appropriately entitled "The Inscrutable Miss Jean Rhys."[2]

Jean Rhys was the daughter of a Welsh doctor and his English Creole wife. She came to England with an aunt in 1910 to attend school in Cambridge; from there she went on to the Royal Academy of Dramatic Arts. When her father died — she was then seventeen — she went to work as a chorus girl in a theatrical troupe which toured the provincial theaters, living between engagements in London. In 1918, then twenty-four years old, she "married a Dutch poet and for ten years lived a rootless, wandering life on the Continent, mainly in Paris and Vienna."[3] In these years she began to write; and in 1922 or 1923, when she was living in Paris, Mrs. George Adam, wife of the French correspondent of *The Times*, brought her stories and sketches to the attention of Ford Madox Ford. Rhys was not happy in her marriage — she and her husband later divorced — and for a time she lived with Ford and his common-law wife Stella Bowen, the Australian painter.

The complex relationships in the *ménage à trois* have been described generally by Bowen in her autobiography, *Drawn from Life*, and obliquely by Rhys in her first two novels. (Ford's biographers have said very little about this particular affair.) Apart from the personal relationship, Ford was probably the most important literary influence upon Rhys. In the last issue of the *Transatlantic Review*,[4] he published under the title "Vienne" a few sections of a novel called "Triple Sec" which she was then writing; and sometime between 1925 and 1927 he arranged for her to translate Francis Carco's novel *Perversité*, involving himself in the project to such an extent that both Carco and the American publisher, Pascal Covici, thought Ford himself was the translator.[5] He also wrote a lengthy preface to Rhys's first book, a collection of short stories entitled *The Left Bank*, which Jonathan Cape published in 1927. In the same year Ford broke off his relationship with Rhys, and she returned to England. She married again (her second husband died in the mid-1940s, whereupon she married his cousin, who has since died); and between 1928 and 1939 she wrote four novels: *Postures, After Leaving Mr. Mackenzie, Voyage in the Dark,* and *Good Morning, Midnight.*[6]

Although each novel centers upon one woman, the four individuals are manifestations of the same psychological type — so much so that if we read the novels in the order of their internal chronology, we find in them one, fairly sequential story, albeit the principal figure suffers a change of name from novel to novel. This story begins in *Voyage in the Dark*, in the autumn, 1912. The narrator and central figure is Anna Morgan, a chorus girl in a touring company at Southsea. She is an orphan, having been brought from her home in the West Indies two years earlier by her stepmother. In Southsea she is picked up by Walter Jeffries, an older man, who meets her later in London and seduces her. He takes care of her, and she falls desperately in love with him. Their liaison lasts until October, 1913, when Walter breaks it off. Anna drifts from one man to another in the demimonde of prewar London. In March, 1914, three months pregnant by an unknown man, she begs money from Walter for an abortion. She almost dies from the bungled operation; but as the novel ends, the doctor who has been brought to her assures her friend Laurie that "She'll be all right. . . . Ready to start all over again in no time, I've no doubt" (*V*, p. 159).[7]

The story resumes in *Quartet*. The year is now 1922, and the heroine, twenty-eight years old, is named Marya Hughes. She is married to a Pole, Stephan Zelli, and they live in Paris. Stephan, a mystery man, appears to be a fence for stolen *objets d'art*. In September, 1922, he is arrested for larceny, and the destitute Marya is taken up by a British couple, Hugh (H. J.) Heidler and his wife Lois. She lives with the Heidlers, and soon H. J. makes love to her with the knowledge and connivance of his wife. But Lois' permissiveness is only a matter of necessity, and she becomes so unpleasant that Marya is repulsed by the situation, she transfers her love-dependency from Stephan to H.J. and cannot break away from him. When Stephan is released from prison, he has to leave France; but before he leaves, Marya sleeps with him. Heidler, because she has "betrayed" him, breaks with her and sends her to Cannes on a pension of three hundred francs a week. The novel ends in a flurry of melodrama: Stephan and Marya return to Paris; he threatens to kill H.J.; she cries out that she will betray Stephan to the police; Stephan throws her aside and goes off with another woman of the district, thinking to himself, "*Encore une grue*" (*Q*, p. 227).

In *After Leaving Mr. Mackenzie* the central figure is named Julia Martin. The place is Paris; the time, April, 1927. Since the previous October when her lover Mr. Mackenzie left her, Julia has been living on the weekly three hundred francs which his lawyer sends her. (This sum for an ex-mistress seems fixed in Rhys's mind.) Now the allowance is stopped with a final payment of fifteen hundred francs. Julia in a fit of rage returns the check to Mackenzie; on the same night she meets George Horsfield. He gives her money and persuades her to return to London. She does so in order to meet her first lover, W. [?Walter] Neil James — who gives her money — and to see her sister Norah and her mother, an invalid who dies while Julia is in London. Norah and her paternal Uncle Griffiths send Julia away after the funeral; she takes Horsfield for her lover and then returns to Paris. The novel ends with her begging one hundred francs from Mr. Mackenzie.

The story reaches its conclusion in *Good Morning, Midnight*. Sacha Jansen, living in bitter retirement in Bloomsbury on a pension from an unidentified person (it is now two pounds ten a week) and trying to drink herself to death, is sent to Paris for a visit by her friend Sidonie. Sacha walks through the streets she knew in earlier days, the familiar places and even remembered faces bringing back events of the past. Her memories sound a bittersweet melody above the harsh, inescapable present, for Paris is unchanged, while she has aged and faded and become a mere shell of hate. In a cruel, reversed mimicry of her own life, a young gigolo attaches himself to her. She tries to persuade him that she does not want him and that she is not wealthy. He attempts to make love to her in her hotel room, and she wounds him as she herself has been wounded by offering him money as a bribe to leave her alone: "You can have the money right away, so it would be a waste of time, wouldn't it," she says (*G*, p. 183). But he leaves without forcing himself on Sacha and without taking her money. His not making use of her, which negative act is a recognition of her as an individual whose wishes are to be respected, brings her out of the isolation and hatred which have for so long surrounded her; and out of compassion she gives herself to the man in the adjoining room whom she has previously despised. The story in the four novels is that of the spiritual progress of a woman from the joy of childhood into the ordeal of adolescent love and sexual experience, through a resulting bitterness, grief, and selfish isolation, toward a position which will allow her to develop a compassionate understanding of the human situation.

In his *New York Times* review of *Wide Sargasso Sea*, Walter Allen pointed out that Charlotte Brontë's Mrs. Rochester summed up "the nature of the heroine who appears under various names throughout Jean Rhys's fiction."[8] Remembering the early novels not quite accurately, he continued, "she is a young woman, generally Creole in origin and artistic in leanings, who is hopelessly and helplessly at sea in her relations with men, a passive victim, doomed to destruction."[9] The woman upon whom Rhys centers her attention is indeed always a victim. Stella Bowen saw this quality in the novelist herself and described her as being "cast for the rôle . . . of the poor, brave and desperate beggar who was doomed to be let down by the bourgeoisie."[10] There is never an escape for the Rhys heroine: happiness is always followed by sadness, and her last state is always worse than her first.

Yet we must qualify these generalizations. This figure of degraded womanhood is not static, but develops from novel to novel, the development being, at least in part, Rhys's movement away from autobiography toward an ever more complete, imaginative rendition of the single character. Thus, in the first novel, *Quartet*, Marya Zelli, unlike the later heroines, has a strength and a vivacity that are sapped but not completely perverted because she is an autobiographical projection, so much so indeed that she fails as a fictional creation: the novelist bestows qualities upon Marya that she would not actually have possessed. Rhys seems only gradually to have learned which of her own experiences properly belonged to the character whom she was to sketch over and over in her novels. She also learned to conceal this recognition and, in a calculated play for verisimilitude, to give the impression of complete subjectivity. If we wish to appreciate Jean Rhys, we must sidestep our first impression that we are reading her autobiography and examine the novels as imaginative works. Only then can we see her most important literary achievement: the portrayal of a psychological type never before so accurately described. These *complete* descriptions make the character more than a psychological type: she is rather woman in one of her archetypal roles.

The most basic experience treated by Rhys concerns the woman's childhood. Its peace and security are associated with a warm climate, in contrast to her adult insecurity in a cold northern world. This pattern is most obvious in *Voyage in the Dark*: Anna constantly shivers and suffers in the English climate. Her love affair with Walter Jeffries springs from an adolescent desire to find that warmth and security which she knew in childhood in the game of sexual love with a partner old enough to be her father. This theme is tentatively announced in several of *The Left Bank* stories, while in *Wide Sargasso Sea* it becomes a poignant memory of the frustrated nymphomaniac who is brutally restrained in the cold isolation of Thornfield Hall.

This archetypal woman never finds a man who will faithfully continue to fulfil her needs. Marya know such happiness longer than any of the other women, but even Stephan, her older, lover-husband, eventually fails her. Her need is both psychic and physical (Rhys was one of the first women writers to express an unabashed, direct acceptance of woman's desire for sexual love); and when Stephan is imprisoned for a year she must allow herself to be taken by another man who is, as always, older and, as always, a brute. Instinctively knowing that her man will desert her, the woman increasingly debases herself in a desperate attempt to hold on to him, the inevitable result being that her abandoned position increases his revulsion. The Rhys woman may be a mistress in name, but in fact she is always a victim of love because she is at the mercy of her controllable desires.

An adjunct theme has to do with woman as creator. These tortured women cannot reach maturity by giving birth to a child which, depending on them, will force them into adulthood; and, having no husbands to provide for them and with no way of earning a living other than by selling their bodies (which must be kept free of a dependent child), they must abort any life that may spring in their wombs. If they do give birth, as Julia Martin does, then they are unable to keep the child alive. Woman as creator and sustainer of life has no part in this archetypal figure.[11]

These women are forever alone outside the realm of everyday society and cut off from the ordinary patterns of life. In them we see a literal meaning of the term *demimonde*, for theirs is only a partial existence. They know that they are alive because they suffer and because money passes through their hands. The respectable world views such women as commodities to be bought and as hostages who must pay their way. As Maudie says in *Voyage in the Dark*, "Have you ever thought that a girl's clothes cost more than the girl inside them? . . . People are much cheaper than things" (*V*, p. 40). In this understanding of life lies the origin of one of Rhys's most important themes, that personal identity is determined by economic wealth. This attitude appears to link Rhys with that realistic tradition which Defoe and Richardson represent, and certainly her stress upon this theme brings her obvious romantic impressionism into line with the harsh realities of modern economic life. But she goes further than any of her predecessors. In her novels all of the prevailing moral values come solely from this single standard, with no attention given to any of the other arbiters of morality which earlier authors recognized, if only to apply lip service to them. The Rhys woman reasons that, since her physical existence depends upon money, everything else does too — character, morals, ethics, even religious values. And since she knows too that money is merely an artificial thing, that which men give to women when they make love to them, or when they send them away, she cannot respect that respectable society which values it: she describes those persons who have a devil-may-care attitude to money as *chic*. Herein lies Jean Rhys's twentieth-century development of the realistic tradition. Her women do not identify themselves as the owners of plantations in Virginia, or as the mistresses of the squire's household, positions valued by a money-minded society no matter how they may have been gained. Rather these women find their identity and a truth for themselves by flaunting their disdain for the money upon which society is based. Julia Martin throws away the check and, aware of her sister's and uncle's absolute disapproval of her, spends her last shillings on roses for her mother's cremation, while Marya and Stephan recklessly spend their last francs on an unneeded, luxurious meal. Stella Bowen wrote about this attitude in reference to Rhys herself, and her comments quite accurately describe Rhys's fictional world:

> All the virtues, in her view, were summed up in "being a sport," which meant being willing to take risks and show gallantry and share one's last crust; more attractive qualities, no doubt, than patience or honesty or fortitude. She regarded the law as the instrument of the "haves" against the "have nots" and was well acquainted with every rung of that long and dismal ladder by which the respectable citizen descends towards degradation.
>
> It was not her fault that she knew these things, and the cynicism they engendered had an unanswerable logic in it. It taught me that the only really unbridgeable gulf in human society is between the financially solvent and the destitute. You can't have self-respect without money. You can't even have the luxury of a personality.[12]

While Rhys's novels are thus linked one to another not only by the central character but also by this harsh, economic view of life, they are not merely psychological studies or economic tracts, but carefully designed dramas of character development. In *Wide Sargasso Sea* this growth is obvious — after all, Rhys chose to enter a progression of events with a predetermined ending (that is, the novel *Jane Eyre*); but this novel is a special case, and the earlier ones present more typical situations faced by the novelist. Although character development is less accomplished in *Quartet* and *After Leaving Mr. Mackenzie* than in the next two novels, by the end of *Quartet* Marya has changed to the extent that she admits her love for Heidler and reshapes her relationship with Stephan. In the second novel there is a more significant change: initially Julia is smartingly alive to the cruelties of life. Then, after a not too subtle flashback to the first time she was "happy about nothing; the first time [she was] afraid about nothing" (*A*, p. 211), a memory which is linked to her catching butterflies which broke themselves to pieces in trying to escape from the box in which she imprisoned them, there follows the incident of George Horsfield touching her arm as they sneak together up the dark stairs of her Notting Hill boardinghouse. She screams and awakens the landlady and of course is asked to leave. She is the butterfly broken by her own struggles against the imprisoning walls of her society and — no less — of her defenseless sensitivity. But at the end of the novel she is rejected by a young man who, having followed her on a dark street, sees her revealed by a street lamp:

> He gave her a rapid glance.
> "*Oh, la la,*" he said. "*Ah, non, alors.*"
> He turned about and walked away.
> "Well," said Julia aloud, "that's funny. The joke's on me this time."

> (*A*, p. 247)

She no longer *feels* the criticism which would have destroyed her earlier, nor does she feel any pity for a starving man whom she sees; and she realizes that she is ending "where most sensible people start, indifferent and without any pity at all" (*A*, p. 248).

Perhaps it was this dead end of emotion in her second novel which caused Rhys to turn away from a biographical chronology in her third, *Voyage in the Dark*. It chronicles Anna's never-ceasing descent on the scale of personal and social values, a history of degradation all the more chilling because so obliquely told. Not for Rhys the gloating of the pornographer over salacious incidents: such matters may be the stuff of life, but she is the artist concerned with character portrayal, her style being completely shaped by its demands. We experience only what Anna experiences; and if we want to see her in the eyes of the world, we must make our own deductions and extrapolations.

But while there is more action in *Voyage in the Dark* than in any of the other novels, *Good Morning, Midnight* is actually the most accomplished of the four novels in terms of character development. Marya and Julia both come to terms with themselves, Anna is a drifter who is shaped by the persons whom she meets, and none of the three ever truly achieves an adult relationship with another person. It remains for Sacha Jansen, the longing-for-death dipsomaniac, who has deliberately frozen over the wellsprings of love to live only through her memory of the past, to develop into an adult by going beyond her adolescent hate-fear of other human beings Yet this change comes only on the last page of the novel and is more suggested than defined. Having wounded the Russian gigolo as deeply as she herself has ever been wounded, and having seen him turn the other cheek, Sacha leaves her door open, inviting the man next door whom she has so long avoided into her bed. The novel ends as she looks up at him:

> He doesn't say anything. Thank God, he doesn't say anything. I look straight into his eyes and despise another poor devil of a human being for the last time. For the last time. . . .
> Then I put my arms around him and pull him down on to the bed, saying: "Yes — yes — yes. . . ." (*G*, p. 190; exact punctuation)

I think that these echoes of Molly Bloom's voice are deliberate and that they serve to tell us more about Sacha than Rhys was willing to state directly. Sacha overcomes the drift toward death that obsessed the earlier manifestations of the Rhys woman by finding this compassion, and in some way it so alters her character that she is no longer a subject for the novelist. The four novels work as a unit which (like certain other contemporary, quasi-autobiographical novels) ends because the material has been brought to a logical conclusion. Significantly Rhys's subsequent novel, *Wide Sargasso Sea*, is set in a distant land in a noncontemporary time.

Reviewers of Rhys's books, even of her first, praised her technique,[13] although none realized that it is based on the consciously manipulated point of view. Like her contemporary Ernest Hemingway, Rhys learned to allow her characters to create themselves through their own narration of their stories. The technique derives of course from Browning's dramatic monologues — Jake Barnes comes to life in the same way that the Duke of Ferrara does — and in the more successful stories of *The Left Bank* Rhys makes a comparably adroit use of the narrator. In "Illusion" the "exceedingly nice" Miss Bruce,[14] an English artist resident in Paris, is stricken with appendicitis and rushed to a hospital. The narrator, in searching out personal necessities for Miss Bruce in her apartment, comes upon the sensible lady's secret, and armoire of bright frocks. The story is only an amusing vignette with overtones of Krafft-Ebing — until one realizes that the author has caught one's attention because she has made the narrator so ambiguous that not even his sex can be determined. Similarly in "The Blue Bird" Carlo (*née* Margaret Tomkins) tells her story of hopeless love for a "Bad Man" to the narrator who is certainly female but whose exact relationship to Carlo is never explained.

The stories of *The Left Bank* are generally told by a sexually ambiguous persona who is alive to pathos, keenly aware of her own sensibilities, generally conscious of the emotions of others, and always completely amoral in her evaluations. They are experimental pieces, and one would like to know how much Ford worked with his young protegée on them. He commented in his "Preface" that, when he tried to get Rhys to introduce topographical details into her writings, "she eliminated even such two or three words of descriptive matter as had crept in. . . ."[15] If she refused direct suggestions, she profited however from Ford's example, particularly in that technique which he called "*progressive d'effet*," the idea "that every word set on paper — *every* word set on paper — must carry the story forward and, that as the story progressed, the story must be carried forward faster and faster and with more and more intensity."[16] In *Quartet* the forward movement is so fast that Rhys loses control and the ending degenerates into melodrama. But in isolated passages we can see her discarding every word that does not contribute to the total effect, as in Marya's confession to Stephan of what happened while he was in jail:

> "Yes. There was a letter from [Heidler] at the hotel to-day. But
> first . . . I must tell you. . . When I'd been there with them . . . a

> little time, Heidler started making love to me. . . . And so I went to her,
> to Lois, and I told her what was happening and I asked her to let me
> have the money to go away. . . . And she said . . . that what was the
> matter with me was that I was too virtuous and that she didn't mind.
> . . . And that I was a fool not to trust Heidler. . . . And that night she
> went out somewhere and left me alone with him. . . ." (*Q*, pp. 218-19;
> punctuation exact)

The passage also illustrates the distinction which Ford made between the
spoken languages and "English-literary jargon."[17] Marya, Julia, Anna, and the
other characters speak or think in the language appropriate to their individual
voices, but when Rhys is outside the character, giving us, as in this passage from
*After Leaving Mr. Mackenzie*, the character's inarticulated and actually unrecog-
nized feelings, she uses a literary language which is unrelated to the character.
Julia sets off for Montparnasse with high hopes, but (as we saw in the passage
quoted above) a young man turns away from her in repugnance, and after this
rebuff she begins to feel a total indifference to humanity:

> The place du Châtelet was a nightmare. A pale moon, like a claw,
> looked down through the claw-like branches of dead trees.
> She turned to the left and walked into a part of the city which was
> unknown to her. "Somewhere near the Halles," she thought. "Of
> course, at the back of the Halles."
> She saw a thin man, so thin that he was like a clothed skeleton,
> drooping in a doorway. And the horses, standing like statues of patient
> misery. She felt no pity at all. . . .
> It used to be as if someone had put a hand and touched her heart
> when she saw things like that, but now she felt nothing. Now she felt
> indifferent and cold, like a stone. (*A*, p. 248)

In these passages there is a device which Rhys probably picked up from Ford:
the use of the ellipsis to indicate those pauses which are a part of the spoken
language, or to show a sequence of events or ideas, or some type of change, which
the novelist does not want to follow through in detail. The technique is appropriate for the inarticulate, drifting heroine, but is much less satisfactory for such
characters as Lois and Heidler, who are always self-conscious and aware of
themselves.

But Rhys only gradually learned her technique, and her first two novels are
flawed by her failure to control the point of view. In both she is omniscient, third
person author, even pausing — in the Ford manner — to address the reader
directly, as here at the opening of the second chapter of *Quartet*: "Marya, you
must understand, had not been suddenly and ruthlessly transplanted from solid
comfort to the hazards of Montmartre" (*Q*, p. 13). But Rhys's point of view is so
patently that of the main female character and so biased in her favor that the
abrupt shifts into the thoughts of another character — often the one against whom
the heroine is reacting — destroy the continuity of the narrative and weaken its

psychological verisimilitude. *Quartet* is the worst offender because Rhys alternately uses the views of Marya, H. J., Lois, and Stephan, and even enters into the consciousness of strangers passing by. The problem is less critical in *After Leaving Mr. Mackenzie* since the cast of characters is smaller, yet the movement from Julia's thoughts to those of the persons whom she meets distracts the reader, not least because these characters enter the narrative only because they have some relationship with Julia; they do not exist in their own right.

The solution to this narrative problem comes in *Voyage in the Dark*. In it Rhys realized that her concern with one character demanded that she write in the first person, utilizing only those sensations, impressions, and experiences which the first person narrator could reasonably have had. Anna Morgan and Sacha Jansen know only that they suffer and that therefore they exist; anything outside themselves exists only because they happen to think about it, or because it impinges upon their consciousness. The controlled point of view which holds to the consciousness of the central character is not only a functional way of telling her story, but also expresses her solipsistic philosophy. The aesthetic value of both *Voyage in the Dark* and *Good Morning, Midnight* is raised because the first person point of view is the technical correlative of Jean Rhys's understanding of life.

I have delayed looking at *Wide Sargasso Sea* because it is a masterpiece that need not be discussed except on its own terms, as well as the logical outgrowth of the developments in the previous four novels. In it Rhys supplies the stories which Charlotte Brontë did not tell of Rochester and his first wife prior to (as well as during) the time period of *Jane Eyre*. Rhys gives her own account of their early lives, their marriage, and Bertha's subsequent madness and incarceration at Thornfield Hall, ending this "secret history" with the death of Bertha in the fire.

*Wide Sargasso Sea* is composed of first person narratives by Antoinette Cosway Mason Rochester (only her husband calls her Bertha) and by Edward Fairfax Rochester, along with a one-page conversations between Grace Poole and Leah, the maid. The sections narrated by Antoinette — the first, part of the second, and the third — are in the past tense and appear to have been written at Thornfield Hall; or, perhaps more logically, to be Antoinette's recollections during her moments of lucidity at Thornfield Hall. The last section takes us through Richard Mason's visit to the attic room to the moment before Bertha-Antoinette slips out of the attic with the lighted candle to set fire to the Hall. The sections narrated by Rochester are also in the past tense, but are subtly different. The whole story is known to Antoinette as she writes, and we, knowing its end but not its progress, must accept the workings out of its details because we recognize the inexorable conclusion looming before us. Rochester's narration however takes place at the moment that events occur, and consequently we share with him his revelations and growing horror. Thus the two voices tell us one story, giving us not merely the contrast of their attitudes, but more important for the effect of horror which it produces, the contrast of the victim who knows her fate with that of the victim who must gradually learn his. Antoinette knows from the start that she is doomed and that any act is futile, while Rochester imagines, even as his destiny bears down upon him, that he is a free agent.

The biographical details which Rhys provides for Charlotte Brontë's characters are as complex as any actually given by the Victorian novelist. Annette Cosway, an English Creole in Jamaica who is widowed about the time of the Emancipation (1834) when her daughter Antoinette is ten years old, lives with her daughter and imbecile son Pierre for five years on the rundown plantation Coulibri, an object of ridicule and hate to the free Negroes. Finally she manages to marry the wealthy Mr. Mason; they live together in the refurbished plantation house until they are driven out by rioting blacks. The house is burned, Pierre is killed, Antoinette is injured and becomes seriously ill, and Mrs. Cosway-Mason goes mad. She is kept in private confinement where she is the sexual prey of her Negro attendants. She dies while Antoinette is at convent school, as does Mr. Mason, but not before he settles thirty thousand pounds on Antoinette. Richard Mason, her stepfather's son, arranges for Rochester, the impoverished younger son of Thornfield Hall, to marry Antoinette; he comes out to Jamaica and is married after only a few weeks' acquaintance. Antoinette gives herself body and soul to him, Richard having already given her money to him with no settlement made in her behalf. Rochester realizes that he does not love Antoinette, although he is sexually infatuated by her. Her passion for him corresponds — so much so that his basically Puritanical nature is revolted, and he is ready to turn away from her in disgust when he is told by her colored half-brother that he has been tricked into marrying the daughter of a mad nymphomaniac. His sudden revulsion throws Antoinette into a sexual panic; we gather that she is indeed unfaithful to him; and to protect his "honor" as well as to "punish" Antoinette, Rochester brings her to England and imprisons her in Thornfield Hall, his own father and elder brother having died and the estate having devolved upon him, ironically removing the necessity for his marrying the heiress. During the voyage to England Antoinette actually goes mad and subsequently knows only intermittent moments of sanity in her garret prison.

Here, then, spelled out clearer than in any of the previous novels, are the details of life of the now familiar Rhys heroine: a happy childhood in a tropical state of nature, growth into adolescence without the presence of a father, a complete submission to physical love, the inevitable loss of that love, and the consequent misery. In one sense, then, as Walter Allen noted, Antoinette Cosway *is* the embodiment of Marya, Julia, Anna, and Sacha. On the other hand, however, her character lies in a somewhat different sphere from theirs. They are shadows of an archetypal figure, and their precise outlines (because we see them always from the inside, so to speak) are often indistinct. Their indefiniteness contributes not a little to their universality. Antoinette, while a manifestation of the same archetypal figure, is however a positive character who is not to be confused with anyone else. She may be representative of nineteenth-century Creole girls at the mercy of fortune-hunting younger sons, and she may even be an example of tropical hot blood reacting to the icy restraint of the north, but she is not, like the other Rhys heroines, Woman with a capital *W*.

Interestingly enough, Rochester does not share this individuality. Rhys's men all have basically the same psychology: they are creatures with physical desires who have the power of simple, logical thinking. Rochester differs very little from Stephan Zelli (the outcome of both stories results from their notions of honor), while his ability to separate physical relationships from psychic ones parallels this trait as it appears in Heidler, Mackenzie, and even Anna's first lover, Walter Jeffries. A man's heart, according to Rhys, is never much involved with his physical desires.

The technique of the novel reinforces the different approach to the male and female characters. The man considers himself to be a free agent in the present moment, not fearing the future and not completely at the mercy of the past. But the woman knows instinctively that she must act out a preordained role and that, no matter what present events may indicate, her end is inevitable. While the first four novels incorporate these psychological concepts, only in *Wide Sargasso Sea* is the technique completely appropriate to the author's basic concept of life. This harsh, realistic view is at times heavily Freudian, the spectre of Nietzsche being never far away; and it appeals only to the strong-minded reader who, like the author herself, can look directly at the human comedy. Because this attitude to life is so convincingly presented through all the means at the novelist's command, we realize that while *Wide Sargasso Sea* captures us initially because of our interest in the story — its explanation of events about which we have always wondered — and because of its ability to provide that *frisson* that readers can never resist, its ultimate aesthetic value comes from its complete unity. Technique, content, and characterization work together to delineate a mature artist's view of life.

It is perhaps too soon to assign Jean Rhys a definite place in literary history, although we can notice her relationship to her contemporaries. The story of her life inevitably makes us compare her to Katherine Mansfield. Both women were ex-colonials who never forgot the islands where they were born. Both of them — like many another colonial newly come to London or Paris — discovered a madder music in a bohemian life morally more lax than that which the natives of Swiss Cottage or the Boul' Mich ever enjoy. And although both Mansfield and Rhys frequently wrote about the helpless woman who needs the love and protection of a man, they were themselves solitary artists who knew their true life best when they were seated at the lonely writing desk. Yet the differences in their personal attitudes make their writings quite different. Katherine Mansfield, in spite of her labors to master the Continental tradition of writing *contes* and her desire to be like a Chekhov or a de Maupassant who could fleetingly turn the brilliance of his genius upon prosaic events, illuminating and fixing them forever as he saw them, never departs from the traditional moral stance of the British novelist, except, from time to time, to slip from it into sentimentality. Jean Rhys, in contrast, employed not only the *mise en scène* of the Continent, but also the

European *Zeitgeist* — its new ideas in psychology, its aesthetic application of certain philosophical ideas, and, most of all, its between-the-wars appreciation of the plight of the individual, the isolation of existentialism. Caught up in such ideas, she quickly leaves behind her the traditions of realism as practiced by earlier British novelists and, neither commenting upon nor manipulating her characters according to any moral pattern, allows them (or more accurately, the single character) to express what is. Relentlessly she develops her single vision of a world in which free will is a myth and the individual has no power to control his destiny. She pays little or no heed to the reader's resulting depression or occasional mystification and never, like Mansfield, utilizes an irony to exalt the reader. Katherine Mansfield often puts him on the side of the gods where he can feel superior to the self-deluding Miss Brills who flounder before him; Jean Rhys does not salve our pride, but aims through her various technical devices to make us experience the degradation and humiliation of her characters. In the Rhys world is no superior vantage point for anyone.[18]

Comparisons with such female writers of the period as Virginia Woolf and those whom Lionel Stevenson has aptly named "A Group of Able Dames" in *The History of the English Novel: Yesterday and After*[19] offer little help in defining Rhys's place in literary history. There are certain similarities between the content of Rhys's novels and those by Djuna Barnes, particularly in the post-war Parisian setting and in the fascination with bizarre psychological types, as indeed there some resemblances between Rhys's novels and those by Radclyffe Hall. The stress which Jean Rhys and Radclyffe Hall gave to misunderstood and socially unacceptable aspects of female psychology helped open the way for that un-abashed treatment of all types of characters which we accept and even demand from novelists today. Of course Hall's evangelical intentions of propagandizing for oppressed women put her novels in a different class from Rhys's; and certainly Radclyffe Hall, in spite of her flaunting of sexual mores and her sophistication, never departs from her traditional — even county-English — morality: she is always concerned with her characters as moral entities. Such a concern is of course completely missing from Jean Rhys's fiction. In it we find a portrayal of human beings, particularly of one type of woman, functioning in an economic society, who are seen from a physiological and psychological point of view. Whatever moral values are present are derived from the characters themselves.

These types and their world are now perhaps commonplaces of contemporary literature. Even in 1940 Stella Bowen could write that "this world . . . has . . . found an impressive literature in the works of writers like Céline and Henry Miller."[20] We might now add to this list such names as Tennessee Williams (his novel *The Roman Spring of Mrs. Stone* reads in some ways like a slick-magazine version of *Good Morning, Midnight*); "Pauline Réage," author of the porno-graphic story of a woman's complete debasement, *The Story of O*; as well as others. Most of these authors would be European or American, rather than British. In spite of all the changes which have taken place in literature and in the other forms of our modern culture, the contemporary British novelist has not completely abandoned traditional moral values. Perhaps the literary heritage of the "great tradition" of morality is sufficient to outweigh the new forces in society.

Yet if Jean Rhys's philosophy has not been adopted by other British novelists, that fact says nothing about her abilities as a novelist. Her five novels are models for anyone who wants an original understanding of life and of human nature, and who desires the aesthetic pleasure one finds in a perfect correlation between technique and content.

*Duke University*

Footnotes:

[1] *La Nouvelle Revue Française*, 202 (Oct. 1969), 481-507, esp. 481-83.
[2] (1 June 1969), 40-42, 49-50. This interview and Francis Wyndham's "Introduction," *Wide Sargasso Sea* (Harmondsworth: Penguin, 1968) are the sources of the biographical information given here. I completed this essay before the publication of Arthur Mizener's *The Saddest Story: A Biography of Ford Madox Ford* (New York and Cleveland: World, 1971), where Mizener refers to Rhys on pp. 344-50 without adding any significant details to those which were already available.
[3] Wyndham, p. 5.
[4] (Dec. 1924), 639-45.
[5] During "the winter months of both 1924-25 and 1925-26, Ford and Stella" lived in Toulon where one of their friends was Francis Carco (Frank MacShane, *The Life and Works of Ford Madox Ford* [New York: Horizon, 1965], p. 194). Always the entrepreneur of literary talent, Ford evidently wanted to help bring Carco's novel *Perversité* (Paris: J. Ferenczi et fils, 1925) before the English-reading public. At any rate, on 7 January 1926 Carco wrote to Ford thanking him for his interest (David Dow Harvey, *Ford Madox Ford, 1873-1939, A Bibliography of Works and Criticism* [Princeton Univ. Press, 1962], p. 97; and in 1928 Pascal Covici published an English translation with Ford's name given as the translator. But in letters to Edward Naumburg, Jr. (Harvey, p. 97) and Isabel Patterson (Richard M. Ludwig, ed., *Letters of Ford Madox Ford* [Princeton: Princeton Univ. Press, 1965], pp. 176-77), Ford declared that the translation was actually made by Rhys. To the latter he wrote, "I could not have done it myself half so well if at all because translating is not one of my gifts and I do not know the particular Parisian *argot* that Mr. Carco employs." In March, 1972, Rhys told me that she translated both *Perversity* and Edouard de Nève's *Barred* (London: Desmond Harmsworth, 1932).
[6] *Postures* (London: Chatto and Windus, 1928; American title — which Rhys prefers — *Quartet* [New York: Simon and Schuster, 1929]), *After Leaving Mr. Mackenzie* (London: Jonathan Cape; New York: Knopf, 19310, *Voyage in the Dark* (London: Constable, 1934; New York: William Morrow, 1935), and *Good Morning, Midnight* (London: Constable, 1939; New York: Harper, [1967]). Page references with abbreviations are noted parenthetically in the text and are to the following editions: *Q—Quartet, A—After Leaving* (London). *V—Voyage* (Harmondsworth: Penguin, 1969), *G—Good Morning* (New York).

[7] The story, "Till September Petronella" (*London Magazine* [Jan. 1960)], 19-39; rpr. *Tigers Are Better-Looking, with a selection from* The Left Bank [London: André Deutsch, 1968]), set in London, 28 July 1914, gives a less desperate picture of Anna — here named "Julia Petronella Gray" — as she encounters various men. Rhys fuses several periods in this story: the description of Petronella's lover "Marston" corresponds to descriptions of Ford, while the French girl who helps Petronella choose her dresses is named Estelle. Obviously it is more than a mere coincidence that Ford's *New Poems* (New York: William Edwin Rudge, 1927) contains a poem commemorating a past love affair — "There shall no refuge be for you and me/Who haste away . . ./But in the deep remoteness of the heart,/In the deep secret chambers of the mind /. . ./ Lo! you, enshrined." — which is entitled "To Petronella at Sea" (p. 35).

[8] 18 June 1967, p. 5.

[9] *Ibid.*

[10] *Drawn from Life, Reminiscences* (London: Collins, 1940), p. 167.

[11] Here is one of the clearest distinctions between Rhys and her heroine: Jean Rhys gave birth to a child (is indeed a grandmother) and also created the fictional character who is the subject of this discussion.

[12] Bowen, pp. 166-67.

[13] D.B. Wyndham-Lewis, "Hinterland of Bohemia," *Saturday Review*, 23 April 1927, p. 637; "Miss Rhys's Short Stories," *New York Times Book Review*, 11 December 1927, p. 28; among others. *The Left Bank* was widely and favorably reviewed.

[14] *The Left Bank and Other Stories*, with a Preface by Ford Madox Ford (London: Jonathan Cape, 1927), p. 30.

[15] Ford, Preface to *The Left Bank*, p. 26.

[16] Quoted from *Joseph Conrad, A Personal Reminiscence* (London: Duckworth, 1924), p. 210, by Frank MacShane, ed., *Critical Writings of Ford Madox Ford* (Lincoln: Univ. of Nebraska Press, 1964), p. 87.

[17] In his letter to Anthony Bertram, 14 Aug. 1922. *Critical Writings*, p. 100.

[18] While it is not perhaps surprising that the more palatable tales by Mansfield have gained a wider circulation than Rhys's gloomy novels, we should also note that the grieving Middleton Murry was a better publicist for the dead woman than Ford was for the live— and still publishing—woman.

[19] *The History of the English Novel: Yesterday and After*, XI (New York: Barnes, 1967).

[20] Bowen, p. 167.

# SUN FIRE — PAINTED FIRE:
# JEAN RHYS AS A CARIBBEAN NOVELIST

*by Louis James*

"For if this novel does not occupy a central place in the growing body of West Indian literature — if it is not a touchstone against which we assay West Indian fiction before and after it — then West Indian literature is in a bad way."[1] John Hearne's comment on *Wide Sargasso Sea* (1966) was not characteristic of earlier criticism of the novel, and it would not be universally accepted in the Caribbean today. Jean Rhys had earlier been considered a European novelist. She had left Dominica, where she was born into a white Creole family, in 1911 when she was sixteen, and her writing was largely set in Europe where, with one short return to the West Indies, she has lived ever since. Although *Wide Sargasso Sea* was set almost entirely in the Caribbean, its first critics were more interested in its links with the Victorian classic, Charlotte Brontë's *Jane Eyre* (1847), for it told the story of Rochester's mad wife kept in the attic of Thornfield Hall. The point that Jean Rhys' book was a radical *revaluation* of *Jane Eyre* and its European attitudes from the perspective of a West Indian Creole was largely missed.

In 1968 Wally Look Lai, a Jamaican, claimed the novel belonged to West Indian literature. This was not because of its West Indian setting, but because the setting and the characters were used as a poetic dramatization of basic Caribbean concerns — the conflict between European and West Indian consciousness, the roots of Caribbean society and history. *Wide Sargasso Sea* was different in kind from Jean Rhys' previous explorations of isolated womanhood — here the individual concerns were symbolic of the West Indian predicament. The poetic intensity with which this was done "must surely place this novel among the major achievements of West Indian literature."[2] Some six years later both the novel and Look Lai's claims were attacked by Edward Brathwaite in a monograph *Contrary Omens* (1974). For Brathwaite, the real centre of West Indian culture is that of the folk: a novel dramatizing the dilemma of a white Creole cannot penetrate the experience of the predominantly black and poor West Indian peoples.[3]

As Kenneth Ramchand has noted, Brathwaite's criticism indicates "the danger of prescription that exists whenever we attempt to base definitions upon social and political content."[4] As Proust knew, memory can intensify and make clearer childhood experience, and it is no paradox that Jean Rhys' novel furthest in time from her Caribbean life should also be her most profoundly West Indian. The speech rhythms, the total imaginative context, from the sense impressions to the minutiae of social relationships, have an accuracy that give particular pleasure to those intimate with the Caribbean, and this is validated by the relevance of the themes to aspects of West Indian culture. Jean Rhys' vision is not that of Edward Brathwaite, although in important ways the two do overlap — notably both reject European materialism in favour of the vitality of the black folk culture. Yet Caribbean culture can never be narrowed to one perspective. Coupling Jean Rhys with the Guyanese writer Wilson Harris, Hearne writes "They *belong* [to the West Indies]; but on their own terms. Guerrillas, not outsiders."[5]

Jean Rhys was born in Roseau into a large family, the daughter of a Welsh doctor, William Rhys Williams, and Minna Lockhart, a third-generation Dominican Creole.[6] The house in which she was brought up — on the corner of Cork and St. Mary's Streets — and the family holiday house Dr. Williams built in the hills above Massacre, can be seen today. Jean, then Gwen Williams, was a sensitive, frail child, overshadowed by her elder brothers and by her vivacious younger sister, Brenda. Her mother largely left her to herself. Her profound link was with her father, a romantic figure — not only in Gwen's imagination — who loved venturing into high seas in a rowing boat, and shocked the local white population by his relaxed attitudes to the blacks, whom he accepted as equals.

Gwen's childhood days formed the basis for her imagination (as surely as Wordsworth's mountains and Dickens' early memories of London haunt their best work). They reappear intermittently throughout her writing, and sometimes the same details recur. Her great love was the mountain house — transformed into the honeymoon house of Granbois in *Wide Sargasso Sea* — "very new and very ugly, long and narrow, of unpainted wood, perched oddly on high posts." On the verandah was an "enormous brass telescope," upon four legs. She would lie in the hammock and watch the sea. In the early morning the sea was a "very tender blue, like the dress of the Virgin Mary, and on it were little white triangles. The fishing boats." By midday the sun could only be looked at by screwing up the eyes for the glitter. "Everything was still and languid, worshipping the sun." When the sun slipped below the sea, night came suddenly, "a warm, velvety sweet-smelling night, but frightening and disturbing if one was alone in the hammock."[7] Her nurse, Meta, added to the intuitive fear of the other world of the night. She must not sleep in the moon. She was terrified by stories of jumbies, *soucoyants* (vampires), and great spiders that would creep above the sleeping child and drop onto its face.[8] She gained her imaginative understanding of *obeah* that give such hallucinatory vividness to the love potion scene of *Wide Sargasso Sea*.

Jean Rhys' early writing about the Caribbean has a wide range. Some of it is vivid recreation — mixing cocktails for her father in the holiday house,[9] or portraying an illiterate Roseau newspaper editor.[10] Other pieces are short stories, Chekhovian in their depth and economy. "The Day they Burnt the Books'[11] encapsulates not only a conflict between mulatto and European, but between two ways of life. Mr. Sawyer, settled in Dominica with private means, tries to preserve his old way of life by filling his house full of books. He resents and insults his mulatto wife, and she, silently, resents and hates him. After his death, years of subdued anger explode. She builds a fire and has a ritual burning of his books, leaving for sale only those with fine bindings — and where the writer was a woman, even leather binding cannot save it. The scene is counterpointed against the attitude to the burning of their son — himself culturally divided — and the white girl who loves him. The relationships of white Creole and expatriate Dominicans with the black community are explored with even greater complexity in two more recent stories, "Oh Pioneers, Oh, Pioneers"[12] and "Fishy Waters."[13]

Imaginatively, perhaps the most remarkable achievement among her Caribbean stories is "Let them Call it Jazz", which appeared in *The London Magazine* for 1962.[14] In it, Jean Rhys writes — in dialect — from the point of view of a black girl from Martinique, living in Notting Hill, London. She finds herself estranged and friendless. Her Caribbean sensibility makes England alien: "not much rain all the summer, but not much sunlight either. More of a glare." Her easy attitude to money makes her an easy prey to her landlady, who robs her of her savings, then ejects her for not having money. She finds temporary refuge in an otherwise empty house speculatively bought by a shady property developer, but growing tensions with her "nice' neighbours explode when she finally gets drunk and answers their insult by breaking a hideous stained glass window. She ends in gaol, a shock of final rejection that destroys her spirit. "It all dry up hard in me now. . . . There's a small looking glass in my cell and I see myself and I'm like somebody else."

One way in which she maintains her identity in prison is through her Caribbean songs, and her singing is one habit particularly annoying to her white neighbours: "I'm here because I wanted to sing," she thinks in prison. In gaol she hears a song composed by her fellow prisoners — the prison song. Hearing it she feels the relief and release slaves must have felt hearing negro spirituals at another time and place. It becomes her adopted song. Released from prison, pursuing a series of jobs, she allows a white composer to hear the tune, and he makes it a hit song. At first she feels betrayed and desolate; then realises that nothing can take away what the song means to her, just as the exploitation of black music cannot remove the black sense of jazz. In its evocation of black emotional warmth and essential awareness of musical rhythm, the story has an unassuming relationship to the insights of *negritude*.[15]

The range of Jean Rhys' writing about the Caribbean has not been previously fully noticed, and when it has been taken into account at all, it has been seen as the primary material from which the masterpiece *Wide Sargasso Sea* was to be fashioned. Kenneth Ramchand's recent essay on the subject,[16] for instance, while noting that Jean Rhys' *Voyage in the Dark* (1934) is "one of the most moving of the West Indian novels of exile," considers how the later work distances and develops the "too simple" divisions of *Voyage in the Dark*. While this is largely true, it can lead to a diminution of the importance of the earlier book. It was the first-written of all Jean Rhys' novels, and is still her favourite. It bears the same kind of relationship to *Wide Sargasso Sea* as Dickens' autobiographical *David Copperfield* bears to *Great Expectations*. Not only is one the mature reworking of the other, but what the earlier work lacks in symbolic objectivity, the first-written makes up in the freshness and poignancy of the personal element. *Voyage in the Dark* was composed from exercise-book diaries kept by the young Jean Rhys when living the desolate life of a chorus girl touring minor theatres in England.[17] As it is less known than *Wide Sargasso Sea*, I intend to explore its achievement in the remainder of this essay.

*Voyage in the Dark* concerns Anna Morgan, a fifth-generation Creole, with a Welsh doctor as a father, cast adrift in England and struggling for a living in a third-rate touring theatre company. She is from Dominica. The story is in four parts. In the first, she enters into a relationship with a young man, Walter Jeffries; when he nurses her through a minor illness there is a brief flowering into love; when he leaves her, she is broken. In a short section, we see Anna footloose in London. She sets up as an assistant to a one-time chorus girl friend, now a form of prostitute, operating a "massage" clinic in Bird Street, London. This venture is likewise doomed. In the third section, Anna conceives a child by an American, Carl, and finally has to appeal to Walter for money for an abortion, an agonizing and sordid operation in which the baby, killed within her, is still-born. In the final terrible climax she has the dead child, and the doctor says briskly, "She'll be alright. . . Ready to start all over again in no time, I've no doubt."[18]

Such a summary does essential violence to the book, which is a delicate counterpoint of Anna's London experiences against her inner memories of the Caribbean. The skill with which this is done defeats analysis. According to Diana Athill,[19] Rhys' method of composition is the painful writing and rearrangement of "an almost incredible mass of tangled notes and drafts" which continues until the work "feels" right. The process suggests, on one hand, a form of self-analysis, and on the other hand a kinship with musical composition. Ford Madox Ford accurately called it Rhys' "singular instinct for form."[20] Each emotion and theme has to have its appropriate and unique rhythm. This process is vividly described in a short story, "Tigers are Better-Looking,"[21] in which the writer, Mr. Severn, finds he cannot write about the Jubilee until he has spent a dissolute night experiencing the mixture of celebration and despair. Then, and only then, do the style and the experience coincide. "The swing's the thing — otherwise the cadence of the sentence . . ." Sitting down to his typewriter the morning after he finds himself released, he "has got it."

It is this sensitivity of style that makes what may appear a simple contrast between England and the Caribbean so moving. Anna, on coming to England, writes: "It was as if a curtain had fallen, hiding everything I had ever known. It was almost like being born again. The colours were different, the smells were different. Not just the difference between heat, cold; light, darkness; purple, grey. But a difference in the way I was frightened and the way I was happy" (p. 7).

The difference not only in what is felt, but in the *ways* of feeling, is crucial to the effect of *Voyage in the Dark*. When Jean Rhys recreates the West Indian house with its verandah and latticed jalousies, dazed by the sun at noon, haunted by the moon at night, the prose itself becomes luminous. We see through the eyes of a child, reacting with responses of wonder and fear to a moonlit boat-ride; and to the discomfort of Sunday, prickly in starched white drawers tight at the knees, white petticoat and embroidered dress, with brown kid gloves ordered from England and, by the time they arrived, one size too small — "Oh, you naughty girl, you're trying to split those gloves; you are trying to split those gloves on purpose" (p. 36). There is the misery of feeling the perspiration trickling under the arms and knowing that there will be a wet patch under the armpit, "a disgraceful thing to happen to a lady" (p. 36). Then, after the boredom of the service, a moment of release walking through the still palms in the churchyard. "The light is gold and when you shut your eyes you see fire-colour" (p. 38). In the passages of memory the senses are all fully alive — sight, smell and touch.

> And the sky close to the earth. Hard, blue and close to the earth. The mango tree was so big that all the garden was in its shadow and the ground under it always looked dark and damp. The stable-yard was by the side of the garden, white-paved and hot, smelling of horses and manure. And then next to the stables was a bathroom. And the bathroom too was always dark and damp. It had no windows, but the door used to be hooked a little bit open. The light was always dim, greenish. There were cobwebs on the roof. (pp. 36-37)

By contrast, descriptions of England are lacking in these qualities. The fields are "squares like pocket-handkerchiefs; a small tidy look it had, everywhere fenced off from everywhere else." The few sensuous details of England express alienation: "The streets like smooth shut-in ravines and the dark houses frowning down." There is monotonous sameness. "There was always a little grey street leading to the stage-door of the theatre and another little grey street where your lodgings were, and rows of little houses with chimneys like funnels of dummy steamers and smoke the same colour as the sky" (p. 8). In the Caribbean, even a cobweb was a significant detail.

The lack of warmth and detail in the English landscape is echoed, for Anna, in the people. English people "touch life with gloves on,"[22] Jean Rhys was to write elsewhere. There is little concern for other human beings, and in particular for women. "Most Englishmen don't care a damn about women" (p. 70). Values are focussed on money and clothes. "You can get a very nice girl for five pounds," one man explains to Maudie, "a very nice girl indeed; you can even get a very nice girl for nothing if you know how to go about it. But you can't get a very nice costume for her for five pounds. To say nothing of underclothes, shoes, etcetera and so on" (p. 40). The evaluation is that of an exploited, single girl in London. But extreme as it is, it is the reflection of a difference between life in a closely-knit island community and the impersonal materialistic life of an English city.

The division, however, is not only between Dominica and London; it existed in Dominica itself. The family circle, ruled over by Aunt Hester, caught in the straight-jacket of being white and respectable, is a cold climate for the sensitive

Anna. So Anna forms her deepest relationships with Francine, the black kitchen girl, a little older than she, and both mother and sister to her. Francine is extrovert, laughing and singing. Anna listens to her songs and joins in the stories. "At the start of the story she had to say 'Timm, timm,' and I had to answer 'Bois sèche'" (p. 61) When Anna has her first period, it is significantly Francine who tells her what is happening, and it all sounds natural; Hester then lectures her on it, making her feel soiled and ashamed.

The white family resents Anna's friendship with blacks. "Impossible to get you away from the servants. That awful sing-song voice you had! Exactly like a nigger you talked — and still do. Exactly like that dreadful girl Francine" (p. 56), explodes Hester. Anna is marooned between being white and being black. (In England, some friends call her a "Hottentot" (p. 12), and she has fantasies of being of mixed blood as she remembers seeing the name of an illegitimate mulatto girl on a slave list, Maillotte Boyd.) She loves Francine, but race dictates that Francine will hate her. She wants to be wedded to the sun, burnt black, or die. She goes deliberately under the midday sun without a hat and waits. "The sun at home can be terrible, like God." The sun punishes her for her presumption, and she is ill with sunstroke and then fever for some months. She turns, not black, but "thin and ugly and yellow as a guinea" (p. 63). The simile identifies her with the European commercial world, in which she is stamped and coined irrevocably.

Throughout *Voyage in the Dark*, the two worlds interweave, the imaginary remembered world more real than the actual present. When Walter takes out the girl he has just met, he opens the door behind the dining room and it is a bedroom. She is shocked and frightened; he covers his awkwardness with forced casualness. She goes in, shutting the door against him. The room, the bed, even the fire, are cold — "The fire was like a painted fire; no warmth came from it" (p. 48). But she is drawn to Walter, and her flickering, incipient emotion is reflected in her observation of the brighter colours, the red of the lampshades. This evokes a sense of the Caribbean, and at the same time, significantly of childhood. It had "a secret feeling — quiet, like a place where you crouch down when you are playing hide and seek." Love, when it comes, brings a web of warm memories. "Thinking of the walls of the Old Estate House, still standing, with moss on them. That was the garden. One ruined room for roses, one for orchids, one for tree ferns." And the sleep that follows is like the little death, sleep, taught in the Convent. "Children, every night before you go to sleep you should lie straight down with your arms by your sides and your eyes shut and say: 'One day I shall be dead. One day I shall lie like this with my eyes closed and I shall be dead.'" Sex brings a flicker of Aunt Hester's condemnation of Maillotte Boyd, the illegitimate slave girl: *"But I like it like this,"* she thinks; *"I don't want it any other way but this"* (p. 79).

The childhood innocence she knew, both in Dominica and in her love for Walter, are betrayed, and the two levels run together in a startling image. Reading the letter in which she learns Walter is casting her off, she thinks suddenly of the verandah at home, and of creeping by her sleeping Uncle Bo to pick up a magazine.

> I got up to the table where the magazine was and Uncle Bo moved and
> sighed and long yellow tusks like fangs came out of his mouth and
> protruded down to his chin — you don't scream when you are
> frightened because you can't and you don't move either because you
> can't — after a long time he sighed and opened his eyes and clicked
> his teeth back into place and said what on earth do you want child —
> it was the magazine I said — he turned over and went to sleep again.

The image comes and goes "What's this letter got to do with false teeth?" (p. 82)
she asks herself. But the relevance is complex. At one level the sudden transformation of her genial uncle into a toothed monster associates her betrayal by
Walter with her rejection by the family, a rejection she may not fully realize as
a child but which becomes clear in a heartless letter he writes later to her Aunt
Hester refusing to help Anna. Deeper, it brings a terrifying crack in her whole
sense of reality. Things are not what they seem. At another time, the image is
reversed: an inanimate mask becomes alive; Uncle Bo's face becomes a hideous
mask. But in the island masquerade, Meta, Anna's black nurse, is wearing a huge
white mask when, suddenly, she looks at the child and thrusts a contemptuous
pink tongue out through the slit. Again, the child is terrified. Both occasions are
moments when the shock breaks out of a conflict of structures of reality, a trauma
seen, in its widest sense, in Anna's confused cultural and racial identity. The
shock splits her psyche at the roots. Her very personality is betrayed. "I saw that
all my life I had known that this was going to happen, and that I'd been afraid for
a long time, I'd been afraid for a long time. There's fear, of course, with
everybody. But now it had grown, it had grown gigantic; it filled me and it filled
the whole world" (p. 82)

Towards the end she has a nightmare of sailing through doll-like islands in a
glassy sea. One of the islands is her island, but the trees are wrong, they are
English trees. Someone has fallen overboard. Drowning appears in the book as
an image of abstraction and spiritual death. Thus, when Walter had ditched her,
"It was like letting go and falling back into water and seeing yourself grinning up
through the water, your face like a mask, and seeing the bubbles coming up as if
you were trying to speak from under the water" (p. 84). When Anna returned to
a party after hiding herself in a ladies' room her friend Laurie had told her, "We
thought you'd got drowned" (p. 103). But this time it is not Anna. Or is it? Is she
dreaming of a scene of her own death? A sailor brings a coffin which opens and
a child rises, a doll-like child-bishop. She wonders if she should kiss its ring. But
it has a cruel face and eyes, and sways woodenly in the grasp of the sailor. Perhaps
her child — her own childhood — is dead and condemns her. She tries to walk
to the shore, thrusting through confused figures, but the deck heaves and she
struggles helplessly.

The images of falling, of violation, of drowning, of the mask, come together
again in the terrifying climax of the book, the birth of her dead child. Physically,
she experiences the giddy sensation of the world heaving and dripping away. The
pains of sex, birth and death merge, and her protests against the fumbling midwife

— "stop, please stop" — mingle with remembered cries against violation by a white-faced lover. The fear, the remembered white face, bring together another moment of terror experienced in childhood in Dominica. She and her family were watching the masquerade of the black community through the jalousie slats. The dancers' masks are painted pink with mocking blue eyes, straight noses and little heart-shaped red lips under which are slits for the dancers to thrust out their tongues. They are masks of mockery and hatred. Ironically, the white onlookers cannot see the satire directed against them — they see the dance only a proof of the blacks' lack of decency and self-respect. ". . . *You can't expect niggers to behave like white people all the time Uncle Bo said it's asking too much of human nature — look at that fat old woman Hester said just look at her — oh yes she's having a go too Uncle Bo said they all have a go they don't mind. . ."* (p. 157) Not only are the maskers imitating white people, one remembers that it was the hideous mask of the sleeping Uncle Bo that terrified Anna.

The remembered scene is punctuated by the cries of Anna — both as the terrified child and as the woman giving birth to her own stillborn baby — "I'm giddy." And the first person "I" of Anna the watcher changes to the "we" of the dancers as she merges, in her imagination, with the dancers. *"We went on dancing forwards and backwards backwards and forwards whirling round and round"* (p. 157). The surging pains intensify, and she is now on a horse, swaying dizzily, with no stirrups to hold to, and the road leading along the sea and up through ghostly shadows to see *"a cold moon looking down on a place where nobody is a place full of stones where nobody is"* (p. 158). She is falling, but still she clings with her knees feeling very sick. She wakes. The dead child is born.

The scene, like that of the nightmare with the doll-bishop, cannot be explained in terms other than itself. It brings together, with terrifying conviction, the actual agony of abortive childbirth and the levels of experience, the qualities of pain, that have emerged through the book, and lead them to the ultimate void, the wasteland in the cold moonlight. The ending echoes the beginning: both describe childhood impressions of Dominica. Her past is her future fate, waiting like a trap to destroy her. But the lonely ruin is not only a profound image of her own desolation. The image reminds us of Eliot's in *The Waste Land*; like Eliot's desert, it is the expression of a spiritual state and the symbol of a culture laid waste by its history:

> In this decayed hole among the mountains
> In the faint moonlight, the grass is singing
> Over the tumbled graves, about the chapel
> There is the empty chapel, only the wind's home.[23]

The haunted, ruined plantation house had appeared earlier in the story, a memory associated with a moment of love, planted with flowers. Anna's tragedy leads her intuitively back in time before even her birth before the ruins were made into gardens. She is led into the collective consciousness of her history, its historical and psychological roots. But for a fuller exploration of this intuition, we must examine *Wide Sargasso Sea*.

For the ruined house not only looks forward to the burning of Coulibri which is a climax of the later book, it looks backwards to a moment in Jean Rhys' personal history. In 1824, John Potter Lockhart of Old Jewry, London — Jean Rhys' great-grandfather — acquired "several plantations and estates in Dominica . . . now known by the name of Genever Plantation," some twelve thousand and thirteen acres and two hundred and fifty-eight souls.[24] The journey to Genever from Roseau then was very like that described in *Voyage in the Dark* in Anna's child-bearing vision: "The road goes along by the sea. The coconut palms lean crookedly down to the water. . . You turn to the left and the sea is at your back, and the road goes zig-zag upwards. . . When you see the sea again it's far below you" (p. 129). There, the other side of Loubière and Morne Eloi would have been the stone plantation house, with its broad verandah, the little wooden slave huts, and the coffee plantations struggling against the encroaching bush. The Lockharts had to face the bitter effects of the Napoleonic wars, which had turned French against English settlers, and the black population against both; the disruption of the Emancipation of the slaves; and the 1829 coffee blight. Personal tragedy also struck. In 1837, James Lockhart died. His wife courageously remained, but in 1844 riots broke out over the census, and Genever Plantation was sacked and burnt. It was rebuilt, and a garden planted in the ruins.[25] The young Gwen Williams visited the plantation and was fascinated by it history. These were the ruins of *Voyage in the Dark*; this was the burning of the Great House that had such tragic results in *Wide Sargasso Sea*.

The point is worth making, not to reduce either book to history — which they are not — but to emphasize the imaginative interfusion of the Caribbean context with the personal themes which are the content of Jean Rhys' books, and to underscore a difference between *Voyage in the Dark* and *Wide Sargasso Sea* that is as important as the fact of poetic reworking of earlier themes: *Voyage in the Dark* ends with the silent agony of the ruined house. *Wide Sargasso Sea* ends with the fire. Fire is the ambivalent symbol of both destruction and passion. The young Anna suffers; the mature Antoinette *rebels* against the life-denying imprisonment of the English Rochester, and asserts her human need for colour, for passion, for love. And this development of theme not only shows Jean Rhys developing her treatment of the white-black dilemma in the West Indies; it also shows a deepening understanding of the West Indian predicament itself.

For in the later novel, Jean Rhys returns to the experience of her grandmother in the burning of Genever, and explores the meaning of the ruins. Her heroine, Antoinette Cosway, is exiled in Jamaica from her homeland on a smaller island in the Antilles. Jamaica is portrayed with the beauty of Eden, but after the fall. "Our garden was large and beautiful as that garden in the Bible — the tree of life grew there. But it had gone wild."[26] The alienation Antoinette senses is caused partly by the social disintegration that follows the breakup of the old slave system — "All Coulibri Estate had gone wild like the garden, gone to bush. No more slavery — why should *anyone* work?" (p. 17). The Creoles face not only hate from the Blacks, but their contempt as well, for they are now powerless and poor.

The racial situation undermines Antoinette's friendship with a black girl, Tia. When Antoinette's mother marries the Englishman, Mr. Mason, who has no understanding of the Blacks, violence breaks out. The ex-slaves burn down the Great House, killing Antoinette's brother. Antoinette runs to Tia, who cuts her head open with a stone, then stands crying. The Creole family is saved only because their pet parrot falls from the house in flames, and the rioters pause in superstitious fear.

The cycle of history holds Antoinette as its victim. When the young Rochester marries her for her money, they return for their honeymoon to the island of Antoinette's childhood; like Jamaica, it is a world of intense tropical beauty, but a garden before the Fall. For a moment they are profoundly happy. But Rochester's cold, materialistic nature is tantalised and tormented by the sensuous warmth and beauty. When he hears allegations that Antoinette's mother was depraved and mad, it confirms his desire to withdraw from what he cannot fully enter. Antoinette, desperate for his love, turns to her black one-time nurse, Christophine, who, against her will, gives her a love potion for Rochester. It is the last thing his cold temperament can take. Driven into depravity and violence, he makes love not to Antoinette, but, with deliberate cruelty, to her maid; he then sets about emotionally killing Antoinette. "I saw the hate go out of her eyes. And with her beauty, her hate. She was only a ghost" (p. 140).

He takes her back to England, ostensibly insane, and imprisons her in the attic of Thornfield Hall. Here, finally she senses that she knows "what I have to do" (p. 156). She goes out with a candle to burn down the house. The end is complex and profound in its meanings. From one perspective, Antoinette has been absorbed into the destructive cycle of Caribbean history: her home was burnt; now she in her turn destroys. From another view, her act is positive: Rochester has not annihilated her, and she asserts her passionate spirit with hot fire. The novel does not show her death: we are left with the image of Antoinette carrying the light through the darkness that cannot overcome it.

*Wide Sargasso Sea* and *Voyage in the Dark* are interrelated. The movement from Anna to Antoinette is a progression in Jean Rhys' heroines from passive suffering to passionate strength, just as the exploration of the cold ruins of Anna's nightmare back to the burning of Coulibri is the deepening of her insight into West Indian history. The one novel lies at the beginning of her writing career; the other at its mature culmination. Yet the early book does not suffer in the comparison. *Voyage in the Dark* remains her most personal and evocative book. Not only does it capture a Caribbean childhood with delicacy; it also intensifies it within a powerful exploration of the experience of exile. And this is an experience known by many West Indians, both white and black.

Footnotes:

[1] John Hearne, "The Wide Sargasso Sea: A West Indian Reflection," *Cornhill Magazine* (Summer 1974), pp. 323-24.

[2] Wally Look Lai, "The Road to Thornfield Hall," *New World Quarterly* (Croptime 1968); reprinted *New Beacon Reviews* I (London: New Beacon, 1968), p. 44

[3] Edward Brathwaite, *Contrary Omens* (Mona, Jamaica, 1974), pp. 34-38.

[4] Kenneth Ramchand, *An Introduction to the Study of West Indian Literature* (London: 1976), p. 99.

[5] Hearne, p. 323.

[6] See, for example, Elgin W. Melown, "Character and Themes in the Novels of Jean Rhys," *Contemporary Literature*, 13 (Autumn 1972), 458-77; for more detail, based on new research, see my study *Jean Rhys*, forthcoming from Longman Caribbean.

[7] Jean Rhys, "Mixing Cocktails," in *The Left Bank* (London: Jonathan Cape, 1927); reprinted in *Tigers are Better Looking* (London: Deutsch, 1968), pp. 173-75.

[8] Personal information.

[9] 'Mixing Cocktails,' *Tigers*, pp. 173-76.

[10] 'Again the Antilles,' *Tigers*, pp. 177-180.

[11] *Tigers*, pp. 40-46

[12] *Sleep it Off, Lady* (London:Deutsch, 1976), pp. 11-22.

[13] *Ibid.*, pp. 45-62.

[14] Reprinted, *Tigers*, pp. 45-67.

[15] Cf. Ramchand's similar point, *op. cit.*, p. 100

[16] *Ibid.*, p. 100.

[17] Personal information.

[18] *Voyage in the Dark* (Harmondsworth: Penguin, 1969), p. 159. All subsequent references will be made to this edition.

[19] Diana Athill, "Jean Rhys and the Writing of *Wide Sargasso Sea*", *Bookseller* (August 20, 1966), pp. 1378-1379. *Wide Sargasso Sea* took nine years to write.

[20] Ford Madox Ford, Introduction to *The Left Bank,* reprinted *Tigers*, p. 148.

[21] *Tigers*, pp. 68-82.

[22] Jean Rhys, *Quartet* (Harmondsworth: Penguin, 1973), p. 9

[23] T.S. Eliot, *The Waste Land, Collected Poems 1909-1935* (London: Faber, 1936), p. 76.

[24] Information, Archives, Roseau, D, no. 5, fol. 600-603.

[25] S.W. Boyd, *Historical Sketch of the Grand Bay Area* (Roseau, Dominica, 1976).

[26] Jean Rhys, *Wide Sargasso Sea* (Harmondsworth: Penguin, 1968), p. 16. All subsequent references will be made to this edition.

# THE EMERGENCE OF A FORM:
## STYLE AND CONSCIOUSNESS IN JEAN RHYS'S *QUARTET*

*Thomas F. Staley*

The curious literary career of Jean Rhys has been well covered by the popular press and weekly reviews. The discovery and rediscovery of "lost" writers and new-found reputations is judged newsworthy, for stories such as hers confirm the collective mythologies of the struggling figure of the writer in the modern world, and thus feature stories with full picture spreads appear in the Sunday supplements of the *Times* and *Observer*.[1] The high and low points of her bizarre life and career have been recorded and misrecorded by nearly a dozen interviewers.[2] In England she became a minor cult figure, posing for fashion shots in the mass media; in American she has been featured in "W," the chic production of *Women's Wear Daily*, and *Ms*.[3] Lurking behind these poses of an eighty-year-old woman commenting on clothes and her own painful hegira from the West Indies, the provincial towns of England, half a dozen European capitals, and finally to a remote cottage in Devon is the novelist who struggled off and on for years with her art against devastating disappointments and what seemed certain failure. These color photographic portraits bring home to me Susan Sontag's accusation that there is something predatory in photography — the subject is somehow violated. Even with success and great age, Rhys has not escaped from her own fictional heroines.

Only after *Wide Sargasso Sea* was published in 1966, when she was seventy-two, and won the Smith Literary Award did any substantial literary recognition come to her.[4] Its success resulted in the republication of her novels by André Deutsch, and, later, the reprinting of them by Penguin, which broadened her reputation and enhanced critical acclaim to the point that A. Alvarez in the *New York Times Book Review* called her, quite simply, "the best living English novelist,"[5] The background of this belated attention is interesting in itself, especially in light of the increasingly serious study of women novelists and the nature of the feminine consciousness, but that is not the task to which I have set myself in this essay. My concern is with Rhys's own self-discovery as a writer as it is revealed at an early stage of her career when she wrote *Quartet* (1928),[6] her first published novel. It is with this work, I contend, that her distinctive style was realized and was brought into subtle harmony with her material and artistic vision. Equally important, an extensive examination of this novel reveals the

129

formulation of the major themes which were to be adumbrated in her subsequent work.

The sketches in *The Left Bank and Other Stories* (1927), Rhys's first book, represented an apprenticeship completed and an initial impulse fulfilled. She had learned from Ford Madox Ford the idiom in which modern fiction was to be rendered effectively, and how personal experience could be transmuted into the subject matter of art. Her instinctive sense of form gave several of these short stories originality, centrality of focus, and unity of theme. The novel, however, created enlarged and different demands; it is a genre more complex, more sustained, and, if it permits less refinement, it also calls for a more substantial rendering of character and a more amplified definition of experience.

Written and published during the height of literary modernism, *Quartet* (1928) had much to commend it as a product of the modernist movement — its sparse style, the author's gift for understatement and irony, the careful rendering of the heroine's preoccupations in a hostile, alienating urban environment. But central to modernist art is the concept best exemplified in English by Joyce and Eliot of the impersonality of the artist, the notion that the artist was to be refined out of the work of art: an art so impersonal that the subject might well follow the contours of the autobiographical self such as Joyce's Stephen Dedalus, but the artist himself remains beyond his handiwork, refined out of existence. For the modernist this concept was neither sleight of hand nor sophistry; it entailed a conscious artistry, a predilection for the formal properties and organic elements of art, a deep commitment to the allusive, the mythic, and a subordination of the traditional narrative concerns of the realistic novel such as plot, event, and resolution of the characters' circumstances.

Rhys's art shares many of these characteristics and impulses of literary modernism, but she was unaware of or removed from many of its preoccupations. Like Virginia Woolf, she had to resolve for herself special problems of authorial control. In her first novel she may occasionally appear to hover too closely over her heroine's misfortunes to achieve complete aesthetic detachment. But her scrupulously disciplined style and adroit rendering of consciousness through imagery and metaphor expand the dimensions of the novel. In short, she creates a form suitable for this close relationship between the self and a fully realized character. Although her later novels succeeded in providing greater aesthetic control and authorial distance, her work was never very closely attuned to the technical innovations of modernism; her art developed out of an intensely private world — a world whose sources of inspiration were neither literary nor intellectual.

Her acquaintance with the modern writers was relatively slight; most of her reading immediately prior to her writing career was in late nineteenth-and early twentieth-century French literature. Ford Madox Ford recognized Rhys's distinctive differences from the beginning when he pointed out her particular preoccupations and influences in his preface to *The Left Bank*. He noted that her literary affinities were not with her contemporaries, but rather with writers such as Anatole France, and he could have added Colette.

Rhys's relationship to the widely varied currents of modernism is difficult to untangle because of her unusual background and the circumstances which brought her to write in the first place. But one important element which she shared with so many writers of her generation was the problem of moral ambiguity. From the beginning of her writing career her work assumed the modifications necessary in describing will and human motivation after Freud. This is in no way to suggest that Rhys was a conscious Freudian, or even that she knew anything about Freud in a formal sense, but rather that her work reflects the modern relativism that had come into being and was central to the shaping forces of modernist literature. Her heroines thus live in a world not shaped by a clear code of social or moral behavior that delineates which actions are "good" and which are "bad." Rhys never probed the unconscious as Virginia Woolf or Marcel, but the world she created is obviously post-Freudian in its treatment of character, arrangement of consciousness, and development of theme. And this intuitive understanding contributed to the modernist character of her work as much as any other single factor.

The importance of *Quartet* in the Rhys canon is difficult to overemphasize, for it reveals not only the discovery and initial development of that original voice and tone which was to characterize and define her fiction throughout the 1930s; it also records the beginning of what was to become that distinctive style. In spite of certain flaws and limitations, *Quartet* initiates most of the major themes that preoccupy Rhys's later fiction. The technical problems, which will be overcome in her later work, also provide clues to the way in which she achieved her later technical mastery.

The earlier part of this essay details the character of the heroine at some length, because *Quartet* also introduces the paradigmatic Rhys heroine, a figure who with only slight transmutation will appear in all her fiction of the 1930s. Julia Martin in *After Leaving Mr. Mackenzie* (1931), Anna Morgan of *Voyage in the Dark* (1934), Sasha Jansen of *Good Morning, Midnight* (1939), all exhibit at various stages of development and in one form or another the general characteristics and attitudes of the heroine in *Quartet*. Although each is a fully drawn and well-defined character in her own right, collectively they form a stunning portrait of the feminine condition in the modern world. Even though these women, because of their similar backgrounds, represent only a segment of women in the world, the depth of their plights and the nature of their struggles reveal many of the broad social and moral issues against which the feminine consciousness must contend. The heroine of *Quartet* is the first figure that goes into the make-up of this sad and woeful portrait of denigration and abuse.

Whatever its limitations, *Quartet* signaled the emergence of a distinctive voice in English fiction. Besides creating a heroine totally innocent of bourgeois values and institutions, Rhys introduced a style — to be perfected and further refined in her later novels — which was admirably suited to the preoccupations of the heroine and the subtle revelation of her nature. Hers is a style which not only reinforces the pressing themes of her novels, but, in fact, it discovers and manifests the themes as it reveals the underlying attitude of the narrative voice toward the heroine, which lies within that surface brittleness of the style itself. As readers, we become increasingly conscious of the nature of her characters, not merely through action, motivation, or exertion of the will on their part, but rather through the rendering of their respective consciousnesses in a style which is always insightful and revealing. Carefully modulated, terse, frequently flat, always understated, the style penetrates surface situations to probe deeply into the underlying relationships and conditions of the characters.

The heroine of *Quartet* is a young woman, Marya, who has married Stephan Zelli, a young Pole who traffics in stolen art works. "On a June afternoon, heavy with heat, they arrived in Paris. . ."[7] from London and have been there four years, except for a long stay in Brussels. Even though Stephan is "secretive" and a "liar" he is "a gentle and expert lover." In spite of their precarious life together, she is happy, for as the narrator tells us: "Marya, you must understand, had not been suddenly and ruthlessly transplanted from solid comfort to the hazards of Montmartre. . . Truth to say, she was used to a lack of solidity and of fixed backgrounds" (p. 15). "She was . . . reckless, lazy, a vagabond by nature. . ." (p. 14). From the opening chapters the rather vague and aimless nature of Marya's character is established; it is suggested that her early disillusionment in trying to become an actress and ending up in a chorus line has made her passive; "she began to live her hard and monotonous life very mechanically and listlessly —" (p. 16). Her passivity explains a great many of Marya's attitudes and reactions and characterizes her personality throughout the novel as she becomes entrapped in a number of situations which she has more or less drifted into rather than decisively chosen. The narrator stresses Marya's passive nature from the beginning, because, among other things, it explains her curious attachment to her husband, and, later, her lover. More importantly, it is the exploration of this passivity which lies at the heart of the novel.

When Stephan is finally arrested and sentenced to prison for one year, Marya is left with no money and must once again fend for herself, a prospect for which she is hardly fit. As she passes through the Paris streets, her walk characterizes her condition: "She spent the foggy day in endless, aimless walking . . . [to] escape the fear that hunted her" (p. 33). Her vulnerability is driven home to her and the world is once again harsh and naked, as she senses it always was: "It was a vague and shadowy fear of something cruel and stupid that had caught her and would never let her go. She had always known that it was there — hidden under the more or less pleasant surface of things. Always. Ever since she was a child" (p. 33). In spite of her fears, she urges herself "to have some guts," but from the beginning we are aware that she is incapable of facing the world without protection. Her premonition in the passage above foreshadows the "cruel" and "stupid" forces which will entrap her.

Protection is offered very quickly, however. A couple whom Marya has met, H. J. and Lois Heidler, suggest that she move into a spare bedroom in their flat. The Heidlers live near the center of the expatriate, bohemian life of Paris; she paints in a dilatory way, and he is an art dealer who champions young painters.

These are the "good Samaritans" of the epigraph toward which the bitterness of the novel is pointed:

> . . . Beware
> Of good Samaritans — walk to the right
> Or hide thee by the roadside out of sight
> Or greet them with the smile that villains wear.
>
> R. C. Dunning

The admonishment in the epigraph, however, is curious, for the weight of the novel is certainly directed to the last line; Marya, unable to hide, is also unable to fix the right smile, or assume the posture, It is in this conundrum that the original title of the novel, *Postures*, could have come to mind, but the later title, *Quartet*, the one which Rhys preferred, suggests a broader scope to the overall theme, and places a more proper emphasis on the complexity of relationships between the Heidlers, Marya and Stephan. Furthermore, to prepare a pose is beyond Marya's scope; she is a creature without guile and her sense of self-preservation grows out of aimlessness. It is not in her nature to assume postures which would require decisiveness and direction. This point is not to suggest that Marya is fundamentally an honest victim of her own moral code of behavior. Survival and protection are the motivating forces behind her actions, and they do allow her to fool herself for a while.

Her helpless situation inevitably draws her to the Heidlers; Marya's need for comfort and any kind of reassurance leads her to create the illusion that Heidler is a strong, security figure; "He was a rock of a man with his big shoulders and his quiet voice" (p. 43). Yet, her instincts are nearly always acute; when she first met Heidler before Stephan's incarceration she saw in his eyes "a curious underlying expression of obtuseness — even of brutality" (p. 11). The center of her restricted world, however, moves closer and closer to the Heidlers; although she professes her love for Stephan when she visits him in jail, she does so "hopelessly," "for she felt that he was withdrawn from her, enclosed in the circle of his own pain, unreachable" (p. 45). The complexities of this potential relationship with the Heidlers are dismissed without a great deal of concern, for, although the prospect fills her with "extraordinary dismay" she thinks: "After all . . . it might be fun" (p. 49). Since she has lost one protector temporarily, and needs another, she allows herself to drift or be taken in without weighing the implications.

Actually, it is Lois Heidler who convinces Marya that she should live with them, by pointing out the limited alternatives for a young woman without money. The prospects are, of course, bleak and this is an important aspect of the entire novel — a subject to be discussed in detail later. Lois, in a sense, has seduced her, but with so few options Marya is willing.The Heidlers attribute higher motives to themselves and are initially half-convinced that they want to protect Marya, but the real truth is they want Marya as a bed companion for Heidler — Lois to keep him from straying permanently, moved by some romantic gesture in his lust, and

Heidler himself, not so much to protect Marya, but to feel the warmth of her small and supple body next to him. From the beginning, then, the motives of both the Heidlers are clear whatever the self-deception or posturing they play upon Marya or upon each other.

Chapter Seven is a deceptively simple transitional chapter, but what it does is complete the prior phase of Marya's life with Stephan and prepare for the inevitable move to the Heidlers. It forms the necessary psychological bridge for Marya. Stephan's insistence that she live with her own "country-people" is the final impetus she needs; more importantly, he also offers some implicit moral justification which is really what she wants, for her financial situation is such that her options are futile ones anyway. Through a clever manipulation of the situation she has forced Stephan to insist she go, and she agrees to do so "to quieten him and make him happier" (p. 57). Having elicited this response, however, she still moves to the Heidlers with a "sense of the futility of all things" (pp. 57-59). These events may seem to contradict my contention that Marya is fundamentally amoral and incapable of posturing. On the other hand, Marya is attempting to remove herself from moral mandates of any kind and whatever machinations she goes through, they are essentially to place the moral issues outside of herself: This kind of action may seem to belie my point, but I would contend that she is not concerned with "good" or "bad" or guilt, but rather with future recriminations.

There is in Marya a sense of a lost past which has been stolen from her, and it is this sense of loss and being plunged into a fearful and "shallow world" that allows her to move from one circumstance to another finding protection from the shadows. The unalterable separation from her past is made abundantly clear in the postscript of a letter from her aunt from whom Marya has requested money: "Have you thought of visiting the British clergyman resident in Paris? He might be able to help you" (p. 58). This suggestion also points to her past, but the force of the six earlier chapters renders the full irony which points up the inseparable gulf between Marya's past and present that can never be bridged. Walking back to the train from the prison. Marya stood for a long time watching a little girl on a merry-go-round, and this picture "made her feel more normal, less like a grey ghost walking in a vague, shadowy world" (p. 57).

Marya's early days with the Heidlers are very deftly drawn and developed through a carefully selected pastiche of scenes which illustrate not only her increasing reliance on the Heidlers but the way in which their world gradually becomes a large part of hers. The domestic scenes which open Chapter 8 reveal the relatively ordered life of the Heidlers and are set in careful contrast to the fear and disruption of Marya's days alone after Stephan was incarcerated. During these early days, amid the routine and order, Heidler assumes for Marya a particular role —protective and paternal— "and it seemed natural that she should wait on him" (p. 59). But whatever the physical comforts of the Heidlers', Marya is more deeply content because she has returned to a small, enclosed world, where Heidler is "the remote impersonal male of the establishment" (p. 59). Lois Heidler, on the other hand, presents a far more complex relationship. Lois uses her as a model for her painting, lectures to her, and does both with confidence. Through her lectures as well as their Cafe lunches, Marya is introduced to the confident sociologist of the entire bohemian scene: "explaining, classifying, fitting the inhabitants (that is to say, of course, the Anglo-Saxon inhabitants) into their proper places in the scheme of things. The Down-and-Outs, the Freaks who never would do anything, the Freaks who just possibly might" (p. 60). Opinions she had on every aspect of this life, and Marya who had seen some of this life herself knew it would be "a waste of time to contradict her. . . She [Lois] gave a definite impression of being insensitive to the point of stupidity — or was in insensitive to the point of cruelty" (p. 60)?

As events transpire this question comes more and more to the surface. The long monologues from Lois gradually drive a wedge between the two women; Marya continues to admire her benefactress during these early days but the initial "soft Intimacy" quickly fades. Lois is also frequently the object of the narrator's irony: "Lois also discussed Love, Childbirth (especially childbirth, for the subject fascinated her), Complexes, Paris, Men, Prostitution, and Sensitiveness, which she thought an unmitigated nuisance" (p. 61). Far more devastating, however, are Marya's own reflections of Lois and their relationship: "'Lois is as hard as nails,' she would find herself thinking. A sentence she had read somewhere floated fantastically into her mind: 'It's so nice to think that the little thing enjoys it too,' said the lady, watching her cat playing with a mouse" (p. 62).

In spite of her growing difficulties with Lois, the world of the Heidlers is for Marya a glittering one, but, at the same time, the chic, intelligent, but seemingly unreal world frightens her and inexorably she is drawn to Heidler. At this stage, however, their relationship is undefined, "but when they danced together she felt a definite sensation of warmth and pleasure" (p. 63). As the days wear on she and Heidler are inevitably drawn together; even before any words are exchanged or any strongly conscious sexual feeling emerges, her senses begin to anticipate the ambivalence of the relationship: "There was a smell of spring in the air. She felt unhappy, excited, strangely expectant" (p. 65). Heidler himself is at first enigmatic and shy, unable to approach Marya. Once again it is necessary for Lois to pave the way for Heidler's advances. In an awkward, rude, and callow manner Heidler tells Marya that he has wanted her from the first time he saw her, and goes on to say in his inimitable charming way that "I know that somebody else will get you if I don't. You're that sort" (p. 72). In spite of their initial row, as they walk out of the Cafe together, he took her arm in his, and "when he touched her she felt warm and secure, then weak and so desolate that tears came into her eyes" (p. 73). This instant flow of mixed emotion depicts clearly Marya's dilemma; she is drawn to Heidler by her need for protection and security, but at the same time she must attempt to reconcile this need with her obligations to the other two members of the "Quartet" — Stephan and Lois.

Stephan is so wrapped up in his own self-torture that he seems to have pulled away from any concern with Marya, and Lois, fearful that Heidler could run off with Marya and aware that his hot lust for her will gradually dissipate, if he can realize his lust while they are under the same roof, encourages Marya to remain in the household as Heidler's lover — the ménage à trois begins with a variety of mixed motives and compromises. Marya's compromise has to do with a certain abandonment of her will; she looks upon her dilemma not so much in moral terms, for she has released herself from that by seeing herself a "a victim." She recalls what a sculptor once told her: "Victims are necessary so that the strong may exercise their will and become more strong" (p. 73). She inverts the Nietzschean cry for self-justification of the strong by applying it to the weak, but having arrived at this position, she still feels the strong urge to retreat altogether, to leave the Heidlers.

Marya does not leave, and, although she has not yet slept with Heidler, the whole nature of their relationship has shifted. She has lunch with a young American writer by the name of Cairn, who expresses concern for her, but is too poverty-stricken himself to help her. He warns her of Heidler, but his inability to give anything but advice brings Marya even closer to a realization that she is trapped both by the Heidlers themselves and by her own lack of will.

Upon her return to the apartment, Heidler pleads his love once more, but Marya forestalls his advances by murmuring that she is afraid of being hurt again. Heidler tries to allay her fears and protests by telling her he wants to make her happy. Perhaps Heidler has touched an important element in spite of his self-interest when he tells Marya: "You tear yourself to pieces over everything, and, of course, your fantastic existence has made you worse. You simply don't realize that most people take things calmly. Most people don't tear themselves to bits. They have a sense of proportion and so on" (p. 77).

The aimless nature of Marya's life has taken the balance and weight from most decisions and as a result panic and fear seize her at all points of conflict. Reasoned decisions emanate from a sense of balance and values which give proportion to alternatives. These are qualities removed from Marya's life.

In this enclosed world of the Heidler's, "little Mado" is the eternal "child," and the values which fashion, rule, and dominate this world opaque to her. As long as she lives in respectful obedience of the laws laid down she will be tolerated, but even here things are capricious and as long as she remains merely an object, she is passive before those human gods who establish the rules and the values by which the rules are laid down.

Lois insists Marya stay where she can watch over the affair, knowing full well that she must ride it out. A candid and revealing point in one of their conversations is Lois's remark, "'D'you suppose that I care what you are, or think or feel? I'm talking about the man, the male, the important person, the only person who matters'" (p. 81). It is to this female self-perspective that all of Rhys's heroines will fall victim — they reject it, but fall victim to its results. In a world where men are so valued, women are inescapably reduced to objects.

We realize that Lois — out of her humiliation and jealousy — has focused her anger on Marya rather than Heidler, for Marya is a female, an adversary. For Lois, in spite of her "advanced" ideas, masculine supremacy is a given, accepted as inevitable. It is this attitude on her part which forces Lois into the further self-humiliations of not only tolerating Heidler and Marya's affair, but condoning it in her presence and cajoling Marya into staying on with them. Lois believes she must help to gratify the male's need whatever the cost to her own person, for he is the superior being; the female must comply. Marya and Lois as females must be subservient to the dominant male, and this subservience is measured by each in different ways: for Lois it brings recognition, position within the art world of Paris, it allows her to be confident and knowing; for Marya it offers a fundamental protection and security, or at least a temporary hospice from concern.

Although certainly no paragon of virtue herself, Marya is befuddled by the entire circumstances of the relationship with the Heidlers and Lois's acceptance of it. Like Heidler, Lois tells Marya she's "making a fuss about nothing at all" (p. 82). After Lois leaves, Marya is possessed with "a profound conviction of the unreality of everything. . ." (p. 83). This dreamlike quality is a part of Marya's nature and it allows her to move from compromising situation to situation without invoking moral judgments. It is through this trance-like quality that she accepts the present in isolation; she drifts into Heidler's arms and in the intensity of the moment immediately feels that "all my life before I knew him was like being lost on a cold dark night" (p. 83). Marya is always ready to settle for the present whatever its ultimate cost especially if it clouds the unpleasant contours of life, but Lois sees the longer shadows and prepares for them. In a male-dominated world, each has different needs: for Lois it is position and respect within the social order, for Marya it is merely protection and some enjoyment of the sensuous pleasures of life. It is in these different worlds that each seeks her own false freedom.

In the early days of the love affair Marya is totally absorbed and happy "for perhaps the first time in her life. No past, No future. Nothing by the present: the flowers on the table, the taste of wine in her mouth" (p. 85). And in a curious way Lois is also happy with the situation. She realizes that people in the restaurant are aware of the ménage à trois, and "instantly reacting to the atmosphere of sympathy and encouragement, sat very straight, dominating the situation and talking steadily in a cool voice" (p. 85).

Lois has adjusted to the relationship far better than Marya; Lois has reduced her to an object — a toy not only of Heidler, but her own toy too. Two remarks to Heidler illustrate how in her clever way she has perched on top of the triangle and made an object out of Marya. First she suggests to Heidler that they must get Marya a new hat, "she must do us credit," Even more devastating for Marya, she suggests to Heidler: "'Let's go to Luna-park after dinner," she said. 'We'll put Mado on the joy wheel, and watch her being banged about a bit. Well, she ought to amuse us sometimes; she ought to sing for her supper; that's what she's here for, isn't it'" (p. 85)?

Marya later protests Lois's treatment of her to Heidler, but he remains delib-erately oblivious to it. It is important for him to do so. He needs both women: Lois for her sense of form and order and independence, Marya for her recklessness and dependence. This crossfire of emotions makes Marya yearn to be free of the Heidlers; she feels caught in an "appalling muddle," knowing she should "clear out," "but when she thought of an existence without Heidler her heart turned over in her side and she felt sick" (p. 89). This turmoil gives her the "fright of a child shut up in a dark room. Fright of an animal caught in a trap" (p. 90). Her dependence upon Heidler increases in direct proportion to her humiliation by Lois. She feels she is a pawn in a game between the two of them — a game played by a set of rules she does not fully understand. Told she won't come out a loser by both sides, she still rightly feels the victim of the mixed desires of both.

One of the many lessons Rhys learned under the tutelage of Ford was the judicious selection of material, a stripping away of all but the essential. This lesson, of course, is of major importance to her style, but it also affects the arrangements of scenes and chapters. In *Quartet* we do not have the precision and synchronization that is a part of the later works, but the clear direction of this important element of her art is established. For example, after the rather full depiction of Marya's early days in the Heidler household with its emerging tensions, there is not a further heaping up of detail. Winter passes into spring and the next scene catches the full impact of the passage of time with a view of the affair from the eyes of an outsider, Cairn, the American writer who has again asked Marya to lunch.

Through the scene with Cairn we are able to see the effects of the Heidlers on Marya after several months. Marya is not naïve and has not been completely taken in by the situation as he had suspected. She is frankly forthcoming with him:

"'Very well then, I will tell you. Listen. Heidler thinks he loves me and I love him. Terribly. I don't like him or trust him. I love him'" (pp. 92-93). Not only does she reveal her own feelings but her acquired knowledge of the game they are all playing.

> D'you get me? And Lois says that she doesn't mind a bit and gives us her blessing — the importance of sex being vastly exaggerated and any little thing like that. But she says that I mustn't give her away. So does Heidler. They call that playing the game. So I have to trail around with them. And she takes it out of me all the time in all sorts of ways. I can just keep my end up now, but soon I won't be able to. And then, you see, I'm conscience-stricken about her. I'm horribly sorry for her. But I know that she hasn't a spark of pity for me. She's just out to down me — and she will. (p. 93).

Marya does not mind Lois hating her, but rather that she pretends she doesn't. Cairn tells her that such a relationship is known as a *Moyen Classique*, and Marya is mildly surprised that the whole thing is so obvious. But Marya is aware that in spite of Cairn's concern he is unable to help her. This scene, however, functions to advance the narrative and move the action from its early stages nearer to the point of crisis, for it summarizes the development and fixes on the present tensions. More importantly, it reveals the transformation in Marya, the protective cynicism, and the new hardness — but it remains to be seen if these new "postures" will lessen her vulnerability.

Much of this new hardness is merely bravado anyway, for when Heidler tells her not to see Cairn again she meekly agrees, and he follows that request immediately with another, not to visit Stephan in prison, and with a meekness that makes for desperation, she responds: "'Yes,' she said. And stopped herself from saying: 'I'll do anything to please you—anything'" (p. 96). But the figure of Lois has become even more imposing for Marya, because it is hardened by hatred rather than softened by love or need.

In fact, the whole arrangement has become for Marya an obsession of love and hatred. She is desolate and desperate, unable to move the relationship in any way. Heidler brings her peace when he makes love to her and comforts her, but these are only temporary respites. As they ride to a summer place in the country, Marya looks across the railway carriage and sees Lois, this "formidable" figure, as "obviously of the species wife" (p. 97). She glances from Lois to Heidler: "and there he was, like the same chord repeated in a lower key" (pp. 97-98). They are inextricably together. Seeing this, Marya realizes that she is only a temporary fixture in their lives, a temporary cross for Lois and passion for Heidler. Soon she would be discarded, no longer to be "taken care of," "and then they wanted to be excessively modern, and then they'd think: 'after all we're in Paris'" (p. 98). Marya is perceptive in her assessment of the entire situation and it is her understanding that makes the whole thing impossible for her. She realizes, too, that she has no weapons to counteract their respective demands upon her: "Of course, there they were: inscrutable people, invulnerable people, and she simply hadn't a chance against them, naïve sinner that she was" (p. 101). "Naïve sinner" — it is from this self-characterization that she justifies her own seduction, her own willingness to play the game at all! "Naïve" because the rules of the game emanated out of bourgeois values — rules too complex for her to grasp in the beginning.

The Heidlers are, of course, content to allow things to continue: Lois confident in her knowledge of Heidler and the nature of his fluctuating passions, Heidler quite happy to have the love object under his roof. Marya, however, brings everything to a dramatic crisis during their visit in the country.

> But every vestige of coherence, of reason had fled from her brain. Besides, however reasonably or coherently she talked, they wouldn't understand, either of them. If she said: "You're torturing me, you're mocking me, you're driving me mad," they wouldn't understand.
>
> She muttered: "I'm not going to live with Lois and you any longer. I — am — not! And You must arrange. . ."
>
> "Ah!" said Heidler, "it's a question of money. I rather thought that was what you were getting at."
>
> She jumped forward and hit him as hard as she could.
>
> "Horrible German!" she said absurdly. "Damned German! Crapule!" She stood panting, waiting for him to drop his arm that she might hit again.
>
> "You're quite right," he muttered, and put his head in his hands. "You're quite right. Oh God! Oh God!"

> Lois went up to him and he lifted his head and looked at her with hatred.
>
> "Leave me alone," he said "I've done with you."
>
> She began to talk in a caressing voice.
>
> "Damn you, leave me alone!" he shouted, and pushed her so that she staggered back against the wall. Then he buried his face in his arms again and began to sob.
>
> Marya's calm came back to her as they disappeared. She began to think how ridiculous it all was, that it was chilly, that she wanted to go upstairs, that she had only imagined the love and hate she felt for these two, that she had only imagined that such emotions as love and hate existed at all. She stood looking at the floor, feeling undecided and self-conscious. (pp. 103-04)

Heidler quickly reverts to his usual defense, pleads drunkenness and retires, saying he'll remember nothing of this tomorrow. The next morning Marya begins to pack and Lois attempts to help her and also apologizes, but Marya has only hatred for her: "She hated her air of guilt. She hated her eyes of a well-trained domestic animal" (p. 107). And it is precisely this aspect of Lois which Marya despises, and yet, Lois's submission offers the security and certitude that Marya knows she will never possess. In spite of her despicable traits these are the very ones which ultimately sustain Lois's place with Heidler and make her a necessary part of his life. As much as Marya, Lois is a victim of male subjugation; she has made herself able to fulfill a greater variety of male needs, but for all of this she is no less violated by masculine domination. Both women are victims of that psychic and physical oppression which Simone de Beauvoir describes in *The Second Sex*, their consciousnesses are not defined in reciprocity with the male but as "the other." In containing only man's "otherness," they are denied their own humanity. And the force of the novel moves increasingly, form this point on, to explore the abyss.

After this rupture Marya's life takes that inevitable downward spiral that fate and poor judgment had prescribed all along. With no other resources, she allows Heidler to set her up in a cheap hotel room, and he comes to visit her in "an atmosphere of departed and ephemeral love [which] hung about the room like stale scent. . ." (p. 111). She tells Heidler during one of his visits after they make love: "'I feel as if I had fallen down a precipice'" (p. 112). The narrative grows increasingly complex as it attempts to register Marya's descent through a series of interrelated images and extended metaphors, developing a structural rhythm that provides a special perspective on Marya's movement and reactions as the events swarm around her. This added dimension is achieved through the style and not only reflects with increasing intensity the full dimension of Marya's destruction, but also renders a deeper thematic resonance to the entire novel as it unfolds a larger vision through this complementary perspective.

Although the narrative focus still moves swiftly through the events, the realistic level is frequently blended with open-ended images and dreamlike flights that are, nevertheless, rigidly controlled by the direct and simple style. The imagery and rhythm of this latter style produce a subtle rendering of a dreamlike quality in Marya's consciousness which breaks from the realistic strains of the narrative and marks the psychological dimensions of her entrapment. These passages reveal far more of Marya's subconscious motives and anxieties than she herself can realize, and thus explore more profoundly the themes of the novel. On one level the narrative force seems to insist that Marya's incapacity to break away from those upon whom she is dependent is justified, but on a deeper level the consciousness revealed to the reader points to a broader framework of human culpability and to the underlying reasons for Marya's desperation, escape from reality, irrational illusions, and amoral posturing.

It is worthwhile to summarize briefly, at this point, the remaining narrative events of the novel which precipitate Marya's eventual fate. Throughout the summer Marya lies in her room, goes out to eat, and once a week to visit Stephan in prison. This routine is interrupted only by Heidler's visits to have sex. By August, however, Stephan is released, but he is allowed to remain in France for only a few days. He must go to Amsterdam to make connections, but he has no money to take her with him. Like a puppet on a string Marya is controlled by who has the money, and Heidler has the money. Torn between love and hate for Heidler, who has forbidden her to see Stephan, and loyalty and despair for Stephan, her choices become more and more restricted and her emotional state less and less stable. Heidler sends her to the south of France to "recuperate" and provides her with only enough money pay for her room and board. She sees her situation growing increasingly desperate, until a letter from Stephan brings "a faint stirring of hope" (p. 165). After their reunion in Paris, Marya realizes that Stephan's situation is such that he must strike out on his own. Marya reveals to Stephan that she had been Heidler's lover during his incarceration. Stephan is curious, but gradually he appears to be infuriated and thus begins a violent scene of cross-recriminations, finally ending with Stephan flinging Marya to the floor and walking out only to meet [fortuitously] Mademoiselle Chardin and go off with her, either for just the night or perhaps to the Argentine.

The imagery in which Marya's sense of her dilemma is framed supports her psychological vacillations and confirms beyond her own awareness the inevitable consequences of her actions. The most persistent image is that of the caged animal, and the arrangement of the image within the fabric of the narrative points out the significance of both the psychological and the problematic elements of the novel. In a wider context, it suggests the implicit post-Darwinian question of just how human beings stand in relation to animals. Are we not after all similarly governed by laws over which we have no control, and are we not with animals brothers together locked in the same struggle for survival? This image with its predatory overtones and depiction of  human confinement also imaginatively accommodates the various forms of conflict within *Quartet*. The first time it appears is after Marya has moved in with the Heidlers, the day after H. J. has made clear to her that he intends for her to be his lover. With this prospect uppermost in her mind, she walks through Paris on a "cloudless, intoxicating day." She thinks of those days after Stephan's incarceration, remembering "her tears and her submissions and the long hours she had spent walking between two rows of street lamps, solitary, possessed by pity as by a devil. 'I've been wasting my life,' she thought. 'How have I stood it for so long'" (p. 74)? Through self-pity she justifies the prospects of her submission to Heidler, excused by weakness and redeemed by helplessness. Although she has not allowed herself to become his lover, she justifies it psychologically as a chance for new birth:

> And her longing for joy, for any joy, for any pleasure was a mad thing
> in her heart. It was sharp like pain and she clenched her teeth. It was
> like some splendid caged animal roused and fighting to get out. It was
> an unborn child jumping, leaping, kicking at her side. (p. 74)

In this early stage the metaphor of the caged animal is not hostile because the entrapped has the resources of escape; it is a bold and natural act, uninhibited and free. Another revealing aspect of the image is that of being acted upon rather than acting. Even joy comes by accepting.

The metaphor is seen in a different context, however, when Marya visits Stephan in prison, and she exhorts him not to be so dejected about his circumstances. She says, "'If anybody tried to catch me and lock me up I'll fight like a wild animal; I'd fight till they let me out or till I died'" (p. 136). Stephan's reaction is unintentionally prophetic for Marya's own circumstance:

> "Oh, no, you wouldn't, not for long, believe me. You'd do as the others
> do — you'd wait and be a wild animal when you came out." He had
> put his hand to his eyes and added: "When you come out — but you
> don't come out. Nobody ever comes out."
> She stared at him, impressed by this phrase. (p. 136)

"Impressed," because on the conscious level she is beginning to transfer his remarks to her own situation. And her "stare" confirms her realization. She quickly changes the subject, for it begins to dawn on her that one does not leave the cage merely by walking out of the unlocked gate. Instincts for survival and lust for life, so natural and pure in animals, are not sufficient protection for human beings with their conflicting motivations and complex feelings of guilt, joy, and despair. More importantly, we are reminded of the larger implications of this metaphor as it applies to the condition of the female generally, for Marya herself earlier referred to Lois as a "well-trained domestic animal" (p. 107). This is the feminine condition in a sexist structure of male physical, social, economic, and psychological dominance. Marya's and Lois's imprisonment is no less real than Stephan's, and, perhaps ugliest of all, this condition makes Lois what she is and provokes Marya to become what she has become. As de Beauvoir has written "It is not nature that defines women: it is she who defines herself by dealing with nature on her own account in her emotional life."[8] But condemned to this oppression she is only an object and since each consciousness must define itself as subject looking for reciprocity of relationship, achievement of freedom in the philosophical sense is impossible, whatever the physical comforts offered to the entrapped. The metaphor of oppression is further extended, however, as Marya's awareness of her dire circumstances increases. During her stay in Nice, she visits the zoo with the Heidlers' friend, Miss Nicolson, and suggests they look at the animals:

> There was a young fox in a cage at the end of the zoo — a cage perhaps three yards long. Up and down it ran, up and down, and Marya imagined that each time it turned it did so with a certain hopefulness, as if it thought that escape was possible. Then, of course, there were the bars. It would strike its nose, turn and run again. Up and down, up and down, ceaselessly. a horrible sight, really. (p. 160)

She sees in the "hopefulness" of the fox that same innocence and daring with which she entered into the affair with the Heidlers (it was with both, psychologically at least). It is through this scene that she sees with far more insight not only the hopelessness of her affair from the beginning, but partially, at least, the horror if its future implications. Although she will continue to raise false hopes and further justifications, as a deeper level she intuits the ramifications of her actions, and this image confirms all the more conclusively the dire consequences of her relationship with the Heidlers.

This extended metaphor of entrapment acts as a barometer of Marya's deepest feelings and understanding of her situation with the Heidlers, but at each instance it carries a suggestiveness beyond her own understanding. There is a clear resonance throughout its early appearance that suggests its benevolence, for the cage is also protective, but as Marya's awareness increases the dominance of its malignancy clarifies. Marya, like the animal, is fed, clothed, and even catered to, but all of this is for the pleasure and whim; of the one who holds the key, and, more particularly, the money — Heidler himself — the male. An important collateral or extension for the cage metaphor throughout the latter half of the novel is the imagery that has to do with the description of hotel rooms which Marya occupies — paid for by Heidler. Although the narrative voice on the realistic level exposes Marya's feelings, the style itself, alternating from direct exposition to a metaphoral language, probes with equal subtlety the underlying conflicts of which Marya is only partially aware. The sentences in this latter mode remain short and direct of simple construction, but a special effect is produced by a staccato force and a sense of space between each construction.

Marya's desperation grows as events keep acting upon her. The metaphor of the caged animal, however, is not sufficiently complex to record her myriad emotions, nor the wider observations of the narrative persona who records her condition in far bleaker terms:

> She was trying to climb onto of the blackness up an interminable ladder. She was very small, as small as a fly, yet so heavy, so weighted down that it was impossible to hoist herself to the next rung. The weight on her was terrible, the vastness of space round her was terrible. She was going to fall. She was falling. The breath left her body. (p. 162)

The cage has given way to a grotesque Kafkaesque image of claustrophobia and vertigo, reflecting Marya's horror, fear, dislocation, and desperation. This mutation of the image with its greater intensity and emotional charge reflects the closing in of the forces against her and her inability to cope with them.

The imagery records with growing forcefulness Marya's disembodiment and defeat; it also points to a condition which the realistic narrative only partially develops. These passages are more engrossing than merely a direct rendering of consciousness, for they are in a sense a stylization of consciousness. This spatial element is further enhanced in the later stages of the novel by a dreamlike quality in the style which pervades the scrupulous surface realism.

Against her fears and the grim sense of foreboding, the narrator records that Marya sets up a number of defense mechanisms based upon fantasies and delusions, driving home the observation that extreme desire turns reality into fantasy. Frequently these fantasies are brought on by more Pernod, "After the fifth Pernod. . . 'Never mind'" (p. 160), or sleeping pills. The narrator tells us that drink brought upon Marya a temporary "irrational feeling of security and happiness" (p. 134), and as her condition becomes increasingly abject, she begins to build on her fantasies. Shunted off by Heidler, she creates an irrational image of Stephan as a savior: "Marya thought of her husband with a passion of tenderness and protection. He represented her vanished youth — her youth, her gaiety, her joy in life. She would tell herself: 'He was kind to me. He was awfully chic with me'" (p. 125). But these projections are desperate escape mechanisms and only serve to increase her despair and gradually give way to a feeling of "sickness" which leaves her lying in bed "huddled with her arm over her eyes" (p. 125). These obsessions become increasingly intense:

> She undressed, and all the time she was undressing it was as if Heidler were sitting there watching her and with his cool eyes that confused and hurt her.
> She lay down. For perhaps thirty seconds she was able to keep her mind a blank; then her obsession gripped her, arid, torturing, gigantic, possessing her as utterly as the longing for water possesses someone who is dying of thirst. (p. 145)

Marya is unable to build any counter-universe against the grim and hostile world of her subjugation; once cut loose by Heidler and uncertain of her position with Stephan she is plunged into darkness. She is now in the world of absurd gestures and purposeless behavior which Kafka describes. Stephan's rejection of her confirms with the most devastating directness her final violation and despair. All of her pathetic efforts to accommodate these opposing forces serve to confirm her own imprisonment and isolation in the masculine power structure.

One may argue that this intense depiction of Marya's obsessional world has blurred the relationship between the narrator and the heroine, closed in on the aesthetic distance, and dismantled the necessary objectivity to render judgment on the world Marya inhabits. Seen in this light the novel is a work marred by self-indulgence and morbidity and offers no enlargement of vision and no real clarity of focus, only a chronicle of a weak victim's inevitable downfall. But to read the novel in this way is to misapprehend grossly the artistry embodied in *Quartet*. Its small canvas, through subtlety of style, probes the meaning of the enclosing world. There is not a single victim in this novel; all four of the major characters are victims; all are motivated by their lusts or needs and driven to a numbness and moral blindness in their hatreds, illusions, and self-pity. The two men are blind and uncaring and the women are little better, because in their desire for protection they become accomplices in the self-destructive and life-denying battle which they wage against each other. The gross and subtle ways in which we hurt each other — it is around this subject that the themes of *Quartet* oscillate, not merely Marya's pathetic downfall.

We become aware of this larger embodiment of theme as we experience the richness of the text and the formal relationship of its parts. For example, there is an adjustment of intimacy between the narrator-persona and the reader. As the relation of incident breaks off and the narrator records certain aspects or features of Marya's present condition, it is done not in a difference stylistic structure, but through a shift in the quality of the tone, usually achieved through imagery of sharp and penetrating focus. Although these images are most frequently realized in the mind of the character, they take on a context beyond Marya as the style in which they are rendered creates this special intimacy between the narrator and the reader. They are disciplined and controlled as they expand through the shaping stylistic arrangement. This technique, which becomes an increasingly dominant characteristic of Rhys's later work, is intricately related to the form of the entire novel, though it is used in a more limited way in *Quartet*. This concentration on the interiority of the text, allied with the brittle surface realism, creates a superimposition of vision on the novel's material and achieves a much deeper engagement between the reader and the work of art. And it is through this unity that the themes of the novel expand and the aesthetic realm is more satisfying. The process for the reader becomes more a sense of shared discovery as the implications of the plot and narrative are embraced through a spatial, thematic, and formal ordering, thus affording an aesthetic whole and a far richer potential text for the reader.

The final scene brings together these various movements of the novel. It focuses on a violent quarrel between Stephan and Marya over her having slept with Heidler and ends with Stephan's departure. Marya is left fallen and battered in what will become her permanent environment, a cheap hotel room — the habitat of the future of all Rhys's heroines, where they sleep, dream, drink, mechanically have intercourse, and are consumed by their helplessness in the world outside. Just before Stephan flings her to the floor, Marya has an epiphany of insight and clarity emanating out of her frustration and anger with Stephan: "She began to laugh insultingly. Suddenly he had become the symbol of everything that all her life had baffled and tortured her. Her only idea was to find words that would hurt him — vile words to scream at him" (p. 184). Terrified by the bleak prospects of her future, and forced to confront them at last, she can no longer recede into a world of false dreams and hopes. Her obsessions are no longer dispelled by her fantasies. Stephan becomes the physical embodiment of all that they symbolize — he represents for her the masculine universe which has used and controlled her. But even now she cannot fully comprehend this sudden revelation of feeling; her anger only searches for words of abuse. Marya remains "baffled' by those who have 'tortured' her and left her pitilessly alone. The monsters who have claimed her, in the end, are without human faces; they are forces endemic to the structure of thought and social order of which Heidler and Stephan are also surely victims, for in the end all of the "quartet" are victims of moral blindness and numbness.

If Marya is hypocritical, self-pitying, and selfish, she is so because of the amoral world which she inhabits. Because she has been reduced to an object, it inevitably comes home to her with an awful force, that her feelings really don't mean anything. There exists in Marya, to use Therese Benedek's term, a "negative narcissism," where the female, treated exclusively as an object, reaches an emotional state in which the exclusive object of her psychic energy is the self and the emotions depressive and painful. In a society which provides such easy victims, there can be no victors. Stephan is left to wallow in his self-pity, seeing women as "loathsome" and "horrible," "soft and disgusting weights suspended round the necks of men, dragging them downwards. At the same time he longed to lay his head on Mademoiselle Chardin's shoulder and weep his life away" (p. 186). Out of this unhealthy mixture we find no capacity to form true relationships with women, and it further reminds us of the flimsy nature of Marya's hope in the first place. Stephan is the embodiment of male weakness and self-pity, but Heidler is a kind of incubus projection of the male species in his dominance and abuse of the female. With typical male hubris he laid out the rules of the game, and when Marya couldn't keep to them, she was merely released from her cage and left to stray as a wounded animal whose pleasure was no longer sought. Lois accepts the world of artificial rather than natural feelings; she bases her entire life on whatever the masculine code imposes upon her and as a result is a dehumanized accessory, who must play the servant's role at best, and at worst the pimp. Her debasement is more complete; she is an active agent, and aggressor toward her own sex.

*Quartet* is a novel deeply suspicious of all human motivation; its themes center around deception, weakness, helplessness, and the cross-purposes of human beings as they seek their satisfactions or protection in a world that is at best apathetic, but, more frequently malignant. If the severely constricted world depicted in *Quartet* offers too limited a vehicle to explore the implications of these broader themes, the novel nevertheless achieves harmony through its penetrating vision of the central character and the world which she inhabits. Rhys's ample achievement in this novel can be too easily overlooked, and her characters and themes judged too morbid. The economy of language and directness of style can lead us to underestimate the range, depth, and quality of feeling in her work, but her narrative focus and technique relieve the intense subjectivity in *Quartet* and offer a dramatic, human portrait of the female consciousness in the modern world.

Footnotes:

[1] See Hunter Davis, "Rip Van Rhys," *Sunday Times Atticus*, 6 Nov. 1966, p. 13. Marcelle Bernstein, "The Inscrutable Miss Jean Rhys," the *London Observer*, 1 June 1969, pp. 40-42, 49-50.

[2] The *Bulletin of Bibliography* is publishing a primary and secondary bibliography of Rhys by B. J. Murray and R. C. Reynolds. The titles of several of these articles and interviews are interesting, for example: "The Sly Lady Novelist Who Went Missing for 20 Years," *Daily Express*, 1 Sept. 1976; "I'm a Person without a Mask," *Mademoiselle*, 79 (Oct. 1974), 170-71; "Fated to be Sad," the *Guardian*, 8 Aug. 1968, p. 5.

[3] Julie Kavanagh, "Rhys-Cycled," *W*, 15 Nov. 1974, p. 6; Judith Thurman, "The Mistress and the Mask: Jean Rhys' Fiction," *Ms*. 4 (Jan. 1976), 50-54.

[4] For a brief discussion of Rhys's literary discovery see Elgin Mellown, "Character and Theme in the Novels of Jean Rhys," *Contemporary Literature*, 13 (1972), 458-72.

[5] A. Alvarez, "The Best Living English Novelist," *New York Times Book Review*, 17 Mar. 1974, pp. 6-8.

[6] *Quartet* was originally published by Chatto and Windus under the title, *Postures*, in 1928, but Simon and Schuster issued it in 1929 as *Quartet*, the title which Rhys preferred. Subsequent British publication by André Deutsch and Penguin (both in print) use *Quartet*.

[7] Jean Rhys, *Quartet* (New York: Vintage Books Edition, 1974), p. 19. This edition is the most readily available in the United States, and pagination is the same as the André Deutsch hard-cover edition published in England in 1969 and still in print. Subsequent references are from the Vintage edition and will be cited parenthetically.

[8] Simone de Beauvoir, *The Second Sex* (London: Jonathan Cape, 1953), p. 65.

# THE ARTIST EMERGING

## by Helen E. Nebeker

In her second novel, *After Leaving Mr. Mackenzie,*[1] Jean Rhys presents a work so complex that it defies discussion. This complexity has led critics to a consistent oversimplification and misconstruing of the novel's impact. The plot is at once deceivingly simple in thrust and complicated in detail. The setting is April in Paris, the heroine Julia Martin, the time some ten years after World War I. As the story opens, Julia is living in a cheap room, recovering from psychic wounds incurred six months earlier, when Mr. Mackenzie had ended their love affair. A "decent Englishman," Mackenzie has been sending Julia a weekly allowance of three hundred francs, but now, in April, having sent her a severance check of fifteen hundred francs, he abjures further responsibility. Julia, in a rage, seeks him out in a near-by restaurant and, in an embarrassing public scene, melodramatically returns his check. Later the same evening, she meets George Horsfield, a young Englishman, and accepts from him, during the course of a platonic evening, fifteen hundred francs. George sympathetically encourages Julia to return to London, where she hopes to gain financial aid from her first lover, W. Neil James. The rest of the plot concerns Julia's ten-day sojourn in London, where she visits James and her family — a sister, a paternal uncle, and an invalid mother who dies during the visit. On the night of the funeral, after having buried her mother and quarreled with her sister and uncle, Julia sleeps with George for the first and last time. Then, having received twenty pounds as a brush-off from the ex-lover, James, Julia returns to Paris. Ten days later, roused from a lethargy of despair by George's gift of ten pounds, ecstatically planning the new wardrobe she will buy with it, Julia goes out into the evening, encounters Mackenzie, and on the spur of the moment borrows from him one hundred francs.

This meager plot belies the novel's aesthetic complexity. The major difficulty — and perhaps defect — lies in Rhys's seemingly diffuse thematic purpose, a confusion which reflects her struggle to construct a viable, personal philosophy within the changing social framework of her time. Actually, once sorted out, one sees that Rhys has managed to evoke in the complexities a panoramic view of changing twentieth-century philosophy. This changing philosophy, almost imperceptible in Rhys's own life, was rising phoenix-like from the ashes of a dying, patriarchal social structure. In this Victorian milieu, man's superior role was clearly defined. Woman, man's adjunct, was at once his creation, his wife, his servant or his mistress. Man's role was certain, secure; woman's was predictable, but tenuous and stifling.

Rhys's main problem in this, her second novel, was to find the means of communicating both the reality she saw and her feelings about that reality, without risking contemptuous denial. She had attempted this difficult communication in her first novel, *Quartet* [2]. Marya, her protagonist, facing the problem of revealing the starkness of woman's life — a revelation for which she anticipated either vehement repudiation or vilification — repeatedly questioned: "How can you understand? What can you know?" But, in *After Leaving Mr. Mackenzie*, Rhys, the emerging artist, chances upon the archetypal metaphor. Through that metaphor, she can express what was formerly inexpressible. Combining a basic mythic pattern with a shifting narrative focus — a focus criticized by many as a disturbing defect, because they do not understand its purpose — Rhys reveals the truth as she sees it, even as she honestly acknowledges that "truth" must always be suspect, multifaceted as it is.

2

Rhys's archetypes are immediately obvious in the details of Julia's hotel room in Paris. The room is "sombre," with a "one-eyed aspect," because the solitary window "was very much to one side." The wallpaper depicts a large, open-beaked bird on the branch of a tree, faced by a "strange, wingless creature, half-bird, half-lizard," also open-beaked and belligerent. The branch on which they perch sprouts "fungus and queerly shaped leaves and fruit." Alerted to the purpose of the story by these images, we know that from the "room" of her private thoughts, Rhys is going to communicate through her "window" — off-sided though it may be — her vision of woman, the strange wingless creature undergoing metamorphosis, threatened by man, the large bird (a symbol of transcendence) with open beak. Perched together on the phallic branch of the tree (a tree is an archetype for life) which sprouts only fungus and *distorted* fruits and leaves (all sexual symbols), the wingless creature, driven by its instinct for survival, faces the larger menace belligerently.

Further archetypes emerge in the red plush sofa, the spotted gilt-framed mirror, which reflects the bed and an "unframed oil-painting of a half-empty bottle of red wine, a knife, and a piece of Gruyere cheese." The reflection is "slightly distorted and full of obscure meaning. The picture and the sofa were linked in her mind. . . The picture stood for the idea, the spirit, and the sofa stood for the act." The reader now sees, far more clearly than can Julia, the essence of reality of her life. Julia links the economics of life (food, drink, the phallic blade) with the "spirit" or essence and knows they are achieved by the act (everything associated with the red-plush sofa). Thus Julia, prostituting herself for the necessities of life, sees the distortion of her life and hates it, but, in the end, she will be unable to reject it.

Archetypes continue to unfold in details of Julia's life. Financially secure, physically unexploited during the six months of Mackenzie's support, Julia is "not altogether unhappy." "Locked in her room," she feels safe. But sometimes she is confused and frightened by her thoughts. Lying in bed, she hates the world and everybody in it. She feels "horribly fatigued." The "rumble of life [is] like the sound of the sea . . . rising gradually around her." Her memory is filled with images of trees, dark shadows, dark, purple seas. (p. 12). Critics have seen in these details only Julia's submersion in her sexual urges. But Rhys's muted strokes deny such simplification, evoking awareness of deeper significance. These are Jungian images of the primal consciousness, the collective-unconscious archetypes of sea and shadow and tree and sunshine. The conflict within Julia is her "unconscious" urging her toward psychic illumination, toward the process of "individuation" in which the conscious comes to terms with the inner center or SELF. This unconscious yearning of Julia for psychic wholeness pains the reader. He senses the implicit irony and pathos as Julia, unconsciously yearning for identity, constantly powders her face, grieves over her fatness and her old coat, plans a new wardrobe. Woman's only sense of worth, implies Rhys, is in terms of physical attractiveness and sexual desirability. But, as Julia sits in a cafe drinking Pernod, planning her "new clothes with passion and voluptuousness," her vision of Mackenzie's "cool and derisory smile" fills her with "dreary and abject humiliation," and we know that Julia, too, is aware of the degradation she suffers.

3

Having examined, if only superficially, Rhys's emerging mythic patterns, we can turn our attention to her use of a multiple narrative focus, through which she develops levels of characterization and, by extension and implication, levels of truth. Furthermore, through this focus, all characters emerge as archetypes, reinforcing her mythic framework. Thus, in the character of Mackenzie, Rhys delineates the prototype of the economically secure, upper-middle-class, late-Victorian male. His mind is "tight and tidy . . . adapted to the social system." He lives by a "certain code of morals and manners from which he seldom departs." Nevertheless, he, too, is undergoing metamorphosis: he has published in his youth a book of poems; he is drawn to "strangeness and recklessness;" he feels haunted by "ungenerous action;" and he pities Julia, even though he rejects her irresponsibility and her lack of self-control. If one remembers Heidler in Rhys's first novel, *Quartet*, Rhys's artistic growth is obvious. For in permitting Mackenzie these contradictory qualities — a consideration Rhys was unable to extend to her earlier arch-villain — Rhys suggests that man, like woman, is vulnerable and a product of his social system, though he struggles against it.

Parenthetically, it is through Mackenzie that Rhys will develop a major theme which she has been intellectually formulating since her first novel. That is, the seeds of man's essential hatred and fear of woman lie in the financial and emotional demands which she makes upon him. The burden of these demands is powerfully demonstrated in a scene where Julia is berating Mackenzie over the unfairness of woman's life. Helplessly he mentally expostulates: "'No, of course life isn't fair. It's damned unfair, really . . . but what does she expect me to do about. I'm not God Almighty.'" (p. 30). And, in the end, abjuring responsibility for her situation and rejecting her emotional and financial pleadings, Mackenzie has "no pity for her; she [is] a dangerous person." Only after she leaves and he has eaten hot food and drunk good wine, secure in his unthreatened world, is he again able to pity her. "'Poor devil,' he thought. 'She's got damn all.'"

Because we are permitted to view Julia and her existence from a shifting vantage point, Rhys convinces us that communication is a many-leveled process and that the "truth" of any communication must be highly suspect. Although Julia reveals to Mackenzie the tawdry facts of her life — marriage, the child that dies, divorce (though perhaps she had never been married at all, as Mackenzie thinks to himself) — one questions the truth. We are aware that Julia recites the script she thinks Mackenzie expects from her "sort of woman" who, he knows, "would be certain to tell you lies anyhow." Typically, Julia mistakes her script for tragedy, but Mackenzie sees only comedy. Rhys's multiple narrative voice operates further to show that men, as well as women, play predetermined roles, which in turn condition their response to others.

Having introduced Julia and Mackenzie, Rhys continues both character development and mythic reference, as she contrasts Mackenzie with young George Horsfield. Both are English, but Mackenzie is of medium height and coloring, whereas George is "the dark young man." While Mackenzie is the stock "capitalist," wealthy and retired at the age of forty-eight, George seems to have inherited only a temporary financial windfall which has permitted him to spend six months kicking up his heels. Unlike cynical Mackenzie, George is romantically sensitive, pitying Julia. George senses that much of life is fantastic, dreamlike, distorted, as in a poor looking-glass, like Julia's vision in the opening scene of the novel. He is tolerant, not a "cold hypocrite" like Mackenzie. He is cautious, ponderous, childish, but, at root, genuine. Having known disillusionment and poverty, George can sympathize with Julia as Mackenzie cannot. Thus his vision of life permits Julia to confide details of her life — real or imagined — which she could not voice to Mackenzie. She can play to the hilt, with George, her role of impotent, suffering womanhood. To him she reveals her wanderings with men, her experience with an older woman, her youthful desire for adventure — and in her adventure, "men were mixed up, because they had to be." And hearing all these details of her life, George oozes warm humanity, thinking, "'Hang it all, one can't leave this unfortunate creature alone to go and drink herself dotty." (p. 54). But even as he listens to Julia's rambling, sentimental story, he is irritated by her vagueness concerning her role: ". . . She spoke as if she were trying to recall a book she had read or a story she had heard and Mr. Horsfield felt irritated by her vagueness, 'because,' he thought, 'your life is your life, and you must be pretty definite about it. Or if it's a story you are making up, you ought at least to have it pat.'" (p. 50). Ironically, at the end of their evening together, George's last thoughts of Julia are in terms of a bawdy song: "Roll me over on my right side, "Roll me over slow; Roll me over on my right side, cause my left side hurts me so." (p. 56). Thus, through Horsfield, Rhys reveals a sympathetic but sharp perception of Julia: she gets kicked around like a dog, but she keeps asking for it!

Unfortunately, George cannot fully transcend the hold of the past, so even as Julia unfolds the supposed reality of her life, we are left unsure of its veracity. Because everything revealed by Julia is filtered through the mirror of George's comprehension, flawed as it is by the myths which work upon him as a male, all that he understands must be questioned. To emphasize the specious nature of George's perception, Rhys introduces the sculptress, Ruth, Julia's older female friend. Through Ruth, Rhys suggests that the "female perception" can be understood only by another sensitive, artistic female. In Julia's seeking communion with another woman — an archetype for the unconscious — we are returned to Rhys's theme of the symbolic search for the SELF. But in Julia's account of her attempt to tell Ruth the truth about herself, that it had been as if she were standing before a judge who didn't believe a word she had said, Rhys suggests two more diffuse but basic themes: (1) that women cannot really hope for rapport with other women, antagonists that they are; (2) at a deeper level, that one cannot fool the unconscious with conscious rationalization. In Rhys's extended imagery, "real" or archetypal woman lies couched, "like an utterly lovely proud animal," behind a mask-like, long, dark face with blank eyes. And in this introduction of the mask image, to be explored at both the literal and the mythic level, Rhys's emerging aesthetic and technical power cannot be challenged.

4

Before Julia can address the mystery of woman's mask, she must make the archetypal "journey of discovery" from Paris to London. Rhys prepares us, as she has done before, for the ultimate results of that experience. Archetypally, the usual "journey into awareness" is a night sea journey from west to east (a symbolic journey from death to life). But Julia's journey is from east to west and Rhys emphasizes the train journey, avoiding completely the sea crossing. In this way, she foreshadows Julia's inability to effect change in her life.

Julia's return to her old haunts in London discloses details of her former life as well as her meetings with five significant people who fall into recognizable patterns. The former lover, W. Neal James is typical Victorian-male stereotype. Preparing for their meeting, Julia remembers that when he had ended their affair, James had been "eternally grateful" for her "sweetness and generosity" and had subsequently "lent" her a "good deal of money." He is, she thinks, "so kind, so cautious, so perfectly certain that all is for the best." But meeting him seventeen years later, Julia realizes the truth. "Because he has money, he's a kind of God. Because I have none I'm a kind of worm." (p. 112). For Julia, James now represents the system which corrupts and the sex which exploits, the male "capitalist" who has created her reality, who controls her vision of herself. With him there can be no communication, no playing the role of impotent, suffering womanhood, no sentimentalizing of her dead little son — real or imagined. His only response would be — and as Rhys structures it, this may well be Julia's dialogue with herself — "Look here, I don't believe that; you're making it up." As Julia admits to Horsfield later, "'I was for sleeping with — not talking to. And quite right, too, I suppose.'" (p. 114). So in the face of her knowledge, Julia plays yet another role, the role in which she believes James has cast her. Good sport, corruptible woman. Then she lapses into her role of helpless, fatalistic woman: "She said: 'Anyhow, I don't know how I could have done differently. . . Do you think I could have done differently?'" (p. 114).

Surprisingly, James, by implication a believer in the Victorian view that working women are naturally corruptible, that they inevitably seek out their own fate as surely as good women control their destiny, replies: "'Don't ask me. I'm not the person to ask that sort of thing, am I? I don't know. Probably you couldn't.'" (p. 114). Then we find that the war has changed James, given him the perspective to understand that some "really decent guys" don't "get on," simply because of "bad luck": "'. . . some women too.Though mind you, women are a different thing altogether. Because it's all nonsense; *the life of a man and the life of a woman can't be compared*. They're up against entirely different things the whole time. What's the use of talking nonsense about it?'" (pp. 116-17. Emphasis added.) Which shows that James understands everything and understands nothing!

That James is a predecessor of Mackenzie is obvious in his age, his attitudes, his affluence which is seemingly not rooted in the competitive capitalistic system. In the same way, Uncle Griffiths, older than James — sixty-five, though he looks much younger — represents an older, patriarchal order from which James, Mackenzie, and George derive. Almost Norse in description, broad, short, unwrinkled, red complexioned, "solid and powerful," Uncle Griffiths represents to Julia and her family "the large and powerful male," Because he is practical, self-concerned, Julia feels contempt for him, perhaps unjustly. For Julia has violated the order in which he is rooted — the patriarch family. In his rational view, Julia has made her bed and must now lie in it. Rhys does not condemn Uncle Griffiths, as does Julia, for being unfeeling, hard. She permits him a sense of humor, love for his wife, whom he had married, impulsively, without subsequent regret. She emphasizes that he provides for himself and his wife, a burden upon no one, and would help Norah, Julia's sister, if he could. Furthermore, he knows a truth of life: "'Of course, everybody has to sit on their own bottoms. I've found that out all my life. You mustn't grumble if you find it out too.'" (p. 84).

But wise though he appears, Uncle Griffiths is at best a benevolent despot. After the funeral of Julia's mother, comfortable, well-fed, surrounded by his "audience of females": ". . . He talked and talked. He talked about life, about literature, about Dostoevsky. He said: "Why see the world through the eyes of an epileptic?'" (p. 133) or of a "woman" he might just as easily have substituted. And when Julia mechanically says, "'But he might see things very clearly, mightn't he? At moments.'" (p. 133), Griffiths can only reply: "Clearly? Why clearly? How do you mean clearly?" To which, of course, there is no answer.

Patriarchal Uncle Griffiths can, however, understand and approve of Julia's younger sister, Norah, who has chosen to stay within the family framework, to measure up to the responsibility of caring for her invalid mother, "making do" as best she can, expecting no better life. Cliché though her type might be, Norah emerges in the capable hands of Rhys as a sympathetic character for whom we have compassion and even hope. Since Norah represents that which Rhys rejected in her own life, one must admire both her artistic control and her intellectual maturity in developing the character.

Norah, dark like Julia, is tall, strongly built, straight-backed. Her face wears an expression of endurance and her voice is sweet "with a warm and tender quality," although Julia sees her face "cold as though warmth and tenderness were dead in her." She is, in Julia's eyes, plainly labelled "middle class, no money . . . all the daintiness and prettiness perforce cut out . . . brought up to certain tastes, then left without the money to gratify them . . . [forbidden] even the relief of rebellion against her lot. . ." (p. 74). Norah is similarly shocked by Julia. She thinks, "'She doesn't even look like a lady now.'"

At the meeting of the sisters in the home of the dying mother, the pull between compassion and hatred is masterful. Julia's visible emotion for her sister touches us. Her gentleness with Norah — now on the defensive about the sordidness of her own life — is in sharp contrast with Norah's desire to see Julia hurt and humiliated. But the reader understands Norah's need to strike out when the starkness of her life unfolds. She reads from a book: "The slave had no hope, and knew of no change . . . no other world, no other life. She had no wish, no hope, no love. . . The absence of pain and hunger was her happiness, and when she felt unhappy she was tired, more than usual after the day's labour. . ." (p. 103); we realize that this is the truth of Norah's existence. But when Rhys forces upon us, through narrative manipulation, the knowledge that this is also the reality of Julia who has sought to escape the fate of her sister, we feel a stab of pain for woman's lot. This is narrative focus employed at its best.

Norah, however, has no room for compassion. She only knows that she is "tall and straight and slim and young — well, fairly young," and that her life is "like being buried alive." "It isn't fair, it isn't fair," she sobs. Julia's return home has forced Norah to realize that in the nine years of caring for her mother, her youth has vanished, her soft heart grown hard and bitter and that the only voices of approval are those of "beasts and devils," the same "beasts and devils" that torture Julia in her vastly different life.

But at least, for Norah, there will be recompense for her years of duty; the will her mother has made will make her financially secure — *the sine qua non* of both men and women in Rhys's view — and at the death of her mother, Norah will begin her own quest for fulfillment. But before this, she and Julia have a fight in which all the animosities of their lives are unleashed in verbal violence. In that scene, which follows the funeral, Rhys reveals, as she has done before, the irony of women able to see each other only in those stereotypes *created by men*. Hence, women cannot reach out in sisterhood, understanding the pain and frustration they all endure as women. Rather, they must seize arms, do battle against each other, engaged as they are in the fight for economic survival. "Good" Norah, once without financial hope for herself, must triumph over penniless Julia, provoking her to anger and incoherence, even though inwardly both sisters desire communication. "Bad" Julia must hate and rage against her sister, who symbolizes the "mean beasts," the good, respectable people" whom she at once envies and hates.

5

It is in the relatively minor character of Julia's mother that Rhys completes her theme of woman's search for SELF or archetypal woman — the creature behind the mask. Brazilian born, "transplanted" from a warm world of "orange trees" to the "cold, grey country" of England, the dark-skinned, high-cheek-boned, dying mother seems to Julia "still beautiful as an animal would be in old age." In sorrow and confusion, she remembers when her mother had been "the warm centre of the world," only to change and become "a dark, austere, rather plump woman . . . worried," unreasonable, whom Julia had grown to fear, dislike, ignore, tolerate, and finally, to sentimentalize as her mother. In the final look at her now dead mother, who had struggled and fought for every tortured breath, Julia senses that "something in the poise of her body and in her serene face was old, old, old. . . [The] sunken face, bound with white linen, looked frightening — horribly frightening, like a mask. Always masks had frightened her." (p. 124.)

With the reference to "masks," all Rhys's overtones coalesce. This "beautiful" woman — "more beautiful than either of us," as Julia has said to Norah — emerges as a mother archetype, Earth-Mother, bearer of life and source of love, the female principle personified. But though she was "old, old, old" (timeless, that is) and had fought long after her body was paralyzed and useless, she is now dead. And her only offspring are Norah — symbol of a kind of light or virtue — who had done the best for her mother that she could; and Julia, at whom the dying woman had looked with "recognition and surprise and anger." These two "realities" — the one rooted in a kind of depressing "duty" and deprivation (the results of the pressures of the superego or the Zeitgeist), the other in egocentrism and an aline, distorted vision (the manifestation of the ego) — will never measure up to the progenitor, the great archetypal woman. As Norah has said: "We're soft, or lazy, or something." But Rhys knows the problem is deeper than that. Ancient, archetypal woman, long since an anachronism (just as is patriarchal Uncle Griffiths), is dead. There is no return to the security of that "sweet, warm centre." If there is to be any hope for woman at all, says Rhys, she must throw off her paralysis and face life without dependency, void though it may seem.

But Julia, on the verge of recognizing the truths synthesized in the person of her mother, is ultimately frightened by the "mask" and all that it entails. Her final gesture of unconscious understanding is the bouquet of roses she buys for her mother's funeral with her last ten shillings;, a token of love for that which was beautiful but, like the roses, fragile and transitory. From this point on, Julia can only grapple with the idea of "nothingness," that is for her the truth of existence.

Although the theme of nothingness is central to understanding the intellectual complexity of this novel, unfortunately, limitations of space prevent discussion here. Suffice it to say that Rhys wrestles masterfully with existentialism, that canker in the soul of twentieth century man: the realization that "*nothing* matters" because "nothing *matters*."[3] This agonizing awareness dominates Julia's final evening with Horsfield, finally overwhelming her so that she sends him away. But as Julia lies on her bed, cold and hostile, hating him, Rhys lets us know that George Horsfield is not the enemy. An enlightened male, he understands Julia's misery and he hates the people and the system which control both their lives. Returning to his "pleasant, peaceful, spacious" book-lined room after leaving Julia at the hotel, he sees with startling clarity what the reader must also see if he is to avoid a grievous over-simplification of Rhys's art: ". . . 'I don't see how I can bring her here exactly. . . I can't bring her here.' Suddenly he saw Julia not as a representative of the insulted and injured, but as a solid human being. . . She must have a bed to sleep in, food, clothes, companionship — or she would be lonely; understanding of her own peculiar point of view — or she would be aggrieved." (p. 168).

Horsfield knows, as does Rhys, at least unconsciously, that woman cannot be transported into a world of peace and order simply because one pities her, as we have seen George pity his cat. She is not a pathetic abstraction; she is an individual, a human being who wants the same things George wants: economic security, friendship (not sexual exploitation). Above all, an understanding of her "reality" as valid.

But just as Rhys will not make George the villain, neither will she give him the role of Saviour. Though he symbolizes enlightened, evolving man, and though he sympathizes with Julia's plight, it is "in a cold and theoretical way." Seeing all that he has with "great clarity," he is nevertheless "appalled" and ultimately will not "be rushed into anything." Rhys seems to tell us that man's own need for survival precludes involvement beyond a sentimental pity and a gratuitous handout. From this point, Rhys never again in her novels takes up the iea of man's evolution.

The final section of *After Leaving Mr. Mackenzie* is anticlimactic. Julia returns from her journey, having changed not at all. She still sees woman as prisoner, confined to her bedroom. Contemplating employment for which she has no references and is in no way prepared, she receives a letter from George containing ten pounds and another brush-off. She leaves her confining room to walk the streets thinking of new clothes, of "love," denying "age." Later she sees a "slim woman with full soft breasts" to whom she longs to talk — again the symbolic urge to communicate with the unconscious. Later still, she thinks, "After all, what have I done? I haven't done anything," which is, for the true existentialist, the only sin. All of this we have heard before.

Then Rhys makes a final mythic statement, in a tense scene between Julia and a young man who stalks her on the street. Wanting to tell the "boy" to leave, she cannot and they "walk on side by side — tense like two animals." In the light she sees that he is a . . . boy — wearing a cap, very pale and with very small, dark eyes set deeply in his head. He gave her a rapid glance, *"Oh, la la,'* he said. *"Ah, non alors.'* He turned about and walked away. 'Well,' said Julia aloud, 'that's funny. The joke's on me this time.'" (p. 187). She walks on seeing nothing but the "young man's little eyes, which had looked at her with such deadly and impartial criticism. She thought again: 'The joke was on me that time.'" (p. 188).

Patently this scene has more significance than just a rejection by a "boy" walking the streets looking for a pick-up (particularly in view of the brief scene which follows where Julia gazes "indifferent and cold, like a stone," on a poor, drooping skeleton of a man). This 'boy" is both Julia's "animus" (that masculine half of the soul image) and, more importantly, the archetypal "trickster," who though dominated by physical appetite, often evolves to become a guide, an initiator into the unconscious. Julia, however, is not yet ready for initiation into even limited truth and the "boy" must reject her, his eyes "deadly and impartial" in their perception. As Rhys has foreshadowed in her first pages, Julia must continue to believe that woman is victimized by man's sexual demands. She will be unable to admit that it is woman who seeks sexual attention; that it is woman who demands both sexual abasement and economic support, protesting all the time, "'That is not what I meant at all, that is not it at all.' YOU BEASTS!"

Rhys concludes this statement in Julia's' final scene with Mackenzie, where she takes him for another hundred francs and goes out into the streets at "the hour between god and wolf, as they say."

To summarize further the ideas suggested in *After Leaving Mr. Mackenzie* is impossible; the complexity of Rhys's vision is yet to fully emerge, both intellectually and technically. But the power is there; each detail in this novel works to purpose; her myth is assuming outline. The later novels will refine and process the wheat from the chaff. This process is discussed in totality in my book: *Jean Rhys: Woman in Passage*, Montreal, Canada: Eden Press, 1981.

Footnotes:

[1] *After Leaving Mr. Mackenzie* (London: Jonathan Cape; New York: Knopf, 1931). Citations in this article refer to the New York: Vintage Books, 1974, edition because of its more general availability.

[2] *Quartet* (New York: Simon and Schuster, 1929).

[3] In an article for *The Times*, 17 May 1975, p. 16, Rhys wrote: "If you've often tried in the past to put yourself to sleep by repeating 'nothing matters at all,' it's a relief when few things really do matter any longer. This indifference or calm, whatever you like to call it, is like a cave at the back of the mind where you can retire and be alone and safe. The outside world is very far away."

# SYMBOLIC IMAGERY AND MIRRORING TECHNIQUES IN *WIDE SARGASSO SEA*.

*Veronica M. Gregg*

Jean Rhys's letters document the rigorous creative process involved in the weaving of the story told in her most accomplished work, *Wide Sargasso Sea*. A collation of aspects of literary techniques can help to produce a complex reading of some of the artistic skills used to tell a story and to create a text. Colour symbolism and nature imagery are cross-referenced to form a patchwork of incremental patterning and correspondences which coalesce in the protagonist's final dream.

Flow imagery is used to underline and carry forward the theme of the fundamental incompatibility of the two major characters. While she is in the convent, Antoinette speaks enthusiastically of colouring her silk roses for needlework class: "We can colour the roses as we choose and mine are green, blue and purple. Underneath, I will write my name in fire red. . ." (44). When the husband arrives in the West Indies and is on his way to the honeymoon house, he moans that everything is too intense: "Too much blue, too much purple, too much green. The flowers too red" (59). By establishing these colors as an integral part of Antoinette (she colors them according to emotional, not natural, coloring), and then showing the husband's powerfully negative reaction to exactly the same colors, the text underscores the crucially different formation of the Englishman and the West Indian woman.

The flower imagery recurs the first night of the honeymoon at Granbois:

> I . . . took the wreath off. It fell on the floor and as I went towards the window I stepped on it. The room was full of the scent of crushed flowers. I saw her reflection in the glass fanning herself. . . (62).

The husband's crushing of the wreath, though not deliberate, suggests the way in which he will later crush Antoinette. The mirror which shows him her reflection reinforces the meaning. The image is further extended when Christophine, Antoinette's maid and protector, warns him against the danger of damaging the flowers: "I send the girl to clear up the mess you make with the frangipani. . . Take care not to slip on the flowers, young master" (71). The reverberations throughout the text are largely achieved through this kind of cross-referencing of imagery.

Antoinette's destruction and the roles of the husband and his alter ego, Daniel, are also suggested by another flower image:

Then I passed an orchid with long sprays of golden-brown flowers. One of then touched my cheek and I remembered picking some for her one day. 'They are like you,' I told her. Now I stopped, broke a spray off and trampled it into the mud (82).

This scene follows the husband's reading of Daniel's letter insidiously suggests that Antoinette is genetically predisposed to madness and badness. The husband's sense of anger and betrayal is not narrated but rendered through his intense reaction to the spray of orchids, another metonym for his wife.

The patterns of imagery are carefully and systematically cross-fertilized to plot Antoinette's end. Amid the overpowering (to him) smell of tropical flowers, the husband recalls a song he thought he had forgotten and sings it to her: "Hail to the queen of the silent night, / Shine bright, shine bright, Robin, as you die" (70). The robin shining brightly as it dies prefigures Antoinette's leap into the flames when she sets her husband's house on fire. The allusion to fire and death echoes and deepens the image of the burning parrot during the fire at Coulibri and adumbrates the novel's end. Coco, the green parrot, belonged to Antoinette's mother, Annette. The bird's wings were clipped by her English husband, Mr. Mason. It is the clipping of the bird's wings which leads directly to its painful and dramatic death when the black people fire the house at Coulibri. The startling image of the parrot being burned to death amid the barely restrained violence of the angry crowd foreshadows Antoinette's own end in her husband's house. The rebellion and hatred, which cause the people oppressed by Coulibri to burn it down, mirror the rebellion and hatred which cause Antoinette to fire her husband's house.

Other nature images are interwoven with religious symbolism. The religious overtones are introduced at the beginning of the novel through the allusion to the Garden of Eden: "Our garden was large and beautiful as that garden in the Bible — the tree of life grew there. . . The scent was very sweet. I never went near it" (17). The garden in Rhys's work is an ironic allusion to Paradise. In the apocalyptic post-Emancipation days which provide the social and historical framework of the West Indian novel, the image suggests Paradise gone wild.

The Biblical allusions also draw on the New Testament and the theme of Christ's betrayal. The husband receives thirty thousand pounds for his marriage to Antoinette. In an ironic redoubling of events the husband is seen to have bought her. It is her step-father and half-brother who use the money as an inducement to the husband to relieve them of the West Indian woman. The number thirty evokes Jesus's betrayal and this is sustained by the image of the crowing cock, which recurs at sensitive points throughout the text. The agent of Antoinette's destruction, the nameless husband, hears the cock crowing shortly after he marries her: "A cock crowed loudly and I remembered the night before which we had spent in the town. Antoinette had a room to herself. . . I lay awake listening to cocks crowing all night. . ." (158) Antoinette's removing herself from her husband and the sound of the crowing cock suggest the pre-crucifixion scene when Christ withdraws from his disciples and one is about to betray him.

The connection between the Biblical story of betrayal and the protagonist's fate is even more effectively dramatised when Antoinette goes to Christophine (the Christ bearer) and begs for a love potion to win her husband's love. After her passionate and desperate entreaties, Christophine gives her a potion. As she leaves the older woman's house, Antoinette hears the cock crowing:

> Nearby a cock crew and I thought, 'That is for betrayal, but who is the traitor? She did not want to do this. I forced her with my ugly money. And what does anyone know about traitors or why Judas did what he did? (97)

When Antoinette poses her rhetorical question — who is the traitor? — the text suggests that she is at once traitor and victim. She betrays Christophine's (and her own) cultural practices by seeking to use obeah as a means of winning back her husband's love. However, she will be victimised herself when the husband uses his own brand of obeah in trying to change her identity by changing her name to Bertha and removing her to England.

After the irretrievable breakdown of the marriage, precipitated by the use of the obeah which went wrong, the image of the cock is re-introduced, side by side with a sleeping Antoinette:

> All the time . . . a cock crowed persistently outside. I took the first book I could lay hands on and threw it at him, but he stalked a few yards away and started again.
>
> Baptiste appeared, looking towards Antoinette's silent room. . .
>
> "What's that damn cock crowing about?'
>
> "Crowing for change of weather.'
>
> Because his eyes were fixed on the bedroom I shouted at him, "Asleep, dormi, dormi" (134).

Baptiste's eyes are fixed on the room in which Antoinette is sleeping because he understands that the cock's crowing symbolises the husband's ultimate betrayal. The crowing of the cock for change of weather suggest that the weather will change for Antoinette, who will be removed to another climate — England.

The manipulation of Old Testament and Christian myths and archetypes is also suggested in the ironic use of the colour white. White in Christian and Western cosmologies often suggests purity, innocence and virtue. In Rhys's novel, white is linked to destruction, betrayal and death. Myra, the housemaid at Coulibri, is portrayed as a creature of doom. The story of her pivotal role in the fire at Coulibri is told in part through the insistence on her white headdress. In front of Myra, Aunt Cora specifically warns Mr. Mason against discussing his plan to import cheap labour for his plantation instead of improving the working conditions of the ex-slaves. But he dismisses her warning as ignorance of the laziness and passivity of black people. Myra, who is nearby, appears at the dinner table

> "looking mournful as she always did though she smiled when she

> talked about hell. . . [T]he handkerchief she wore round her head was
> always white never striped or a gay colour" (30).

Myra's mournful looks, her preoccupation with hell, and her perpetual white headdress presage tragedy. The carefully selected description of Myra suggests that she is listening to the conversation at the dinner table, and she will tell the other black people of Mason's intentions. The deliberate manner in which she betrays the family is suggested, not stated. When members of the household become aware that the ex-slaves have surrounded the house on the night of the fire, Myra is still present. However, when the fire starts, and Annette goes to Pierre's room, she realizes that Myra has abandoned the sick child and disappeared. Annette cries in anguish: "The little room was on fire and Myra was not there. She has gone. She was not there" (38). When Cora replies aphoristically, "That does not surprise me at all," the reader recalls her insistent warning to Mason and the images which shaped the portrayal of Myra as she came to the dinner table.

White as a symbol of death and betrayal stands in dramatic contrast to the red, which is a symbol of passion, liberation and life. The last section of the novel opens with a fire motif:

> The paper shrivels, the sticks crackle and spit, the coal smoulders and
> glowers. In the end flames shoot up and they are beautiful. I get out of
> bed . . . to watch them and to wonder why I have been brought here.
> There must be a reason. What is it that I must do? (153)

The juxtaposition of the questioning of her fate and the fire image signals Antoinette's ultimate purpose. When Grace Poole observes pityingly that Antoinette has no idea of the length of time she has been in the attic, she responds that her reality and fate cannot be measured in sequential time. She apprehends her life and her suffering through memory senses and experience:

> On the contrary . . . only I know how long I have been here. Nights
> and days and days and nights . . . slipping through my fingers. But
> that does not matter. Time has no meaning. But something you can
> touch and hold like my red dress has a meaning (151).

The substance of Antoinette's reality is captured in the red dress, "the colour of fire and sunset. The colour of flamboyant flowers." The red (of the dress) also suggests passion, anger, and ultimately a death-defying leap into the flames, which will liberate her from the prison. It is through the motif of the red dress that the text builds a sense of Antoinette's reality in the attic and dramatises her destiny: "I looked at the dress on the floor and it was as if the fire had spread across the room. It was beautiful, and it reminded me of something I must do. I will remember I thought. I will remember quite soon now. That was the third time I had my dream, and it ended" (153). In Antoinette's dream, all aspects of her life coalesce and the dream prepares her for her final act. The persistent fire motif, implicit in the use of red, anchors all the other images and patterns which are used as variation on the central theme — Antoinette's life and death.

Symbolic imagery and colour symbolism are complicated by a complex and reiterative use of mirroring techniques. One of the central mirror images in *Wide Sargasso Sea*, as most critics have observed, is the relationship between Antoinette and Tia. As Coulibri burns, Antoinette thinks that she will seek comfort in her friendship with Tia. The other girl, however, rejects her brutally and scars her for life, by throwing a stone which hits Antoinette in her face:

> I looked at her and I saw her face crumple up as she began to cry. We stared at each other, blood on my face, tears on hers. It was as if I saw myself. Like in a looking-glass (38).

Tia represents the mirror returning the gaze.

The use of mirror imagery is linked to and feeds into the dream/reality dialectic in the work, and together (the mirroring and use of dreams) the become another of the key organizing principles of *Wide Sargasso Sea*. Tia's role as Antoinette's avatar begins even before the crucial encounter at Coulibri. The episode in which Tia switches dresses with Antoinette introduces the connection between the two:

> I looked round and Tia had gone. I searched for a long time before I could believe that she had taken my dress. . . . She had left me hers and I put it on at last. . . (21).

When Antoinette arrives home in Tia's shabby dress, her mother is horrified, especially because she has made new friends after a long period of being a social outcast. She insists that the dress be burned.

As Christophine forces another dress on the child, she observes that the coming of the new neighbours means trouble. Antoinette also feels frightened and recognizes that her old life is changing. It is immediately after this incident that she has the first installment of her dream. (It is one dream repeated with variation and extended throughout the text in progressive sequences.) The dream in its first appearance hints at the danger which awaits the protagonist, as she is in a forest being followed by someone who hates her.

It is the second installment of the dream, however, which fleshes out the character's dilemma. It is placed immediately before the husband's voice takes over the narrative. The motifs are of sex, death, terror and fascination which are all features of the nightmare reality of Antoinette's life with her husband. The dream is set partly in *hortus conclusus*. The text deliberately uses the term 'enclosed garden' which alludes to the myth of Narcissus and reinforces the mirroring imagery which runs the dream and reality theme in the work. In the enclosed garden, as Gayatri Spivak asserts, Antoinette finds not love, but a strange, threatening voice inviting her into a prison which masquerades as a love. The sexual imagery is conveyed through the reference to the beautiful white dress and thin slippers, symbols, of virginity about to be deflowered. (White, as suggested before, reinforces the theme of death). The forest as a symbolic geography of sex and death is linked to Antoinette's ultimate destruction. The connection to death is made through the sexual love for her husband. It is this love which leads to her betrayal. In her dream, 'the tree jerks and sways'. The swaying tree suggests the phallocentric sadism embodied in the character of the husband. When she wakes, Antoinette she says she dreamed she was in Hell. Hell describes precisely the kind of life which she will endure in England. (The reference to Hell is also a gloss on Rochester's perception of the West Indies as hell, Charlotte Bronte's *Jane Eyre*.)

The connection between sex and death is far more than the usual preoccupation with sex as a kind of symbolic death. The novel's technique points to the destruction and the terror which manifest themselves when sexual contact is based on exploitation and gross abuse of power. The text reinforces this concern by using Antoinette's dream experience as a point of recall for her mother's tragic life and death. As Antoinette recounts her dream to the nun in the convent school, the nun chides her, insisting that she put the dream out of her mind. Yet, Antoinette is unable to forget. As she drinks the chocolate that the nun offers her, it triggers memories of her mother:

> I remember that after my mother's funeral, very early in the morning, almost as early as this, we went home to drink chocolate and eat cakes. She died last year, no one told how, and I didn't ask. Mr. Mason was there and Christophine, no one else. Christophine cried bitterly but I could not. I prayed, but the words fell to the ground meaning nothing.
>
> Now the thought of her is mixed up with my dream.
>
> I saw her in a mended habit riding a borrowed horse, trying to wave at the head of the cobblestoned road at Coulibri, and tears came to my eyes again. 'Such terrible things happen,' I said, 'why? Why?' (51)

The explicit connection between the second installment of Antoinette's dream and Annette's end directs the reader back to the episode with Tia's dress. After observing her daughter wearing the shabby dress which Tia left behind, Annette works desperately to change their clothing, symbol of social status and of sexual attractiveness. Annette buys several yards of muslin and within a week both she and her daughter have new clothes. With her new attire comes a new lifestyle for Annette. Her new neighbours lend her a horse (the reference to the borrowed horse in Antoinette's reminiscences) and she becomes a part of their social world. It is her entry into and acceptance by that new world which leads to her marriage to Mason, which is her disaster. The narrative arrangement, through dreams and mirror imagery, and symbolism, connects the contents of Antoinette's dream with the shape of her mother's life to show how one's experiences reflect the other's. Each woman's life is a mirror image; a redoubling of the other.

Another character who mirrors Antoinette is Amelie. The text insists on their connection through an examination of gender relationships which suggests that the oppression of women is continuous with imperialism and slavery. When Antoinette attacks her husband for sleeping with the maid, she makes an explicit parallel between his exploitation of the servant and the planter's exploitation of slaves. Her husband responds that slavery was a question of justice. Such an assertion further inflames Antoinette:

'Justice,' she said.'I've heard that word. It's a cold word. . . I wrote
it down several times and always it looked like a damn cold lie to me.
There is no justice. . . .My mother. . . what justice did she have? My
mother sitting in the rocking chair speaking about dead horses and
dead grooms and a black devil kissing her sad mouth. Like you kissed
mine (121).

The referencing and cross-referencing of the women's experiences with men,
each life repeated with slight variation, suggests a splintered mirror, each life
with slight distortion, representing part of the mosaic.

The mirror image becomes increasingly significant as the story moves toward
its end. Imprisoned in her husband's house in England, Antoinette meets Bertha
face to face. However, before she actually confronts the other self which her
husband had begun to create even in the West Indies, she flees from the image:
"It seemed to me that someone was following me, someone was chasing me
laughing. Sometimes I looked to the right or to the left but I never looked behind
me for I did not want to see that ghost of a woman who they say haunts the place"
(153). Despite the husband's avowed intention to destroy Antoinette by creating
another identity for her, and despite her being treated as if she were insane,
Antoinette maintains her integrity. She apprehends Bertha as a external to her
own experienced reality and sense of self.

Although Antoinette flees from Bertha at first, she gains strength after she
enters the Red Room and observes the wealth accrued by husband through his
trading in her life. She comes back into the hall ready to confront her doppelgänger:

It was then that I saw her — the ghost. The woman with streaming hair.
She was surrounded by a gilt frame but I knew her. I dropped the
candle I was carrying . . . and I saw flames shoot up. As I ran or
perhaps floated or flew I called help me Christophine help me and
looking behind me I saw that I had been helped. There was a wall of
fire protecting me. . . (154).

(The reference to the gilt frame is the clue to the reader that Antoinette is looking
in a mirror).

The fire as an instrument of liberation is what frees her from the distorted
mirror image of Bertha, the madwoman in the attic. When she cauterizes by fire
the imposed identity, she thereby creates her own.

At the end of her dream reality, Antoinette is beckoned by both the husband
and by Tia. The husband is calling her by the name he has destroyed. Tia, on the
other hand, challenges her mockingly to jump. That Tia is in fact her mirror image
is further reinforced by the reference to the pool at Coulibri ". . . I saw the pool
at Coulibri. Tia was there" (155). The pool invokes again the Narcissus image.
When Antoinette calls Tia by name and jumps, she is reconnecting with her own
identity, her self. The fracture is healed. The scar when Tia's stone had left on
Antoinette's face and on her life will now be removed.

Rhys's sophisticated use of mirror imagery and symbolism, her precise artistry and crafting, make *Wide Sargasso Sea* a work which reverberates with meaning at several different levels. In this paper, I have tried to demonstrate the ways in which Rhys uses images and symbols to render rather than tell (through straightforward narrative alone) the story of Antoinette Cosway.

Works Cited:

Rhys, Jean. *Wide Sargasso Sea*. 1966. Harmondsworth: Penguin, 1968. Subsequent references to the work will appear parenthetically in the text.
____. *Jean Rhys: Letters 1931-1966*. 1984. Harmondsworth: Penguin, 1985. Jean Rhys's letters to her editors, especially those of the last ten years preceding the publication of *Wide Sargasso Sea*, provide an invaluable record of the technical and artistic energies which she used to shape the novel.
Spivak, Gayatri. "Three Women's Texts and Critiques of Imperialism" *Critical Inquiry* 12 (1985): 243-61.

Works Consulted:

Rhys, Jean. *Wide Sargasso Sea*. 1966. Harmondsworth: Penguin, 1968.
____. *Jean Rhys: Letters 1931-1966*. 1984. Harmondsworth: Penguin, 1985.

Secondary Sources:

D'Costa, Jean. "Jean Rhys 1890-1979." ed. Daryl Dance, *Fifty Caribbean Writers*. New York: Greenwood Press, 1986.
Miller, Jane. *Women Writing About Men*. London: Virago Press, 1985.
Spivak. Gayatri. "Three Women's Texts and Critiques of Imperialism" *Critical Inquiry* 12 (1985): 243-61.

# WIDE SARGASSO SEA AND THE GOTHIC MODE

## Anthony Luengo

Critics have so far failed to place *Wide Sargasso Sea* within its proper literary context, the Gothic mode of fiction.[1] This is not to say that it should be considered a Gothic novel in the traditional and strictest sense of the term. More than time separates its author from the late eighteenth century world of such quintessentially Gothic novelists as Ann Radcliffe and "Monk" Lewis. Nowhere as sentimental as Radcliffe, much less sensationalistic than Lewis, Rhys moves much deeper than either into the unstable mental world of her characters, much as Charlotte and Emily Brontë were to do when they helped to transform the tired clichés and conventions of the Gothic into powerful tools for exploring the turbid depths of the human spirit.[2]

One might perhaps hazard the term "neo-Gothic"[3] to describe novels such as *Jane Eyre*, *Wuthering Heights*, *Wide Sargasso Sea* and the numerous American writers of fiction from Charles Brockden Brown through Hawthorne, Poe and Melville to Faulkner, Capote and McCullers who, as one important commentator on the "American Gothic" sub-species puts it, deal:

> . . . with the exaggerated and the grotesque, not as they are verifiable
> in any external landscape or sociological observation of manners and
> men, but as they correspond in quality to our deepest fears and guilts
> as projected in our dreams or lived through in "extreme situations."[4]

It is tempting, of course, to use the term "Caribbean Gothic"[5] with reference to *Wide Sargasso Sea* but in the absence of a body of West Indian writing in a similar vein,[6] the term remains largely meaningless. The novel must therefore be discussed within the wider context of the Gothic tradition. While no definite sources can be accurately pinned down, one finds in Rhys much that is reminiscent of writers as widely separated in time and place as Emily Brontë and William Faulkner. In recognizing such similarities, one is simply recognizing the literary richness of the novel.

Like all novels in the Gothic and neo-Gothic mode, *Wide Sargasso Sea* is remarkable in its evocation of landscape. Both narrators of the novel evince, to slightly paraphrase Ramchand,[7] a "sensuous feel" for a land that is at once overpoweringly beautiful and mysteriously menacing. At the most superficial level this makes the work intoxicatingly "atmospheric." Colours and smells predominate as indeed they do in the many scenes of pastoral charm strewn

throughout Radcliffe's writings. Compare, for example, Rochester's account of
his sensations as he stands on the veranda of the honeymoon retreat at Granbois
for the first time with one of Radcliffe's typical descriptions of the Mediterranean
lowlands at the foot of the Alps. Here is Rochester:

> Standing on the veranda I breathed the sweetness of the air. Cloves I
> could smell and cinnamon, roses and orange blossom. And an intoxi-
> cating freshness as if all this had never been breathed before. (p. 61)

Here is Radcliffe's more mannered prose:

> The gay tints of cultivation once more beautified the landscape; for the
> lowlands were coloured with the richest hues, which a luxuriant
> climate, and an industrious people can awaken into life. Groves of
> orange and lemon perfumed the air, their ripe fruit glowing among the
> foliage; while, sloping to the plains, extensive vineyards spread their
> treasures.[8]

But even as unprofound a writer as Radcliffe attempts to make her carefully
wrought landscape pictures perform more than merely a decorative function. In
short, her landscapes are made to convey, in however uncomplex a way, the
subjective states of her characters, especially those of her overly sensitive young
heroines such as Emily (*The Mysteries of Udolpho*): gloomy, precipitous heights
reflect her terror, sunlit, gentle valley slopes and pasturelands her peace of soul.
This "projective method" of landscape description, as we have already noted
above, becomes a valuable tool in the hands of neo-Gothic writers in England and
American, and Rhys, working in the same tradition, uses it to great effect. As
Rochester ascends towards Granbois (shades of Emily ascending to the gloomy
pile of Montoni's castle!, pp. 224-27), the sense of impending danger is conveyed
thus:

> The road climbed upward. On one side the wall of green, on the other
> a steep drop to the ravine below. We pulled up and looked at the hills,
> the mountains and the blue-green sea. There was a soft warm wind
> blowing but I understood why the porter had called it a wild place. Not
> only wild but menacing. These hills would close in on you. (p. 58)

The subjective nature of landscape description in the novel has been recognized by Ramchand though, ever preoccupied with psycho-historical factors, he
fails to acknowledge Rhys's indebtedness to Gothic and neo-Gothic fiction for
the method.[9] Thus the dense tropical forest which symbolises the increasing
gloom and confusion of Rochester's mind should be seen as a latter-day
descendent of the many dark woods that appear in the novel's late eighteenth and
early nineteenth-century literary ancestors. In desperate search of the truth,
Rochester moves through the forest:

> I had reached the forest and you cannot mistake a forest. It is hostile.
> The path was overgrown but it was possible to follow it. I went on
> without looking at the tall trees on either side. .  How can one
> discover truth I thought and that thought led me nowhere. . . I found

> that the undergrowth and creepers caught at my legs and the trees
> closed over my head. . . (pp. 86-87)

The sense of menace is here more pronounced that it is in similar scenes in
Radcliffe owing, I feel, to the greater importance given the function of the forest
in neo-Gothic fiction, especially as it developed in America. Fiedler makes the
point that the haunted forest provided a handy solution to a basic problem that
faced the Gothic in the New World: what to substitute for the centuries-old castle
of the European Gothic writers?[10] Hawthorne, perhaps the most quintessential of
American Gothic writers,[11] exploits to the full the symbolic implications of the
dark forest in such superb allegories on the nature of good and evil as *The Scarlet
Letter* and "Young Goodman Brown." Rhys's technique is much the same: her
Caribbean jungles at once provide a strikingly visual and textured terror and a
convenient mirror in which to reflect the inner turmoil of her two main characters.
Thus we can trace Rochester's changing moods by his "changing attitudes to a
seemingly changing land."[12] Antoinette, in contrast, is unnervingly consistent in
her view of the forest: it is an absolutely diabolical force that presses close on the
walls of her Edenic garden (her recurring erotic dream at the convent, p. 50), and
which, in fact, is seen at one point early in the narrative to actually overwhelm the
garden at her beloved Coulibri:

> Our garden was large and beautiful as that garden in the Bible — the
> tree of life grew there. But it had gone wild. . . Underneath the tree
> ferns, tall as forest tree ferns, the light was green. Orchids flourished
> out of reach or for some reason not to be touched. One was snaky
> looking. . . (pp. 16-17)

As in American Gothic then, nature, especially in its wilder aspects, takes on
in *Wide Sargasso Sea* the importance that had in original Gothic fiction been
given to architecture. In his vastly informative if not very profound history of the
Gothic novel, Montague Summers rightly stresses the central role played by the
many castles, manors, convents and abbeys in the novels of Walpole, Radcliffe,
Lewis and the many less adept practitioners of Gothic fictional art.[13] By the time
of the Brontës, architecture (Wuthering Heights, Thornfield Hall) takes second
place to the portrayal of character, especially as reflected in the natural landscape.
In America, Poe liberated neo-Gothic fiction even further from the confines of the
original "haunted castle."[14] Not surprisingly, *Wide Sargasso Sea* provides little
in the way of haunted interiors. Coulibri is, if anything, a place of refuge for
Antoinette from the outside darkness, as indeed is the convent in its own morbid
way, ". . . my refuge, a place of sunshine and of death" (p. 47). The shabby
cottage at Granbois is more pathetic than frightening, ". . . more awkward than
ugly, a little sad as if it knew it couldn't last" (p. 60), though at times one can feel
Rhys pushing description in the direction of the traditional Gothic:

> But the feeling of security had left me. I looked round suspiciously.
> The door into her room could be bolted, a stout wooden bar pushed
> across the other. This was the last room in the house. . . I went back

> into the dressing-room and looked out of the window. I saw a clay
> road. . Beyond the road various half-hidden outbuildings. (p. 63)

One quality that Coulibri and Granbois very definitely share is their extraordinary remoteness, a geographical isolation which, of course, symbolises the spiritual separation of the protagonists from the mainstays of normality. Antoinette's mother suffers because of the isolation of Coulibri (her favourite word is "marooned"), and this eventually turns her mad. Granbois is even more remote, high in the hills, shut in by the forest, on an island inhabited, according to Antoinette, by four "hermits" (p. 74).[15]

The presence of ruins in *Wide Sargasso Sea* should also be seen in terms of the book's literary ancestry. As in the European Gothic novel, they are expressive not so much of the end of a feudal order (in the West Indian context, the plantation system) as they are of a romantic statement of deeper, more universal significance of the kind made by Radcliffe in the following passage:

> The view of the ruins was very striking; the three chief masses, great
> and solemn, without being beautiful. They spoke at once to the
> imagination, with the force and simplicity of truth, the nothingness
> and brevity of this life — "generations have beheld us and passed
> away, as you now behold us and shall pass away: they thought of the
> generation before them as you now think of them, and as future ages
> shall think of you. We have witnessed this, yet we remain; the voices
> that revelled beneath us are heard no more, yet the winds of Heaven
> still sound in our ivy."[16]

Much the same kind of romantic, contemplative mood (though much more is left implied than actually stated) descends on Rochester in the midst of his desperate trek through the forest referred to above:

> Here were the ruins of a stone house and round the ruins rose trees that
> had grown to an incredible height. At the back of the ruins a wild
> orange tree covered with fruit, the leaves a dark green. A beautiful
> place. And calm — so calm that it seemed foolish to think or plan. (p.
> 86)

The ruins, to be sure, fulfill a definite purpose in the narrative: they embody the increasingly terrifying enigma of Antoinette, her ancestry and her island which Rochester is finding he cannot solve. At the same time, the almost mind-annihilating calm which they momentarily induce in him broaden the meaning of the scene: what is suggested, I believe, is a Radcliffean or romantic apprehension of mutability.

Brief yet striking, the "ruins scene" in *Wide Sargasso Sea* is typical of the economic and effective use that Rhys makes of the conventional machinery of the Gothic. Her narrative remains uncluttered with the prodigious use of much of the traditional claptrap. Fearsome approaching footsteps; shadowy figures and flickering lights in the dark; strange voices and music from out of nowhere; mysterious portraits; doors suddenly slamming or grating bloodcurdlingly on their rusty hinges: all that is left out. Tempestuous atmospheric conditions in which, as one historian of the Gothic has correctly noted,[17] the Gothic spirit delighted, makes an appearance only once (and this in the hurricane zone!).[18]

One must not forget either the moon which inevitably provided the dim illumination for the Gothic night as, for example, in the following passage from Lewis's *The Monk*, a description rich with the stock ingredients of the traditional Gothic:

> The castle, which stood full in my sight, formed an object equally
> awful and picturesque. Its ponderous walls, tinged by the moon with
> solemn brightness; its old and partly ruined towers, lifting themselves
> into the clouds. . .[19]

Rhys does not indulge in such stagey effects, but rather connects the moon with terrifying intimacy to the subjective states of her two main characters. Thus Antoinette relates to Rochester the incident in which she sleeps in a hammock on the veranda under the full moon. She concludes the account with the question:

> "Do you think that too," she said, "that I have slept too long in the
> moonlight?" (p. 70)

The question is indirect but its meaning is nonetheless clear. Rhys is consistent in her application of the moon image to Antoinette, the climactic and most horrifying flicker (superbly pinpointing her deteriorated mental state) coming when Rochester refers in the final section of his narration to her "blank hating moonstruck face" (p. 136). The same consistency of application holds with regard to Rochester, though the moon takes on a different resonance in his case. It is made to express his sense of desperate alienation, "Not night or darkness as I knew it but night with blazing stars, an alien moon. . ." (p. 74). He also associates it with the heavily scented river flowers which hold promise of an intense, almost self-annihilating dark sexuality:

> I was longing for night and darkness and the
> time when the moonflowers open.
> Blot out the moon,
> Pull down the stars.
> Love in the dark, for we're for the dark
>     So soon, so soon. (p. 139)

Rhys has here moved way beyond the calculated theatricality of the traditional Gothic. To her credit, she comes close in spirit at this point to that outstanding achievement of nineteenth century neo-Gothic, Emily Brontë's *Wuthering Heights*.

Rhys's use and control of the machinery of, what Summers has called,[20] the "terror-Gothic" is even more remarkable in the area of magic and superstition. Here she makes more lavish use of the materials available to her but they are at no time allowed to get out of hand. She completely avoids both the lurid diablerie of Lewis's *The Monk* and the reneging "explained supernatural" of Radcliffe.[21] In *Wide Sargasso Sea* discussion of obeah revolves around the figure of Christophine. As a child, Antoinette hears the talk of the other servants concerning

Christophine's supposed necromantic activities and, not surprisingly, her already
fevered imagination conjures up terrors whenever she enters the servant's room:

> I was certain that hidden in the room (behind the old black press?)
> there was dead man's dried hand, white chicken feathers, a cock with
> its throat cut, dying slowly, slowly. Drop by drop the blood was falling
> into a red basin and I imagined I could hear it. (p. 26)

This is as sensational as Rhys ever becomes in her treatment of obeah (and this
is purely *imagined*). Antoinette sees "the girls from the bayside" bringing
suspicious offerings of fruit and vegetables to Christophine (p. 18), and seemingly more reliable proof of evil doings comes to Rochester in the warning of
Daniel (p. 103) and the letter from Fraser (p. 118). But Daniel's vindictiveness
and Fraser's vague reference to Christophine's "nonsense" make their testimony
not very trustworthy. Even when Antoinette turns in desperation to Christophine
for some kind of magical cure to the unbearable tensions between Rochester and
herself, the reader is not made privy to the consultation; the sly words of
Christophine are calculatedly chosen to create a sense of ambiguity:

> "So already you frightened eh?" And when I saw her expression I
> took my purse from my pocket and threw it on the bed.
> "You don't have to give me money. I do this foolishness because
> you beg me — not for money."
> "Is it foolishness?" I said, whispering and she laughed again, but
> softly.
> "If *béké* say it foolishness, then it foolishness. *Béké* clever like the
> devil. More clever than God. Ain't so? Now listen and I will tell you
> what to do." (p. 97)

We never in fact hear what Antoinette is told. We only know that she departs with
something wrapped in a leaf "cold and smooth" against her skin, some kind of
natural drug as it turns out which she gives to Rochester in a glass of wine. But
this is hardly black magic. Far from being a wicked devil-woman in the mould of
Lewis's Matilda (*The Monk*) Christophine comes across as the most sane,
perceptive and dignified character in the novel. If she does dabble in obeah, we
can surmise that it is mainly for practical purposes, her forte a kind of natural bush
medicine for which the authorities (quite irrationally) have little sympathy.[22]

Obeah is also used in the novel to heighten the enigma of Antoinette and her
island which, as pointed out above, disorients Rochester. Thus when he comes
upon the ruins of the stone house in the forest, he finds propitiary bunches of
flowers strewn on the ground; questioning the unsmiling Baptiste soon after he
receives only brief, elusive answers (pp. 87-88). In this way then Rhys, as with
the figure of Christophine, makes her materials narratively purposeful and
essential to the thematic import of her fiction.

Still drawing upon elements from the realm of magic and superstition, Rhys
puts to good service that eerie visitant to the nighttime world of the Gothic and
neo-Gothic — the ghost. To be sure, she does not, as Lewis does, present us with
actual ghosts. Neither does she follow the practice of Gothic writers like Walpole

and Radcliffe who, as Railo has correctly noted,[23] talk a lot about ghosts
(especially hinting at their imminent appearance), but never actually introduce
them. Radcliffe's ghosts, like so much else that is apparently supernatural in her
work, are either explained away or discussed in the spirit of eighteenth century
rationalism as, for example, in the discussion between the Baron de Saint Foix
and Count De Villefort in the last volume of *The Mysteries of Udolpho* (pp. 549-
50).

For Rhys a ghost is a mental phenomenon, the product, like Macbeth's dagger,
of the "heat-oppressed brain." It thus becomes, like the landscape, and expression
of the anguish of her main characters. In the midst of her recurring dream of
conflagration at Thornfield Hall, Antoinette sees the ghost of a "woman with
streaming hair . . . surrounded by a gilt frame but I knew her [her mother]" (p.
154). Antoinette herself becomes a ghost in the eyes of Rochester a death-in-life
figure as she sinks deeper an deeper into madness:

> She was only a ghost. A ghost in the gray daylight. Nothing left but
> hopelessness. *Say die and I will die. Say die and watch me die.* (p. 140).

In becoming a ghost, she is becoming for Rochester one with her ancestors,
themselves ghosts with their "White faces, dazed eyes, aimless gestures, high-
pitched laughter" (p. 142). It is appropriate that Rochester should end his section
of the narrative with such spectral images as he faces head-on the full horror of
his situation.[24]

In transforming the conventional machinery of the "terror-Gothic" Rhys gives
new life as well to the conventions of characterization (in other words, to the
stereotypes) of the Gothic and neo-Gothic that have come down to her. In her
portrayal of Rochester and Antoinette she works with four important character
types: the Gothic villain, the young hero, the "persecuted woman" or "maiden in
flight,"[25] and the *femme fatale*.[26] We must now discuss her use of these types
before we can reach a conclusion concerning what the novel is ultimately all
about.

The Gothic Villain, as many literary historians and critics have indicated, is
the closest literary ancestor of the type that was to become known in the Romantic
period as the "Byronic Hero."[27] Rochester, as he is portrayed in *Jane Eyre*, comes
definitely out of this mould: he has been a guilt-haunted wanderer, "harsh . . .
grim . . . almost histrionically cynical."[28] his face marked with the standard
features of his type (prominent forehead, full, black well-defined eyebrows and
piercing dark eyes, grim mouth and chin, black whiskers). In *Wide Sargasso Sea*,
Rhys gives us a more youthful Rochester, an initially self-deluding, fortune-
hunting Englishman who comes to a gradual and deeply unsettling realisation of
his Creole wife's mental instability. As he first presents himself to us, he is a
romantic suitor, ". . . I bowed, smiled, kissed her hand, danced with her" (p. 64),
to outward appearances like many another colourless and virtuous young hero
(more calculating than most, perhaps) from the world of Gothic and neo-Gothic
fiction: Theodore and Edmund in *The Castle of Otranto*. Valancourt in *The*

*Mysteries of Udolpho*, Edgar Linton in *Wuthering Heights* but to name a few. They serve in their respective novels as foils to the darker (and more memorable) personalities of Manfred, Montoni, Heathcliff and the many other Gothic villains and near villains who achieve a kind of apotheosis in Byron's work. In *Wide Sargasso Sea*, however, Rochester does not remain the young hero for long, as he pointedly states: "A short youth mine was" (p. 70). Subjected to shock after shock, he goes through a metamorphosis, not only psychologically in the direction of neurosis, but, from a purely literary standpoint, in the direction of the Gothic/Byronic villain/hero type.

A foreshadowing of the transformation that is to take place comes early in Rochester's narration when he sees himself as a Faustian figure:

> I have sold my soul or you [his father] have sold it, and after all is it
> such a bad bargain? (p. 59)

The reference is fleeting but no doubt calculated, introducing as it does the "diabolic bargain" (the willing choice of damnation) which, as Fiedler has perceptively pointed out,[29] is at the center of the Gothic novel and its descendents. Later in the narrative, Christophine, in anger, accuses Rochester of being "wicked like Satan self" (p. 132), an accusation hardly justified in terms of the action itself, but which in the light of the literary tradition in which the author is working is highly connotative. Finally, there is Grace Poole's account of her reaction to Rochester's offer of extra remuneration for keeping the mad Antoinette: "I don't serve the devil for no money" (p. 145). Rochester has by this time become the Byronic figure, "misery in his eyes," who is much more fully developed in *Jane Eyre*. Rhys, it can be seen, had Brontë's Rochester very much in mind as she created her own version of the character. She is careful to have her Rochester anticipate what he is to become in later life and in another fiction. From the viewpoint of characterization then, Rhys's Rochester needs the complement of Charlotte Brontë's if he is to be fully understood.[30]

Rhys's Antoinette, in contrast, has only the most tenuous relationship with the grotesquely insane "Bertha" of Brontë's novel. As depicted in *Wide Sargasso Sea*, she is not the type of raging mad woman, but rather a complex amalgam of two stock figures of Gothic and neo-Gothic fiction: the "persecuted woman" and the *femme fatale*.

The most immediate literary ancestor of the "persecuted woman" of Gothic fiction, as Praz has pointed out,[31] was Richardson's Clarissa Harlowe, the gentle, virtuous, melancholic maiden, pursued, persecuted and seduced by the lecherous Lovelace. Walpole and Lewis retained the frankly sexual nature of the pursuit, though Radcliffe, not surprisingly, considerably tones down the erotic element. Typical of her general method, Rhys internalises the image of flight in order to make it speak of the terrible anguish of her heroine. She begins with the external, objective depiction of persecution and flight, the recurring scenes early in the book in which the hapless Antoinette is harassed by the recently freed blacks:

> I never looked at any strange negro. They hated us. They called us

> white cockroaches. Let sleeping dogs lie. One day a little girl followed
> me singing, "Go away white cockroach, go away, go away." I walked
> fast but she walked faster. "White cockroach, go away, go away.
> Nobody want you. Go away." (p. 20)

As the external menace gives way to a steadily deepening anxiety, the images become charged with eroticism, welling up in Antoinette's recurring nightmare in which she is followed into the forest near Coulibri by one man, "his face black with hatred" (p. 50). Antoinette exists, in effect, in a state of continuous flight, from the blacks, from Rochester himself (her initial resistance to marriage and, later on, her flight to Christophine), from the terrors of her own soul.

To be sure, Antoinette is more than merely a Radcliffean innocent in danger. The complexity of her characterization comes in Rhys showing her to be at once victim and *femme fatale*. In Rochester's eyes she becomes understandably very much the latter, a dangerous woman, like her ancestors before her, who must be watched:

> The way they walk and talk and scream or try to kill (themselves or
> you) if you laugh back at them. Yes, they've got to be watched. For the
> time comes when they try to kill. . . She's one of them. . . (p. 142)

As it is, she robs him of his youth and peace of soul (forgetting for the moment the happiness which he does eventually find in *Jane Eyre*). At one point in the narrative she even mocks his God:

> "You are always calling on God," she said. "Do you believe in
> God?"
> "Of course, of course I believe in the power and wisdom of my
> creator."
> She raised her eyebrows and the corners of her mouth turned down
> in a questioning mocking way. (p. 105)

This is not to call Antoinette Satanic after the fashion of, say, Lewis' Matilda: that would be to exaggerate. Matilda is presented as a witch, a woman actively in the service of the Devil. Rhys, as we have noted already, avoids Lewis' excesses. Her method is much more subtle. She creates around Antoinette, as she does around Rochester, a sense of damnation that grows naturally out of the narrative action. Again, a process of internalisation takes place: Antoinette is first told by the servants (early in the book, first by Godfrey, then by Myra) that she and her kind are destined to hell. In time, she herself comes to believe this, dreaming of damnation at the convent and even embracing it in fits of ecstatic self-condemnation:

> All the same, I did not pray so often after that and soon, hardly at all.
> I felt bolder, happier, more free. But not so safe. (p. 48)

But such moments of desperate, heaven-defying happiness predictably give way to a state of unrelieved inner torment from which her only release can be death:

> "Say die and I will die. You don't believe me? Then try, try, say die
> and watch me die." (p. 77)

In the final analysis, *Wide Sargasso Sea* must be read as a novel about anxiety. This is to be expected. As Praz has commented:

> . . . an anxiety with no possibility of escape is the main theme of the Gothic tales. . .[32]

But the anxiety conveyed in Rhys's novel goes much deeper than the shallow fears and terrors felt by the one-dimensional characters in the novels of Walpole, Radcliffe and Lewis. The anxiety that haunts Rochester and, especially, Antoinette is caused by the disintegration of the self. In Rochester's case an initial self-deluding confidence is rapidly undermined and he feels, for the first time in his life, a dreadful sense of alienation. In Antoinette's case the dilemma is stated specifically in terms of a crisis of identity:

> "It was a song about a white cockroach. That's me. That's what they call all of us who were here before their own people sold them to the slave traders. And I've heard English women call us white niggers. So between you I often wonder who I am and where is my country and where do I belong and why I was ever born at all." (p. 85)

One is reminded here of the character of Joe Christmas in Faulkner's *Light in August* who, like Antoinette, lives in a nightmare world because he does not know who he is or where he belongs. To create this nightmare of identity adrift, both Faulkner and Rhys make imaginatively powerful and deeply meaningful use of the conventions of the Gothic mode. Thus, like all good writers, they at once relate to literary tradition and make a statement that is relevant to their own time.

Footnotes:

[1] See Kenneth Ramchand, *The West Indian Novel and Its Background* (London: Faber and Faber, 1970), pp. 223-36, who sees the novel in psycho-historical terms, a confirmation of Fanon's view of the terror produced in the minds of resident colonisers during the process of decolonisation. For a more literary approach, see Elgin Mellown, "Character and Themes in the Novels of Jean Rhys," *Contemporary Literature*, 13 (1972), 458-75, and Jean Rhys, *Wide Sargasso Sea*, intro. by Francis Wyndham (Harmondsworth: Penguin, 1968), p. 11, the edition from which all subsequent page references will be drawn. Wyndham, however, also becomes somewhat preoccupied with sociological and historical factors and this, to some extent, undermines the validity of his assessment of the novel.

[2] See Donald W. Baker, "Themes of Terror in Nineteenth Century English Fiction: the Shift to the Internal," *DA*, 16, No. 1 (1956), 118-19.

[3] The term "New Gothic" might just as validly be used as indeed I discovered it has been by Robert Heilman, "Charlotte Brontë's 'New Gothic,'" in R. C. Rathburn and M. Steinmann, eds., *From Jane Austen to Joseph Conrad* (Minneapolis, Minn.: The Univ. of Minnesota Press, 1958), pp. 118-32. I discovered this essay after I began my paper and I am more or less in agreement with its ideas though I do feel that the refashioned Gothic conventions play a smaller part in *Jane Eyre* than Heilman makes out.

[4] Leslie Fiedler, *Love and Death in the American Novel*, rev. ed. (New York: Stein and Day, 1966), p. 155. See also James Justus, "Beyond Gothicism: *Wuthering Heights* and

An American Tradition," *Tennessee Studies in Literature*, V. (1960), 25-33, in which
Brontë's novel is compared with the works of Hawthorne, Melville and Faulkner.

[5] Walter Allen in his review of the novel, *New York Times Book Review*, 18 June 1867, p.
5, uses the term though very superficially with reference to the "brooding, sinister"
atmosphere.

[6] H.G. de Lisser's *The White Witch of Rose Hall* (London: E. Benn, 1929), and some of
Edgar Mittelholzer's work, for example, *Eltonsbrody* (London: Secker and Warburg,
1960), and *My Bones and My Flute* (London: Secker and Warburg 1955), come to
mind; but neither writer works anywhere as consciously (if at all) with the conventions
of the Gothic as Rhys does.

[7] Ramchand, pp 232-35.

[8] Ann Radcliffe, *The Mysteries of Udolpho*, ed. Bonamy Dobree (OUP, 1970), p. 55. All
subsequent page references are to this edition of the novel.

[9] Ramchand, p. 255.

[10] Fiedler, pp. 159-160.

[11] See Jane Lundblad, *Nathaniel Hawthorne and the Tradition of the Gothic Romance*
(New York: Haskell House, 1964).

[12] Ramchand, p. 235. I am in full agreement with his discussion of Rochester's changing
attitude to landscape.

[13] Montague Summers, *The Gothic Quest* (London: The Fortune Press, 1937; rpt. New
York: Russel and Russel, 1964), pp. 191-92.

[14] See Eino Railo, *The Haunted Castle: A Study of the Elements of the English Romanticism*
(London: Routledge and Kegan Paul, 1927; rpt. New York: Humanities Press, 1964),
pp. 167-71.

[15] The medieval ring of this word makes it sound out of place in a Caribbean context, but
if one recalls the references to hermits in such early Gothic fiction as Horace Walpole's
*The Castle of Otranto* (in which the hermit of Joppa plays an important role), its
appearance should not be so surprising.

[16] Summers, p. 406. Quoted in the course of his argument with André Breton's interpretation of the meaning of ruins in the European Gothic Novel, pp. 404 ff.

[17] Davendra Varma, *The Gothic Flame* (London: Arthur Barker, 1957), p. 21:
Its [the Gothic] spirit revels in the fierce howling winds, portentous stormy clouds, an
the dark wild imagery of nature. . .

[18] *Wide Sargasso Sea*, p. 135. Rochester's shattered nerves reflected in the increasingly
disjointed movement of the prose of this final section of his narration.

[19] Matthew G. Lewis, *The Monk*, intro. by John Berryman (New York: Grove Press, 1959),
p. 165.

[20] Summers, pp. 28-31. Summers distinguishes three types of Gothic, (i) "terror-Gothic,"
(ii) "sentimental-Gothic," and (iii) "historical-Gothic." He gives handy examples of
each though with the caution that the first two are blended in many novels.

[21] See Summers, pp. 135-40 for a discussion of the "explained supernatural."

[22] That she sees herself as a kind of doctor (or doctor's aide) is apparent in her account to
Rochester of the "old-time doctor" whom she assists in mending a certain woman's
severed nose. (p. 125).

[23] Railo, p. 251.

[24] The method here is similar to that of Emily Brontë who fills the concluding chapters
(from Ch. 29 on) of *Wuthering Heights* with references to ghosts as never before in the
preceding narrative. As in *Wide Sargasso Sea* this is preparatory to the reunion of the
living with the dead.

[25] The "persecuted woman" is the term used by Mario Praz in *The Romantic Agony*, trans. Angus Davidson (London: OUP, 1933), pp. 95-186; the "maiden in flight" is Fiedler's term, pp. 127-32.

[26] Praz, pp. 189-286.

[27] See especially Praz, pp. 53-91 ("The Metamorphoses of Satan"); also Varma, pp. 191-92; Lowry Nelson, Jr., "Night Thoughts on the Gothic Novel," *Yale Review*, 52 (1963), 236-57, especially 251-56.

[28] Heilman, p. 122. He also sees Heathcliff as a descendent of the Gothic villain. Angus Wilson, "Evil in the English Novel," *Kenyon Review*, 29 (1967) 167-94, views both figures in the same light.

[29] Fiedler, pp. 139 ff.

[30] Allen makes this point as well though I find that he goes too far in calling Rhys's Rochester "almost as shadowy a figure as Charlotte Brontë's Bertha Mason."

[31] Praz, pp. 114-116.

[32] Mario Praz, "Introductory Essay to *Three Gothic Novels*" (*The Castle of Otranto, Vathek, Frankenstein*), ed. Peter Fairclough (Harmondsworth: Penguin, 1968), p. 20.

# "THE OTHER SIDE":
# WIDE SARGASSO SEA AND JANE EYRE

## by Michael Thorpe

The crucial question *Wide Sargasso Sea*, as a work of art, might seem to pose is whether it can stand and be judged alone, or whether in the view expressed by Walter Allen it is only "a triumph of atmosphere [which] does not exist in its own right, as Mr. Rochester is almost as shadowy as Charlotte Brontë's Bertha Mason."[1] Jean Rhys's own comment, "She seemed such a poor ghost, I thought I'd like to write her life,"[2] might seem to lend support to Allen's generalization, suggesting as it does that Rhys expended her whole creative effort upon an act of moral restitution to the stereotyped lunatic Creole heiress in Rochester's attic. Certainly, Rhys's Antoinette (Bertha), who tells Edward (Rochester) "There is always the other side, always" (p. 106),[3] is given a passionate voice to make "the other side" felt. Yet hers is still only one side and, though it might be argued of her creator's earlier novels between the wars that Rhys was more concerned to do fictional justice rather to her women than their men, *Wide Sargasso Sea* stands out as her most balanced novel in its even-handed treatment of the sexes. Her inward presentation, in the second part of the novel, of Rochester's viewpoint — complex but not "shadowy" — is unmatched in her earlier work, and its strength is enhanced by our contrasting recollections of *Jane Eyre*.

It is not Rhys's manner to spell out her characters' viewpoints, or to eke them out with detailed authorial commentary on background or theme. For her, as for Hardy, a novel is "an impression, not an argument."[4] Though I have seen people ignorant of *Jane Eyre* respond to this novel as a self-sufficient work, it would be foolish to deny that many average readers come to it with some recollection of *Jane Eyre* and that Rhys relied in a general way on their doing so. Still, she did not assume that her reader's remembrance would be anything but dim and perhaps composed of stereotypes: Rochester recalled as a passionate, Byronically-moody man, his life blighted by the secret existence of the mad wife in the attic, she being little more than a figment of the "gothic" imagination — though the compassionate Charlotte Brontë asks that we pity her, there is no effort to understand. Only in the brief Part Three, the climactic passage set at Thornfield, is some specific knowledge of *Jane Eyre* assumed. This part is introduced by Grace Poole, the woman readers of *Jane Eyre* may remember as looking after the confined heiress. Consistent with her approach, Rhys gives more credibly human

178

substance even to this minor character, Bertha's sullen jailor being presented as another woman as victim, sinking low that she may sink no lower:

> After all the house is big and safe, a shelter from the world outside
> which, say what you like, can be a black and cruel world to a woman.
> (p. 146)

This passage implicitly echoes that which closes Part One, and the security Antoinette feels in the cold "refuge" of her convent is contrasted with "outside" (pp. 47,50): the mad woman and her jailor are, unwittingly, sisters beneath the skin.

Again in Part Three, it is perhaps unlikely that even readers of *Jane Eyre* will recognize that the passage in which Antoinette, holding her red dress against herself, asks if it makes her "look intemperate and unchaste" as "that man" said, calling her "infamous daughter of an infamous mother" (p. 152), closely echoes Rochester's words in his self-exculpatory account to Jane of his relations with his first wife (Ch. XXVII).[5] This is not only an unusually explicit attempt to humanize our understanding of Bertha, but also that of Rochester, for his words are transferred in Rhys's novel to "that man," Antoinette's step-father Mr. Mason in his virulent disapproval of her relationship with her half-cast cousin, Sandi. The remainder of Part Three allows us to see Antoinette's incendiarism, not as a maniac's melodramatic finale, but as the inevitable tragic sequel to what we have learnt, not only of her embittered relationship with Edward, but also of her early life and trials.

An unexpected consequence of re-reading *Jane Eyre* in search of links with *Wide Sargasso Sea* is finding Brontë's novel a more "dated" work, marred by stereotyping and crude imaginings at points where a vaulting imagination such as Emily possessed was needed. I do not refer to the crude "gothic" of Bertha's characterisation, which has been often enough deplored since the novel appeared, but to the coarse assumptions about madness, mingled with the racial prejudice inherent in the insistent suggestion that "the fiery West Indian" place of Bertha's upbringing (Ch. XXVII) and her Creole blood are the essence of her lunacy: "Her mother, the Creole, was both a mad woman and a drunkard" (Ch. XXVI). Later she is "my Indian Messalina" (Ch. XXVII), a byword for debauchery, while Rochester's own confessed peccadilloes go under the milder name of "dissipation." Of course, the blackening of the dehumanized creature from the West Indian past readily serves Brontë's purpose of winning sympathy for the deceived and deluded Rochester from both Jane and those of the Victorian audience prone to racial prejudice.[6]

Radical though she undoubtedly was in her frank portrayal of passion in this novel, Charlotte Brontë observed certain righteous limits, which she spelt out to a correspondent — not without misgivings:

> It is true that profound pity ought to be the only sentiment elicited
> by the view of such degradation [as Bertha's], and equally true is it that
> I have not sufficiently dwelt on that feeling: I have erred in making
> *horror* too predominant. Mrs. Rochester, indeed, lived a sinful life

before she was insane, but sin is itself a species of insanity — the truly
good behold and compassionate it as such.[7]

Evidently Brontë herself felt that she had not sufficiently realized Bertha's
humanity: it was easier to make a mere figure of a character who was, unlike
Rochester and Jane, wholly imagined as a means to an end. *Jane Eyre* itself is
contradictory on the issues the letter touches upon: in his account Rochester
complains that Bertha's descent from "idiots and maniacs through three generations" was concealed from him, but also that her "gross, impure, depraved" vices
"prematurely developed the germs of insanity" (Ch. XXVII). Thus, Bertha must
be congenitally insane and yet depraved *before* that madness shows itself — a
shaky diagnosis but convenient or else it would have been possible to pity her, as
indeed before she knows all Jane once beseeches him to do. Essentially, of course,
our pity is needed for Rochester.

In getting *behind* Bertha's insanity, eschewing the catch-all dismissive generalization — "sin is itself a species of insanity" — Rhys joins those modern
writers, novelists especially, who have sought to win their readers' understanding and compassion for those whose mental state is often, and for deeply complex
reasons, just the wrong side of a thin dividing line from "normality." This concern
was foreshadowed in her earlier novels, especially *Good Morning, Midnight*
(1939). There her heroine, Sasha, is one of Rhys's "weak," to whom the whole
world is alien and menacing; her passions are a clinging to security, her fears of
others' cruelty "imagination" to the strong. A passage in which one of her lovers,
Serge, relates an encounter with a drunk "half-negro — a mulatto" woman who
lives caged with her "monsieur" in the attic of his Paris boarding house prefigures
the plight of Antoinette, everywhere an exile:

> She told me she hadn't been out, except after dark, for two years.
> When she said this I had an extraordinary sensation, as if I were
> looking down into a pit. It was the expression in her eyes. I said: "But
> this monsieur you are living with. What about him?" "Oh, he is very
> Angliche, he says I imagine everything."[8]

This brief episode holds the seeds of the Edward/Antoinette relations, as Rhys
was to treat it twenty-five years later, in what was to be her most fairly and fully
realized analysis of the fatal want of imaginative and emotional understanding
repeatedly presented in her earlier work as "very Angliche." If it may be argued
that she shows some bias in that work, in *Wide Sargasso Sea* she rises above any
temptation to blacken Rochester in his turn. Clearly, she set herself, not only to
humanize the West Indian exotic, but also to portray subtly and sympathetically
its effect upon Edward (an aspect I shall develop later). She does not for her
purposes need Jane Eyre, not merely because this is the story of Edward and
Antoinette, but because in a bold departure she draws implicit parallels, not only
between Antoinette and Jane, so underlining their common plight as women, but
also draws out hidden affinities between Antoinette and Edward, affinities which
are the substance of their tragedy.

The development of Rhys's narrative, where it centres upon Antoinette, bears striking resemblances to Brontë's portrayal of the younger Jane. Both heroines grow up fatherless and emotionally threatened by those who take charge of them; they live much within themselves and in their imaginations, made fearful by emotional and physical insecurity. Jane is an orphan: Antoinette virtually one, losing her father in childhood and seeing her mother marry again, infatuated, only to become insane after the burning of their estate by the emancipated negroes (in the disturbances of the late 1830's). The real life of both, as children, is driven inward by maltreatment or indifference. Life is the nightmare, only in dreams and fantasy do they find relief. In fact, Jane's experience is such that she might have recognized much in Bertha's suffering at Thornfield Hall: her agonies in the red-room, where her aunt confines her, correspond to Bertha's incarceration, while her temptation to a superstitous doubt of her own reality, as when she peers in the looking glass (Ch. II), is counterpointed in Rhys's novel by the looking-glass motif linked with Antoinette, who constantly needs one to be reassured of her identity. Another implicit link between Jane and Antoinette is in the oppressed Jane's search for escape in the "charm" of exotic far places conjured up for her by *Gulliver's Travels* — but her imagination more often torments than consoles her, inflamed by her daily struggles for survival. Those around her set her down as "a mad cat" subject to "tantrums"; before she goes to Lowood she is, like Bertha, virtually confined, and treated as a wild, unstable being. It is hardly surprising that the pictures she paints at school, which she later shows Rochester, recall her fevered imaginings: one, of the "woman's shape to the bust . . . the eyes shone dark and wild; the hair streamed shadowy" (Ch. XIII), might have been an unconscious presentiment of Bertha as she is later shown, but Brontë certainly points no such link.

Re-reading Chapters I to X of *Jane Eyre* one cannot help but notice how much in them corresponds to Antoinette's essential experience as a solitary, unloved child in Part One of *Wide Sargasso Sea*. Both heroines seek imaginative escape, know terrors beyond the common, endure the encroachment of menace that threatens the very soul, and reach out for a seemingly impossible happiness. Jane's Lowood, the school that "excludes every glimpse of prospect" (Ch. V) is nevertheless, like Antoinette's convent, a "refuge" (p. 47) from a harsher world without. But here a crucial difference arises. Jane finds support and inspiration in the example of the saintly Helen: Antoinette can only envy the so well-adjusted de Plana sisters, especially Hélène (p. 45). Antoinette can only learn from her how ill fitted she is to enter life beyond the convent, where she acquires no shield against reality; she will always carry on the surface the ineradicable marks of her harsh early experience. Jane, however, goes forth armed with the saving talisman of Helen's Christian example which keeps her proof at the centre against later misfortune and temptation. The significance of this, which crystallizes clearly when Jane rebuffs Rochester's plea for love after he has confessed his "horrible life" with the words "trust in God and yourself. Believe in Heaven. Hope to meet again there" (Ch. XXVII), may easily be overlooked by modern commentators seeking to define Jane as a free spirit.[9] Jane's severe morality reflects her creator's views — "sin is a species of insanity." Brontë's moral forcing, despite her casting of Jane as a seeker after liberty and self-determination, is reductive and constricting — nowhere is this more clearly shown than in the novel's dehumanizing of Bertha, the hapless creature for whom her own experience might have taught her more than a perfunctory plea for pity, soon set aside by Rochester (Ch. XXVII). Of course, Jane is a child of her author's imagination and of her time. I do not claim that Brontë could have been expected to write the greater, more complex novel potential in the parallel experiences of the early Jane and the imprisoned wife. This, in part, is what Rhys has done, writing clear of the racial prejudices that must have limited Brontë's reach and creating in the affinities between her Antoinette and Brontë's Jane a subtle, implicit comment on the short-comings of *Jane Eyre*.

Helen Burns, Jane's moral exemplar, tells Jane that she cannot believe God's creatures will "be suffered to degenerate from man to fiend" and holds "another creed . . . [which] makes Eternity a rest — a mighty home, not a terror and an abyss" (Ch. VI). Helen's creed is instinctive and positive, a sure stay for Jane and a vanquisher of goblins. Antoinette in her convent would hold to a similar faith, if she could, as taught by the nun who "knew about Heaven and the attributes of the blessed, of which the least is transcendent beauty. . . I could hardly wait for all this ecstasy and once I prayed for a long time to be dead" (p. 48). But to despair is mortal sin, there is also Hell: what has become of the soul of her mother who in her madness had died both of the "two deaths" (p. 106)? Part One ends with Antoinette trembling on the brink of "*outside*" (p. 50); dreading the "security" of the arranged marriage her dubiously solicitous step-father, Mr. Mason, has arranged for her, she dreams of Hell and the menacing male figure who draws her into darkness. She goes forth to meet her fate in Edward (Rochester) unsupported by other-worldly sanctions. All seems prepared for a treatment of Edward that will redress Brontë's bias against Bertha, but instead Part Two, which takes us at once into his consciousness, makes possible a sympathetic insight into him also.

In Brontë's novel, when Jane returns to Rochester after his blinding in the fire Bertha caused, he recognizes her voice and thinks it a "sweet delusion"; but Jane assures him, "your mind, sir, is too strong for delusion, your health too sound for frenzy" (Ch. XXXCII). We can readily believe this, despite Rochester's trials with Bertha and his losing Jane: his account of his marriage and Bertha's "mad" blood comes from one whose reason is always proof against the West Indian "hell" — despite the passing temptation to despair and suicide from which "A wind fresh from Europe" cleanses him (Ch. XXCII). For Rochester's highly coloured and, finally, self-exculpatory account of his hapless marriage Rhys substitutes in her Part Two a more complex, inward account, counterpointing it in many aspects against our prior insight into Antoinette's warped life. She thus achieves a poignant depiction of a mutual incomprehension that rests, in fact, on a closer identity of personal experience than Edward or Antoinette ever imagine. As he rides with her toward Granbois, their honeymoon house, Edward broods upon his invidious position and composes the first of his mental letters of reproach to his father in England:

> I have a modest competence now. I will never be a disgrace to you or to my dear brother, the son you love. No begging letters, no mean requests. None of the furtive shabby manoeuvres of a younger son. I have sold my soul or you have sold it, and after all is it such a bad bargain? The girl is thought to be beautiful, she is beautiful. . . (p. 59)

Edward's dubious bought "security" counterpoints Antoinette's (who is bought, who sold?. . . "The white cockroach she buy young man" sings the half-caste Amélie in his and Antoinette's hearing (p. 83), his inferior position in his family, his exile from what is familiar, the fever he is plunged into on his arrival in Jamaica, these all leave him groping for some sure ground for self; he is sceptical of life's promises and, like Antoinette, of "happiness": "As for my confused impressions they will never be written. There are blanks in my mind that cannot be filled up" (p. 64) — Edward's words, not Antoinette's. Edward, too, is young; and Rhys has built upon Rochester's expressed resentment, in *Jane Eyre*, of his "avaricious" father: "When I left college I was sent out to Jamaica to espouse a bride already courted for me (Ch. XXVII). In her portrayal Edward (a milder name that the formidable "Rochester") is an uncertain, perhaps emotionally crippled young man.[10]

Rhys's counterpointing of Antoinette and Edward is deliberate and hardly to be missed. Their shared desire for "peace" (pp. 58, 66) is disabling, for each demands it of the other, neither can accept the unfamiliar as "real" (p. 67). Their potential mutual dependence is aborted by a deeply shared vulnerability, which Antoinette exposes and Edward conceals: "I thought these people are very vulnerable. How old was I when I learned to hide what I felt? A very small boy. Six, five, even earlier. It was necessary, I was told, and that view I have always accepted" (p. 85). This is an "English" flaw, clearly, but Edward is not incapable of feeling; only in him a genuine emotional susceptibility, distrusted and constricted by a willed morality, has gone dangerously awry. Rhys brings this out in various ways, of which one becomes a persistent thematic contrast — Edward's and Antoinette's conflicting responses to the place, Granbois, and its surroundings.[11] At first Edward goes often to Antoinette's bathing pool, finding there "an alien, disturbing, secret loveliness. And it kept its secret. I'd find myself thinking, 'What I see is nothing — I want what it *hides* — that is not nothing'" (p. 73). His early hopes and promises, to Antoinette, of "happiness" in this inauspicious marriage are as fragile as his sense of his own reality — and little less so than hers. The passion they share at first, sharing the sun, is sure to recoil upon her. It would have taken less than Daniel Cosway's malicious gossip about her mother's madness and her own past relationship with her half-caste cousin, Sandi (of which her step-father so violently disapproved) to harden Edward's habit of repressed feeling into cold alienation. The warmer Antoinette, who "have the sun in her" (p. 130) confronts him too late with her truth. She recalls Coulibri and the garden where she had been "happy": this nakedly-remembered past

merges into the alien place which is "my enemy and on your side" (p. 107). In vain
she tells him, "It is not for you and not for me. It has nothing to do with either of
us. That is why you are afraid of it, because it is something else" (p. 107). Her
risky recognition of non-meaning (there is no moral scheme — contrived by
"people," whom she has learnt to fear) conflicts with that rigid invocation of "the
power and wisdom of my creator" (p. 105) which Rhys's Edward fearfully stands
upon, shunning the freedom of facing the worlds' "dark forest" (p. 137) — which
surely involves passionate relationship — existentially.

Could Edward have acknowledged with Antoinette that dangerous freedom
and have helped her face it, he might have grasped the elusive "secret."
Antoinette gives him passion, a self-abandon in desire he cannot trust: Daniel
Cosway's accusations,[12] Antoinette's foolishly countering use of the love potion
certainly deepen their alienation, but are not essential. Their shared tragedy is that
Edward has never learnt to give, nor Antoinette to receive securely. The "secret"
is denied by their deep, shared incapacity for relationship and love. At the
moment of departure Edward is "suddenly, bewilderingly . . . certain that
everything I had imagined to be truth was false. False. Only the magic and the
dream are true — all the rest's a lie. Let it go. Here is the secret. Here" (p. 138).
The place holds the "secret"; it is Antoinette's, spiritually her only stay: in
carrying her away to England he vents his frustration, rationalized as revenge for
her suspected betrayal, not only upon her but upon himself. He acts with the
calculating cruelty of the sensitive, not the brutal. His romantic desires for a
marriage of self and place — more possible for him, as for Antoinette, than a
relationship with people, for he despises her "savage" people, as she had learnt
from her step-father's example to fear his — ends with "nothing" (p. 142).

At the beginning of Part Three Grace Poole remembers "Mrs. Eff" (Mrs.
Fairfax in *Jane Eyre*) reproving her for her unwillingness to accept Edward's
proposition that she look after his mad wife with this plea for sympathy: "I knew
him as a boy. I knew him as a young man. He was gentle, generous, brave. His
stay in the West Indies has changed him out of all knowledge. He has grey in his
hair and misery in his eyes. Don't ask me to pity anyone who had a hand in that"
(p. 1345). Another side, of course, and a partial one, but by this time Rhys has
allowed Edward claims upon our pity; we have seen him steel himself against pity
(p. 135), fearful of his own disintegration, and thus violate his own soul in
destroying Antoinette's. His future does not concern Jean Rhys (though he could
have none in the Brontëan manner), but his relationship with Antoinette has been
developed into a many-sided and complete study of tragic incompatibilities
retrieved from Charlotte Brontë's workshop floor.

Footnotes:

[1] New York Times Book Review, 18 June 1967, 5.
[2] Interview, *The Guardian*, 8th August 1968.
[3] References to *Wide Sargasso Sea* (Harmondsworth: Penguin, 1968), by page number.
[4] Preface, *Tess of the d'Urbervilles*.

[5] *Jane Eyre* references by chapter number.

[6] Christine Bolt, *Victorian Attitudes to Race* (London: Routledge, 1971), *passim*.

[7] Letter to W. S. Williams, 4th January, 1848: Clement Shorter, ed., *The Brontës: Life and Letters*, Vol. 1 (London: Hodder & Stoughton, 1908).

[8] *Good Morning, Midnight* (Harmondsworth: Penguin, 1969) pp. 79-80.

[9] Cf. Dennis Porter. "Of heroines and Victims: Jean Rhys and *Jane Eyre*", *The Massachusetts Review*, 17, No. 3 (Autumn 1976), 540-551, *passim*; Porter stresses Jane's "strength of character" and "self-esteem" by contrast with Antoinette as passive victim, disabled by her colonial experience and circumstance. He overlooks the religious aspect, vital to Brontë as to her heroine.

[10] Here again I must differ with Dennis Porter, who roundly states "Rochester's failure to care enough for the feelings and the fate of his vulnerable child-bride is represented by Jean Rhys as a paradigm of male cruelty towards women" (*op. cit.*, 543): "child-bride" is hardly apt, not only because Antoinette Cosway is 18, but Edward himself is "young" — he reflects bitterly "a short youth mine was" (p. 70). Porter reduces the novel's complexity, seeing it simplistically as reflecting Rhys's semi-autobiographical concern with women's victimage in a male-dominated world. His paper rests upon the fashionable poles of male chauvinism and women's liberation between which the weak Antoinette fails.

[11] Cf. Kenneth Ramchand's perceptive brief discussion, stressing the "highly subjective landscape", *The West Indian Novel and Its Background* (London: Faber, 1970), pp. 230-36.

[12] Daniel Cosway, not Daniel *Mason* (the name of Antoinette's step-father), as Porter mistakenly calls him, *op. cit.*, p. 544: Daniel claims to be Antoinette's half-brother, her father's illegitimate son by a black woman, and plays in his accusations upon that repugnance toward the darker races and the issue of miscegenation which was as natural to an Englishman of Edward's time as breathing. While it is true that Edward betrays Antoinette with the half-caste servant, Amélie, only to realize in the morning that "her skin was darker, her lips thicker than I had thought" (p. 115), this is no simple case of "male cruelty towards women" (see note 10 above). Edward is reacting from his conviction that Antoinette, who had given him a love-potion in a foolish effort to secure him, had tried to poison him; perhaps too, he is bitterly imitating the affair with her half-caste cousin, Sandi, that Daniel Cosway has broadly hinted at.

# THE WIDE SARGASSO SEA:
## A WEST INDIAN REFLECTION

### by John Hearne

In what may be termed the natural forest of West Indian fiction as it stands now there are two cleared and carefully landscaped areas. These two areas have been pioneered by, and are under the husbandry of Wilson Harris and Jean Rhys. The two have used what is common to all of us between Belize and the Rupununi Savannahs as source material for imaginative literature in a fashion — or, rather, in two fashions — which no none else has attempted. Others abide our question — Lamming, Mais, Reid, Naipaul, even Walrond — these two alone are free fabulists. They *belong*; but on their own terms. Guerrillas, not outsiders. Independent of official supply lines; but perhaps more committed in the gut to the desperate campaign we are waging for identity than many who wear the issued uniforms, and who receive battle orders from the certified commanders-in-chief: whether these commanders be foreign readers; our own established politicians and administrators; the complacent, newly; cultivated West Indian middle class — to whom literacy is not a necessity but a domestic utensil, like a refrigerator; the brand-new university men floating their Ph.D.s on an uncertain academic stock exchange; or the self-appointed high priests of mass culture who somehow manage to reconcile their claims; to the leadership of popular expression with their ownership of three-bedroom, two-bathroom bungalows, 1600 c.c. automobiles, expensive private schools for their children, and all the other perquisites of the good bourgeois life.

I have written of Wilson Harris elsewhere. It is to Jean Rhys, and her elusive, troubling talent, that I should like now to turn my attention. And, at that, to one book: *Wide Sargasso Sea*.

For if this novel does not occupy a central place in the growing body of West Indian literature — if it is not a touchstone against which we assay West Indian fiction before and after it — then West Indian literature is in a bad way. Nobody who has tried to make a bedtime story out of our peculiar experience can afford not to pay special honour to this novel. Not, that is, if he or she is a serious artist; or, at least, a person of serious artistic intention.

Let us get out of the way, the two pillars upon which I. A. Richards said any theory of criticism must rest: '*An account of value and an account of communication.*'

Profound inquiry into sexual relationship and brilliance of technique in 'proving' how subordinate the moral concept is to the sexual imperative make up the given climate of Jean Rhys' extraordinary work.

Our real search is into *what* is being said. And our real duty rests on the openness with which we accept her achievement. We cannot, to paraphrase Conrad, render the highest justice to her visible world unless we are prepared to undertake these two obligations of understanding and celebration.

As a story, it is the account of a marginal community run over and abandoned by History. It is not a documentary of any one place or time. Indeed; Time is treated with such an elastic, arbitrary unconcern throughout the book that enters it into the lists of those dreams in which we spend so much of our life, in which we experience so much of our real suffering. The closest parallel to it in tone, in senuousity, which I can think of is Stephen Crane's *Red Badge of Courage*: that atavistic dream of war from the unconscious memory of a young man who had never seen action, but who yet conveyed — as accurately as any author since Homer — the floating, random and excruciating journey one soul makes when carried into violent, prearranged conflict with another.

And, significantly, at the end of *Wide Sargasso Sea*, it is the heroine in her madness who summarises, with devastating objectivity, the true nature of our relationship with Time:

*Time*, she says, *has no meaning. But something you can touch and hold like my red dress, that has a meaning.*

So might one of Crane's nameless soldiers, wandering across the incomprehensible confusion and pain of the battlefield, have said as he touched and held not his red dress but his red wound.

On the surface, *Wide Sargasso Sea* is a Gothic romance. And like all the great or simply very good stories since we began telling each other stories (because reality is too much to bear without the shield of fiction) it can be reduced to a few lines, almost to a picture, within the scope of a child's understanding. . .

A beautiful, forlorn girl who is very poor becomes rich because her beautiful, forlorn mama marries a rich man, and mama and stepfather both die conveniently, leaving her a good inheritance. Her wicked stepbrother, for his own social advantage, then marries her off to a handsome but cruel stranger, a fortune hunter. She falls in love with the handsome, cruel stranger. Is abused and betrayed by him, and by others she has never wronged. Goes mad. Is carried away to a cold castle in a cold, hostile land and kept a prisoner while her husband enjoys the use of her dowry.

In the end she destroys her prison by fire, herself by a leap from the battlements, and leaves her wicked husband blinded but purified by the fire that nearly consumed him.

As I have suggested, any imaginative child would be able to discern the lineaments of fulfilled morality in this simple tale. Just as it understands what Don Quixote on his lunatic charge against windmills is all about. Or, for that matter, as it knows what is going to be the result if there is a garden, an apple tree, a serpent, a woman and a man.

What it does not fully appreciate, of course, is the art that makes the retelling of these simple encounters necessary. And it is the art and structure behind *Wide Sargasso Sea* — that simple, almost sentimental journey — which I should like to consider.

In form and point of departure, its originality lies in taking the characters from an established work, *Jane Eyre*, back from their literary beginnings and fashioning, credibly, the unwritten history of creatures whom a previous author had invented. Its validity depends on a *book* from elsewhere, not on a basic, assumed life.

And yet, is this not a superb and audacious metaphor of so much of West Indian life? Are we not still, in so many of our responses, creatures of books and inventions fashioned by others who used us as mere producers, as figments of their imagination; and who regarded the territory as a ground over which the inadmissable or forgotten forces of the psyche could run free for a wile before being written off or suppressed?

The story opens, as I have indicated, with a now familiar theme: the crisis of personal and historical identity. Trouble has come to a society that was never truly a polity, an integral part of an assured culture, but only a plantation; and although the white survivors of the catastrophe have closed ranks, the white heroine and her half-mad Martiniquian mother are not really acceptable to the stolid, Protestant Jamaicans who have huddled round the fire they have lit against the dark and chill of Emancipation. Antoinette Cosway and her mother are outsiders; and her only strength lies in her dry acceptance of the pitiless historical fact that not only she and her mother, but the entire society — white and black, and everything on which they had built their pathetic, fragile pretensions — has also been cast out, castaway.

*[They wait] for this compensation the English promised when the Emancipation Act was passed.* Antoinette muses. *Some will wait for a long time.*

The compensation she refers to here is not only financial: it implies in the broadest sense, a cultural recompense that can  never be given from outside.

After the one horse left to them on the ruined estate is poisoned (for no conceivable purpose of gain) by the newly emancipated blacks, Antoinette's mother — whose only remaining pleasure had been aimless rides, dressed in a faded habit — says simply, *Now we are marooned . . . now what will become of us.*

In saying this, the mother speaks not only for herself and her young daughter — the white survivors of a system built on ships: sugar ships carrying investment capital to industrial England; slave ships carrying labour to the West Indies — but for the whole plantation that has been abandoned, left in a state of suspension, by another, confident and burgeoning society that does not understand it, has always had an uneasy conscience about it, and that has seen it drift out of ken with a self-righteous, self-congratulatory conviction of having done good.

It is here that the first of the recurrent mirror images in this intricately fashioned story occurs. For the observation by Antoinette's mother — that they are 'marooned' in an absurd situation of spite and anarchy — is reflected by

Godfrey, the old ex-slave who remains on the ruined estate because he has nowhere else to go, and because the newly freed young men no longer look after old people. *The Lord make no distinction between black and white*, he says after the dead horse is found under a frangipani tree, *black and white the same for Him.* And when Antoinette's mother (because she is still young and cannot bring herself to recognise that the red dress and the red wound are all the same in the register of indifferent Time) calls him a 'hypocrite,' Godfrey answers simply, *The devil prince of this world, but this world don't last so long for mortal man.*

We would mistake Jean Rhys' intention, however if we saw it only as the realistic depiction of a social milieu: black, bewildered ex-slaves against white, bereft ex-slave owners on a useless plantation.

In the long, mostly atrocious history of the human race, there have been countless situations where the tentative, half-ashamed desire to respond with love and understanding and gratitude to the gifts another can bestow has been aborted. American slavery — the nearly incredible record of white cruelty and black misery that lodges in the past of this hemisphere, from just south of Canada to just north of Argentina — is only one of those situations. Jean Rhys' unique contribution to the cautious, painful, damnably dangerous search we make into the human heart lies in her transcendence of the merely political, ultimately banal situation of technologically powerful whites who once oppressed technologically unequipped blacks, but who are now disadvantaged by a change of circumstances.

She adopts the situation, instead, to fashion an enduring symbol of the horrid malformation that occurs when the purely self-seeking ego uses the inarticulate but so essential offerings of the instincts as mere energy, as stacked fuel to be lit or extinguished without regard for their integral significance to our successful functioning as men and women wholly alive.

For what happens between Mr. Rochester, the gentleman adventurer from England where only *Gold is the idol they worship*, as Antoinette Cosway says, and Antoinette, the ignorant Creole, is a sad corruption of the potential love open to any two human beings who approach each other with deference and a sense of awe. It is far more horrible corruption than the mistress-slave relationship between Antoinette and Christophine (who was given to Antoinette's mother as a wedding present), or between Antoinette and all the other blacks in the story, whom neither Rochester, nor the other new men come out to scavenge in the hulk of the West Indies, can begin to understand. It is central to a true appreciation of *Wide Sargasso Sea* to note that, quite early in the book, Antoinette's mother tells her second husband, English Mr. Mason, that he must not refer to the ex-slaves as niggers, nor even as Negroes, but as black *people*.

## II

And it is this regard for the precious and irreplaceable *person* that makes *Wide Sargasso Sea* so West Indian a work of art. From the brutal farce which has passed for so much of what we call our history, the West Indians have managed to salvage this: the man or woman who stands alone, independent of the consoling pomp and title against which individuals from other, richer, more assured societies find their meaning. Men and women, here, are so often sustained by an indomitable self-awareness; yet have, also, the capacity to *give* of themselves without constraint or hypocrisy or heartless formality. Both traits were learned, long ago, as habits of survival. Both traits, to a large extent, still endure.

This, Rochester cannot understand. He cannot understand it about Antoinette whom he marries in contempt, for her money; nor can he understand Christophine and the blacks on the honeymoon island: the boy, for example, to whom he has never spoken, who weeps for love of him on his departure. This presence of love — or, if you prefer, of the open, unpretending heart — disturbs Rochester's sense of values, unsettles him in places where he assumed he was stable. Without the elaborate defences of law, artifice and byzantine custom that have made his English life seem so secure, if not particularly pleasant, he feels naked: threatened by the very spirit of the place to which he has come to market himself as a desirable bridegroom. It is crucial to our understanding of the story to remember that his first thought, on entering his little dressing room in the honeymoon house up in the hills, is that there is a bolt on *his* side of the door into the bedroom he is to share with Antoinette; and that a stout wooden bar can seal the only other door leading on to the verandah. Antoinette is, despite her untouched beauty, malignant: like the land. He resents her, as he resents the place, because he feels that what he sees is nothing. *I want what it hides*, he tells himself. To his Faustian and rapacious mind, the idea of a people — his wife and her savage blackamoors — who ask few questions of each other, who accept the genius of a place without disturbing it for more than will supply their daily needs, is not only disagreeable but nearly terrifying. And in the end, it is his terror of what he feels to be the savagery encompassing him, invading his most cultivated privacies, that drives him to the appalling, calculated cruelty with which he systematically reduces Antoinette to madness.

Against Rochester's terrified, and therefore cunning, consciousness, Antoinette has no effective defences. Her relationship to history, to the world of facts carefully balanced in a double entry ledger, to the landscape she accepts as a nourishing *donné* containing unavoidable possibilities of both pleasure and pain is artless and intuitive. She is no fool (although badly schooled), but as Christophine says of herself, towards the end of the story, *Read and write I don't know. Other things I know.*

This formal insufficiency is what makes her so vulnerable to Rochester's assault: an assault made utterly ruthless by his fear that he too may become like Antoinette, like Christophine, like the blacks of the alien and insiduous land, if he does not act quickly. Antoinette disintegrates under his coldly planned attack — as Coulibri, the fair estate of her childhood, disintegrated when the impersonal currents of a mechanistic, profit and loss culture carried it into a sea of dead clinging weeds.

Coulibri and all that it represented had been based, of course, on the grossest injustice, on abominable cruelties, on monotonous indecencies, but we have to ask ourselves — as we follow Rochester's bleakly egotistic misuse of a generous and passionate creature, his sanctimonious destruction of an eager, loving spirit, his joyless indulgence of the appetites which he has been taught to despise — whether he does not represent a more profound corruption of the whole man alive than ever happened at Coulibri in the days of bondage, of explicit physical torture, and of frankly admitted sensuality.

One of the most powerful and reverberant scenes in the novel is the final confrontation between Rochester and the old nurse, the ex-slave Christophine — after Christophine has given Antoinette an aphrodisiac that has stimulated Rochester into one night of hallucinatory lust, followed by the morning in which he tries to vomit up all those passions in himself which had been released by the love philtre.

There is a moment in this scene where, for the first and only time in the story, Christophine laughs: *a hearty, merry laugh*, as Rochester describes it. She is sharing with him the secret which only they and Antoinette know: that under the influence of the herb, he had been very rough with Antoinette. Christophine had seen the marks on the girl's body when she undressed her the following day. She is acknowledging, with more admiration than censure, that Rochester too can be human, fallible and desperate for contact when he is oblivious of his crippling solemnity. For the first time Christophine can regard Rochester with something like wry affection — as a fellow castaway. The physical bruising he has inflicted on Antoinette while transported by desire is *a little thing*, Christophine says, *[a] nothing*. And she goes on to tell him how she once had to hold a woman's nose to her face, until the doctor arrived to sew it back, after the woman's husband had nearly severed it with his machete during a jealous quarrel.

Anything done in passion, she implies, is better than the isolate sterility of a Rochester who will not, or cannot, acknowledge the divinity that informs our passionate exchanges. She goes on to speak fondly of the white doctor who came galloping up the mountain track to perform the operation:

> an old-time doctor, she remembers, he laugh and laugh . . . {Not like} these new ones. I don't like them. First word in their mouth is police. Police — that is something I don't like.

She is wrong, of course, in her dismissal of reason and discipline as represented by the police. But she is less, much less, false to her integrity as a human being than is Rochester, whose rational *hubris* and heavy, metallic greed have suffocated the essential dualism of his nature. He is dying from lack of fulfilled instinct: as an unhorsed knight of the later Middle Ages died from lack of breath inside the prison of his ornate, overweighty armour.

Antoinette and Christophine may inhabit a world where there are perhaps too few clearly defined boundaries around the passions; a world in which historic references are treated too carelessly; a world in which reflection and moral analysis of action's consequences tend to be subordinate to a purely intuitive reading of a complex but finally unyielding Nature. But yet — Antoinette and

Christophine are closer to more fertile sources of life than is Rochester. They are the carriers of an ancient, enigmatic message he has forgotten how to read, or lost, or thrown away for unsatisfying triumphs. As he rides the bridle path down from the honeymoon house on the mountain top, and the stupid boy who has given his mute, overflowing heart to him weeps for his departure, he has to admit to himself: *Who would have thought that any boy would cry like that [and] For nothing. Nothing. . .*

With the possession of his fortune, gained by a counterfeit love, now secured for his disposal because of his wife's madness, Rochester is forced to recognise that he is a non-person. That the undeveloped child behind him weeps for a *nothing*.

## III

But we should not look at *Wide Sargasso Sea* as simply a brilliant symbolic rendering of the conflicting relationships between the proprietorial metropolis and the abandoned plantation. Nor should we regard it only a study of the collision course between a set of rigid white values and an emerging, insurrectionary black awareness. It is more than these. More, even, than one of recent fiction's most urgent yet objective scrutinies into the stubborn challenge and response struggle between the male, ego-asserting principle of conquest and the female concept of mutual nurture by a co-operative deployment of our instinctive resources.

Its essential inquiry is into the most treacherous, least clearly mapped, most demanding terrain of the human condition. The terrain, I mean, to which we all hope to migrate some day; the big promised land on the other shore of a wide ocean; the place for which we are all headed, and for which journey all our efforts in politics, art, philosophy — any endeavour we can name — are merely means of acquiring capital to equip ourselves. The great good place, in brief, where we can find someone to love who will love us in return.

Most of us will never get there; and only a few of us will ever glimpse the coastline above the horizon. But at least the hope of getting there keeps us alive and functioning: right up to the end when, old and still hoping, we perish in our out of date craft, caught by the matter of the wide sargasso sea.

It is this unflinching examination of perennially reviving, perennially blighted hope that makes Jean Rhys' novel so important, and that places it so dead centre of what we can only term the West Indian perception.

For here we have learned to accept, without disappointment, the fact that most attempts to reach love must fail. (Fail absurdly rather than tragically.) But that the attempt to reach it must be seen, always, as the goal of our other, utilitarian enterprises if we hope to realise our true dimensions of humanity.

'Peace and Love,' for example, is the slogan of Jamaica's most politically radical sect, the Rastafari. As far as I know, such a slogan is unique among the radical groups of the world.

In *Wide Sargasso Sea*, as was suggested at the beginning of this reflection,

Jean Rhys sees this quest for love as taking the form of mirror reflections, of duplicated experience. It is not a new concept. Plato held that every soul born into this world was an entity divided, hungrily searching for the separated half with which it could join to become whole and happy again. Jean Rhys' singular and beautiful achievement is to have discovered fresh images for an idea nearly as old as written thought.

From the black child, Tia, who throws a stone into the child Antoinette's face when the blacks burn Coulibri, and who then bursts into tears because she realises that the blood she had drawn is a part of her own, through the parrot, Coco, whose question *Qui est là* is always answered, by it, with *Ché Coco, Ché Coco* (and whose death, as its singed wings fail to flight it from the burning house, prefigures Antoinette's leap from the roof of Thornfield Hall), to the stark passage when Christophine's exposition on the true nature of love so overwhelms Rochester that he can only echo her words in his mind, the images of reflection are multiple and interwoven with a consummate rightness. . . Until the moment when the mad girl carrying the lit candle sees herself in the corridor mirror in Thornfield Hall, and fails to recognise who is staring back at her.

It is at this moment that Jean Rhys, with courage and an obstinate honesty of vision, gives us the answer to our question about the possibilities of success in our search for love — which is, really, only another term for our question about the possibilities of success in our search for the conquest of Time.

And the answer, to use Forster's great closing phrase, is *No, not yet. . . No, not there.*

There are a few small victories; we carry off, occasionally, a few spoils from minor engagements; at moments we *have* to believe we have reached the further shore that was promised us. Always there is compassion. *All in compassion ends*, as Derek Walcott has told us.

But, finally, there is only the red dress held between a poor mad girl and a cold room; only the red wound clutched by a nameless soldier on a battlefield of which he sees only the trees under which he will lie down and rest. Only the red flames roaring in Thornfield Hall, pulling its vanity down.

# WIDE SARGASSO SEA

## by Kenneth Ramchand

Had rationalisation been necessary, the case for including Jean Rhys's *Wide Sargasso Sea* in a course on West Indian literature would be that this novel challenges us to think a little more carefully about two questions: What makes a novel a West Indian novel? and what do we mean when we say that a writer is a West Indian writer? A safe enough generalisation to begin with is that those literary works are West Indian which describe a social world that is recognisably West Indian, in a West Indian landscape; and which are written by people who were born or who grew up in the West Indies. Where the disruption of intimacy between an author and his native world has not been acute, or where the separation between them has not been absolute and prolonged, our generalisation works satisfactorily. But the case of Miss Rhys, the author of *Wide Sargasso Sea*, is a tempting one.

Francis Wyndham begins his Introduction[1] to this novel with the information that Jean Rhys, daughter of a Welsh doctor and a White West Indian mother spent her childhood in Dominica before going to England at the age of sixteen. Memories from a West Indian childhood float about in her earliest writing[2] and in *Voyage in the Dark* (1934), it is the memory of another life now lost, and another place still felt in the blood which benumbs the heroine and unfits her for existence in the England to which she has been brought: 'hundreds thousands of white people white people rushing along and dark houses all alike frowning down one after the other all alike all stuck together — the streets like smooth shut-in ravines and the dark houses frowning down — oh I'm not going to like this place I'm not going to like this place I'm not going to like this place' *(pp. 15-16, Penguin edition)*. What strikes Mr. Wyndham more strongly about these earlier works of Miss Rhys, however, is their modern urban background and the present plight of their underdog heroines. Accordingly, when he comes to *Wide Sargasso Sea* he can acknowledge that the setting is now the West Indies but yet another nightmare for a beleagured Rhys heroine, and he links the novel closely to the preceding ones by recognising Antoinette Cosway as 'a logical development of Marya, Julia, Anna and Sasha who were also alienated, menaced, at odds with life.'

A West Indian commentator, Wally Look Lai, is ready to concede that Miss Rhys's other works are European, and that in them the author is more a European that a West Indian writer; but for him there is a radical discontinuity when we come to *Wide Sargasso Sea*. It is a West Indian novel, in which the West Indian setting is crucial; 'It is not that it provides a mere background to the theme of rejected womanhood, but rather that the theme of rejected womanhood is utilised symbolically in order to make an artistic statement about West Indian society, and about an aspect of the West Indian experience.'[3] Implicit in Look Lai's contention, and in the method he adopts to support it, is the principle that in trying to judge whether a writer is a West Indian author we must rely on the tale, and allow that to be the source of our most relevant impressions about the teller; if we come to the conclusion that a certain work is West Indian, then it follows that the writer, as author of that particular work is a West Indian writer. Look Lai's discussion is about the novel itself, and not Miss Rhys's colour, class or nationality, because in difficult cases we are driven to fundamentals: we know a writer is a West Indian writer if the work is West Indian. But this leaves us with our original question, 'What makes a novel a West Indian novel?'

To this question, it is tempting to reply that we just know. For to affirm that a work is West Indian is to suggest that a West Indian reader may be more responsive to landscape and setting, more alive to social and political levels, and more caught up in, sometimes, indeed, more caught out by the work's 'buzz of implication' than he would be if reading a non-West Indian work. In *Wide Sargasso Sea* Jean Rhys employs a variety of devices — detailed descriptions of place and weather; casual references to the colour of the sky and degrees of light, heat or shade; allusions to the scents and tints of flowers; and sometimes, as in the following example, observations of a native's behaviour — all of which bring to the reader's senses a landscape felt and recognised by a West Indian as his own.

> We rode on again, silent in the slanting afternoon sun, the wall of trees on one side, a drop on the other. Now the sea was a serene blue, deep and dark. We came to a little river. 'This is the boundary of Granbois.' She smiled at me. It was the first time I had seen her smile simply and naturally. Or perhaps it was the first time I had felt simple and natural with her. A bamboo spout jutted from the cliff, the water coming from it was silver blue. She dismounted quickly, picked a large shamrock-shaped leaf to make a cup and drank. Then she picked another leaf, folded it and brought it to me. 'Taste. This is mountain water.' (pp. 70-1)

Like Wilson Harris and Derek Walcott, Miss Rhys is concerned as much to evoke the landscape as to explore its impact upon human consciousness. The different stages in the changing relationship between English husband and White West Indian wife are marked by the husband's changing and confused attitudes to the landscape; and the difference in temperament between Antoinette and her husband is measured out for us in his reading of the natural world which he identifies with his wife:

> 'You have no right,' she said fiercely. 'You have no right to ask questions about my mother and then refuse to listen to my answer.'

'Of course I will listen, of course we can talk now, if that's what you wish.' But the feeling of something unknown and hostile was very strong. 'I feel very much a stranger here,' I said. 'I feel that this place is my enemy and on your side.'

'You are quite mistaken,' she said. 'It is not for you and not for me. It has nothing to do with either of us. That is why you are afraid of it, because it is something else. I found that out long ago when I was a child.' (pp. 129-30)

As with landscape, so with social background. Jean Rhys's intelligent memory of the West Indian linguistic situation enables her to invent varieties of language to suit respectively, her characters from England; her dialect and French-patois speaking Negro characters; her White West Indian whose language ranges between these two; and the would-be grandiloquent mulatto Daniel Cosway:

Dear Sir,
I take up my pen after long thought and meditation but in the end the truth is better than a lie. I have this to say. You have been shamefully deceived by the Mason family. They tell you perhaps that your wife's name is Cosway, the English gentleman Mr. Mason being her stepfather only, but they don't tell you what sort of people were these Cosways. Wicked and detestable slave-owners since generations — yes everybody hate them in Jamaica and also in this beautiful island where I hope your stay will be long and pleasant in spite of all, for some not worth sorrow. Wickedness is not the worst. There is madness in that family. Old Cosway die raving like his father before him.

(pp. 95-6)

The language in *Wide Sargasso Sea* has an authentic ring to the West Indian's ear, and evokes, in a way no didactic account can, the whole social spectrum in the West Indies. A West Indian reader, moreover, armed with a knowledge of West Indian history, and burdened with attitudes and feelings rooted in the peculiar orderings of the plantation system, recognises the accuracy of the 'factual' data, and responds to nuances in the situation that could easily be missed by a non-West Indian reader. This kind of difference between readers of the novel exists for the fictional characters too. It is brought out with deliberate obviousness in Part I of the work, where Jean Rhys prepares us for the mutual incomprehension of Antoinette and her husband by pre-figuring it in the lack of understanding between the girl's mother and her new husband from England, Mr. Mason. Antoinette's mother senses danger in the stirrings among the Black population and wants to go away, but Mr. Mason's complacency and his prejudices will not be touched by the fear and understanding of the slave-owner's daughter:

'You have lived alone far too long Annette. You imagine enmity which doesn't exist. Always one extreme or the other. Didn't you fly at me like a little wild cat when I said nigger. Not nigger, nor even negro. Black people I must say.'

'You don't like, or even recognise, the good in them,' she said, 'and you won't believe in the other side.'

'They're too damn lazy to be dangerous,' said Mr. Mason. 'I know that.'

'They are more alive than you are, lazy or not, and they can be dangerous and cruel for reasons you wouldn't understand.'

'No, I don't understand,' Mr. Mason always said. 'I don't understand at all.' (pp. 32-3)

Jean Rhys makes Antoinette's husband different from Mr. Mason in that the former is conscious of the cultural difference between himself and his West Indian wife: "I felt very little tenderness for her, she was a stranger to me, a stranger who did not think or feel as I did' *(p. 93)*. He is constantly on his guard with the Blacks: 'She trusted them and I did not. But I could hardly say so. Not yet' *(p. 89)*; and he is appalled at Antoinette's intimacy with them: "'Why do you hug and kiss Christophine?" I'd say' *(p. 91)*. The failure of the two social worlds to come to terms with each other is implied in the failure of the relationship between Antoinette and her husband; and the main elements in this failure are revealed to be the Englishman's inability to accept the White West Indian's attachment to the landscape of her birth; and his unwillingness to take as natural her closeness in sensibility to the world of the Blacks, to which Christophine and Antoinette's childhood friend Tia belong, and which is the life-breath of the novel: 'We had eaten the same food, slept side by side, bathed in the same river. As I ran, I thought, I will live with Tia and I will be like her. Not to leave Coulibri. Not to go. Not' *(p. 45)*.

We jump suddenly from the account of Antoinette's childhood in Part I into the relationship that has come about through an arranged marriage between the girl and a young Englishman come out resentfully at his father's behest to the West Indies to make his own fortune. The change in subject matter is accompanied by a change in perspective that is startling and dramatic. Much of Part II is presented from the point of view of the alien husband: 'everything is purple, too much green. The flowers too red, the mountains too high, the hills too near. And the woman is a stranger' *(p. 70)*. The difference in background and sensibility is immediately felt by the reader but emerging even more importantly from this entry into the husband's consciousness is our sense of the struggle of a certain kind of mind to break free and expose its buried emotions and yearnings:

> My fever weakness left me, so did all misgiving. I went very early to the bathing pool and stayed there for hours, unwilling to leave the river, the trees shading it, the flowers that opened at night. They were tightly shut, drooping, sheltering form the sun under their thick leaves It was a beautiful place — wild, untouched, above all untouched, with an alien, disturbing, secret loveliness. And it kept its secret. I'd find myself thinking, 'What I see is nothing — I want what it *hides* — that is not nothing.' *(p. 87)*

Long before we arrive at anything as definite as the formulation of a theme, the West Indian-ness of *Wide Sargasso Sea* imposes itself upon a responsive reader. But it is difficult to speak about this kind of alertness to a novel's background noises let alone demonstrate it, so it is just as well that we can fall back, in argument, upon a position implicit in Look Lai's discussion: the *theme of Wide Sargasso Sea* is West Indian, and it is this that makes the novel a West Indian novel.

One is inclined, then, to agree with Look Lai that in *Wide Sargasso Sea* there is an exploration of 'the encounter between two whole worlds,' but with reservations. The last two quotations from *Wide Sargasso Sea* were intended to suggest that at any critical approach focusing exclusively on Antoinette must suffer the limitation of being little more than half-satisfactory. For Miss Rhys allows us to explore not just 'the White West Indian's relation to England, the nature and consequences of his involvement with the world from which his ancestors came,' but also, and with just as great relevance to an understanding of our colonial situation, the Englishman/coloniser's psychic relationship to the West Indies. If *Wide Sargasso Sea* has a West Indian theme, its originality arises from the author's peculiar ability to examine 'the encounter between two whole worlds' from both points of view — that of Antoinette, and that of her husband.

Yet to say that a novel is West Indian is not to deny its accessibility to a non-West Indian, nor indeed to deny the validity of a non-West Indian's reading. The differences in emphasis between Francis Wyndham and Wally Look Lai can be accommodated as arising from different cultural/national perspectives, and as another illustration of the many-sidedness or objectivity of a work of art, making it possible for it to mean different things to people from different countries, just as it can mean different things to the same person at different times.

It is interesting in this context to look at the stark differences in interpretation of *Wide Sargasso Sea* between Look Lai, and a fellow West Indian, Edward Brathwaite. Look Lai's explication of the theme of the White West Indian's relation to England is at the same time an appeal to his fellow West Indians to take a less tribal view and to see the experience of White West Indians as an aspect of the West Indian experience. Brathwaite concedes that Jean Rhys's concern was as Look Lai finds it in the novel, and notes with sadness that 'what really interests Look Lai about *Sargasso Sea* is not the deep subtle hopeless black/white "West Indian" relationships'; he dismisses the novel as 'a fictional statement that ignores vast areas of social and historical formation,' and then seems to quarrel with the art of fiction itself. He asserts that Tia the African girl and Antoinette, the White Creole, could not have been friends in real life and therefore could not be in the novel: 'Tia was not and never could have been her friend. No matter what Jean Rhys might have made Antoinette think, Tia was historically separated from her by the impassable boundary of colour distinction.'[4] Brathwaite's account of the wrongness of *Wide Sargasso Sea* is completed and explained by the procla-mation of a kind of 'fact' that should have been less binding to a writer who as poet/historian is often projected as being concerned with ignored and forgotten possibilities for colonised and coloniser in West Indian life:

> Now he was sure
> he heard soft voices mocking in the leaves
> What did this journey mean, this

> new world mean:
> discovery? Or a return to terrors
> he had sailed from, known before?
>
> I watched him pause.[5]

Surely, the poet who could imagine such a possibility of self-discovery for the first coloniser has fallen short of his own intuition when he declares that 'White Creoles in the English and French West Indies have separated themselves by too wide a gulf, and have contributed too little culturally as a group, to give credence to the notion that they can, given the present structure, meaningfully identify or be identified with the spiritual world on this side of the Sargasso Sea?'

A literary work doesn't only say things *through* the elements (people, places, things, etc.) out of which it has been made; it speaks, and it does so in unexpected ways, to native readers *about* those elements. As the native critic's interpretation of social reality may differ from the presentations of his author or from the interpretations of other critics, the work may become contentious in its country of origin, and native readers may appear to outsiders to be battling over shadowy substances around certain texts and authors. Sometimes indeed, the commentator may entirely lose sight of what it is that the particular literary work is trying to do or say because of the burden of his own wishes and theories. The extreme example referred to above helps us to see how easy it is to slip away from literary work when we seek, however legitimately, to extract its social significance; and it calls to our notice the danger of prescription that exists whenever we attempt to base definitions upon social and political content. Even as Brathwaite attempts to persuade us that *Wide Sargasso Sea* is whitewash, however, we can venture to add to our un-theoretical understanding of what makes a West Indian novel West Indian this generalisation relating to understand the world and their social relations better, and with such authenticity that the challenge cannot be ignored even if we want to set it aside.

In arguing for *Wide Sargasso Sea* as a West Indian novel, Look Lai advances its socio-cultural theme as something that 'transcends the purely personal nature' of the encounter between Antoinette and her husband. The general proposition about the relative merits of socio-cultural and personal themes that seems to lie behind this remark is, to say the least, a questionable one. Although, moreover, we recognise the importance of the socio-cultural theme, and in spite of the distancing from the author that is implied in the fabrication of *Wide Sargasso Sea* (historical setting, fictional characters based upon historical types, detailed landscape, narrating characters), we find a lyric intensity in the work which suggests the existence of something much more personal to the author and to the reader imbedded in the fiction. We shall now explore this personal feature, in the belief that we may discover what it is that this West Indian novel is saying *through* the elements out of which it has been constructed. The argument depends upon a recognition of how certain aspects of an earlier novel *Voyage in the Dark* (1934) appear in a new form in *Wide Sargasso Sea* more than thirty years later; and upon an interpretation of the husband's experience in the novel of 1966.

The action of *Voyage in the Dark* takes place in the eighteenth year of Anna Morgan, a West Indian girl who had arrived in England two years earlier. Memories of her West Indian childhood make her experience in England all the more intolerable, but she numbs herself into getting used to a colourless life, slips into prostitution, and the end of the novel finds her almost recovered from an abortion that will allow her a new start. In the circumstances of her exile, it is a new start that can only be a dreary 'starting all over again, all over again. . .' *(p. 159). Voyage in the Dark* is one of the most moving of the West Indian novels of exile; and its critique of English life against the background of a West Indian existence full of warmth, colour and spontaneity brings it very close in temper to the literature of negritude.

After two years in England, Anna finds the small tidy fenced-off fields she had seen on her arrival symbolic of the lives in her new environment; the cold predictable greys of streets and buildings *(p. 8)* only mirror the inhabitants: 'I don't know how people live when they know exactly what's going to happen to them each day' *(p. 64).* Even more oppressive to Anna is the acceptance of this colourless, tasteless life. This is equated by Anna with getting old, and it is illustrated in this snippet from a restaurant scene: 'There were two middle-aged women at our table and a young man with a newspaper which he read whenever he stopped eating. The stew tasted of nothing at all. Everybody took one mouthful and then showered salt and sauce out of a bottle onto it. Everybody did this mechanically, without a change of expression, so that you saw they knew it would taste of nothing. If it had tasted of anything they would have suspected it' *(p. 50).* For Anna, this dreary mode of existence is contained in the word 'whiteness' and she remembers again and again that even before coming to England 'I wanted to be black. I always wanted to be black. . . Being black is warm and gay, being white is cold and sad' *(p. 27).*

The symbolic contrast between whiteness and blackness which develops in the novel is really an extreme expression of a duality which Anna, as a White West Indian trained to think of England as home, cannot reconcile in herself: 'Sometimes it was as if I were back there and as if England were a dream. At other times England was the real thing and out there was the dream, but I could never fit them together' *(p. 8).* For Anna, this duality expresses itself in two contrasting climates, two landscapes, two societies, and two ways of feeling and thinking. *Voyage in the Dark* is more an expression of the pain and confusion arising from this duality, than an artistic exploration of it. But in the following extended quotation we can see in a relatively simple form many of the ingredients that are to be re-worked in *Wide Sargasso Sea.* Anna's lover, a hard young man who exploits her sexually has brought her away from London for the weekend:

> That day it was hot again. After lunch we went to Savernake Forest.
> The leaves of the beech trees were bright as glass in the sun. In the
> clearings there were quantities of little flowers in the grass, red,
> yellow, blue and white, so many that it looked all colours.
> Walter said, 'Have you got flowers like these in your island? These

little bright things are rather sweet, don't you think?'

I said, 'Not quite like these.' But when I began to talk about the flowers out there I got the feeling of a dream, of two things I couldn't fit together, and it was as if I were making up the names. Stephanotis, hibiscus, yellow-bell, jasmine, frangipanni, corolita.

I said, 'Flamboyant trees are lovely when they're flowering.'

There was a lark rising jerkily, as if it went by clockwork, as if someone were winding it up and stopping every now and again.

Walter said, as if he were talking to himself, 'No imagination? That's all rot. I've got a lot of imagination I've wanted to bring you to Savernake and see you underneath these trees ever since I've known you.'

'I like it here,' I said. 'I didn't know England could be so beautiful.'

But something had happened to it. It was as if the wildness had gone out of it. (p. 67)

*Voyage in the Dark* is a fictional work so it would be foolish to believe that all the things that happened to Anna happened to Miss Rhys. But is worthwhile noticing a number of details in the novel which correspond to some of the few facts we have about the author. Like Miss Rhys, Anna came to London as a young girl after a childhood in the West Indies, and both the character and the author have a Welsh father. Neither these similarities nor the recurrence in different works of the same names, places and events in a West Indian childhood would justify us in making a direct connection between the author and any of her fictional characters. But the veranda with its enormous brass telescope standing on a wooden table which appears in the early fragment 'Mixing Cocktails' in *The Left Bank* (1927) helps us to a useful realisation. It is brought into *Voyage in the Dark* when Anna tells Walter about the skill the 'I' in 'Mixing Cocktails' also boasted of *(see Voyage, pp. 44-5)*; and it seems to come alive dramatically with the spirit of Antoinette in *Wide Sargasso Sea* when the husband goes there after a violent outburst from her: 'My arm was bleeding and painful and I wrapped my handkerchief round it, but it seemed to me that everything round me was hostile. The telescope drew away and said don't touch me' *(p. 149)*. We can trace in Miss Rhys's use and re-use of the same material, a progressive distancing *in the art* of autobiographical fragments and pressures which nevertheless account for the intensity of feeling in all her works.

In *Wide Sargasso Sea*, Jean Rhys discovers a form that allows her to return to the relationship between those qualities that had been too simply categorised as whiteness and blackness in the early novel: and the duality that had baffled Anna is now given full exploration by the invention of two separate characters. They are credibly presented in the first place as individuals, then as representatives of two different worlds. But at the same time they stand for two sets of human qualities which in combination make for wholeness in the person. It is not to *Wide Sargasso Sea* as a historical novel relevant to our understanding of West Indian society today (although it certainly is that), that we respond with such a sense of personal involvement, but rather to *Wide Sargasso Sea* as an exploration of the possibilities of bringing wholeness to the divided self of modern times.

The Antoinette we meet in Part I of *Wide Sargasso Sea* suffers from a world weariness and a desire for death like Anna of *Voyage in the Dark*, but it is a measure of Miss Rhys's success in creating character in the later novel that Antoinette's death-wish springs logically from her desolating experiences, and carries no traces of a mood that might be being undergone by the author. The revival that takes place on the journey to Gran Bois and during the early days of the honeymoon shows Antoinette to be gay, spontaneous, trusting, responsive, incapable of pretence, vulnerable; she only wishes to die if happiness is not possible:

> 'Why did you make me want to live? Why did you do that to me?'
> 'Because I wished it. Isn't that enough?'
> 'Yes, it is enough. But if one day you didn't wish it. What should I do then? Suppose you took this happiness away when I wasn't looking. . .'
> 'And lose my own? Who'd be so foolish?'
> 'I am not used to happiness,' she said. 'It makes me afraid.'
> 'Never be afraid. Or if you are tell no one.'
> 'I understand. But trying does not help me.' (p. 92)

The portrayal of Antoinette may appear less impressive an achievement than it really is, but Miss Rhys's impersonation of the husband, her ability to enter into the masculine consciousness of the secret sharer at the sweet honeymoon house is a feat that should suggest something more than a tour de force of imagination. It is, accordingly, on what happens and what nearly happens to the husband that it seems useful to concentrate now.

The husband chosen for Antoinette Cosway by her step-brother Richard Mason is a young man embittered by the ill-treatment he has received from his father, resentful of the fact that this marriage has been arranged for him too, as an economic proposition, and suspicious of a place and a people he does not understand. Because of the narrative technique employed, we are able to contrast the feelings and attitudes he keeps to himself with the behaviour his tight suppression permits him to show: 'How old was I when I learned to hide what I felt? A very small boy. Six, five, even earlier. It was necessary, I was told, and that view I have always accepted. If these mountains challenge me, or Baptiste's face, or Antoinette's eyes, they are mistaken, melodramatic, unreal. . .' (p. 103). This representative of 'whiteness' is not, as he might have been in *Voyage in the Dark*, incapable of feeling but he fears to be vulnerable; and the smooth face that can hide its feelings can, more sinisterly than in the earlier novel, pretend that the object which challenges it to feel does not exist.

The hardness of the young man contrasts with the vulnerability of Antoinette, and the reserve that his intellectual approach brings him allows him to police his own emotions, while observing ironically the surrender to feeling that he engineers in his wife:

> I'd remember her effort to escape. (*No, I am sorry, I do not wish to*

*marry you).* Had she given way to that man Richard's arguments, threats probably, I wouldn't trust him far, or to my half-serious blandishments and promises? In any case she had given way, but coldly unwillingly, trying to protect herself with silence and a blank face. Poor weapons, and they had not served her well or lasted long. If I have forgotten caution, she has forgotten silence and coldness. (p. 91)

As the days and nights of the honeymoon pass, however, we see him succumbing more and more to 'a music I had never heard before,' still analysing his wife ('She was undecided, uncertain about facts — any fact,' *p. 87*), still measuring his emotions and fearing them ('It was at night that I felt danger and would try to forget it and push it away,' *p. 93*) but giving in, nevertheless, learning the songs that Antoinette sings and allowing himself to think of entities his background and training would have told him were too nebulous to pursue: 'What I see is nothing — I want what it hides — that is not nothing' (*p. 87*).

It is this process of dissolution which is checked when Daniel Cosway's malice arrives at the honeymoon house, to bring those concrete realities back that had previously regulated the husband's life: 'As I walked I remembered my father's face and his thin lips, my brother's round conceited eyes. They knew. And Richard the fool, he knew too. And the girl with her blank smiling face. They all knew' (*p. 104*). What follows in *Wide Sargasso Sea* is a compassionate presentation of a mind trying to convince itself that a confidence trick has been played upon it, but never quite finding peace until it agrees to play a trick upon itself. The husband's mind will not open itself up to the harsh truths of a furious Christophine, yet it parodies its former method of operation by substituting for ironic commentary a self-inflaming repetition of the old woman's charges (*pp. 153-4*). It undermines Antoinette's faith in words ('I will tell you anything you wish to know, but in a few words because words are no use, I know that now') yet by calling her 'Bertha' it hopes to use words in an incantatory way, as Antoinette recognises later, to dispel the magic it had once ratified: 'Names matter, like when he wouldn't call me Antoinette, and I saw Antoinette drifting out of the window with her scents, her pretty clothes and her looking-glass' (*p. 180*). For all his show of coldness and control, our feeling that in the long conversations with Antoinette (*pp. 126-37*) and Christophine (*pp. 150-61*) the husband is a struggling soul becomes a conviction as we follow his vacillations in that interminable period when he is waiting to take Antoinette on the long ride away from Gran Bois.

If in the exchanges with Antoinette his words and his actions seem to suggest that his mind is in control of his emotions, it is 'all the mad conflicting emotions' that take drunken charge of him in the long reverie (*pp. 164-73*). At the silent centre he broods, thinking of his 'revenge and hurricanes' but he is besieged by supplicating memories of Christophine's pleas, and of the joys he has shared with Antoinette. He steels himself against the sadness he feels about leaving the honeymoon house to the desolation ('the long slow death by ants'), feeds on bitter phrases from Daniel Cosway to push Antoinette from his mind, and yet bewilderingly finds himself overcome by the conviction 'that everything I had imagined to be truth was false.' Swiftly in his mind he lives the rest of his life at the sweet honeymoon house with Antoinette, and the words he thinks of saying to her slip out, too late to reach Antoinette:

> No, I would say — I knew what I would say. 'I have made a terrible mistake. Forgive me.'
> I said it, looking at her, seeing the hatred in her eyes — and feeling my own hate spring up to meet it. Again the giddy change, the remembering, the sickening swing back to hate. They bought me, *me* with your paltry money. You helped them to do it. You deceived me, betrayed me, and you'll do worse if you get the chance. . . (That girl she look you straight in the eye and talk sweet talk — and it's lies she tell you. Lies. Her mother was so. They say she worse than her mother.)
> . . . If I was bound for hell let it be hell. No more false heavens. No more damned magic. You hate me and I hate you. We'll see who hates best. But first, first I will destroy your hatred. Now. My hate is colder, stronger, and you'll have no hate to warm yourself. You will have nothing. *(p. 170)*

Antoinette's glazed eyes drive him back to a safer resolution, and now freed of his conflicting emotions he can carry out the plan he has prepared.

Miss Rhys shows the husband sliding back into being the person who has learnt to hide what he feels, and whose mind could ignore and deny the existence of any challenge to its certainties. He is able to admit to himself now that Antoinette has left him thirsty, 'and all my life would be thirst and longing for what I had lost before I found it'; yet deliberately he consoles himself with the thought that he will soon have made her into one of those with 'white faces, dazed eyes, aimless gestures, high-pitched laughter' who know truth but cannot tell it. As for himself, he is prepared to wait until the mind can complete its reversion to normality and change the truth that was Antoinette, finally, into a lie: 'I too can wait — for the day when she is only a memory to be avoided, locked away, and like all memories a legend. Or a lie. . ' *(p. 172)*

The mode of experiencing the world that we see in Antoinette's nameless husband is one which we cannot in the twentieth century associate with any one nation or race. The force of materialism, social aspiration and the operations of mechanical intellect radically separated from true feeling are features of the dehumanisation of man in many modern societies. It is part of Miss Rhys's achievement that we should understand the frustration, the longing to escape buried within the Satanic destructiveness and the cruel exercise of power when this mode comes into full confrontation with that other represented by Antoinette:

> Everybody know that you marry her for money and you take it all. And then you want to break her up because you jealous of her. She is more better than you, she have better blood in her and she don't care for money — it's nothing for her. Oh I see that first time I look at you. You

young but already you hard. You fool the girl. You make her think you
can't see the sun for looking at her. . . But all you want is to break her
up. *(pp. 152-3)*

But Antoinette's suicide, and her burning down of Thornfield Hall which we see
through her dream to be a return to the warmth and colour and innocence of her
childhood world *(p. 189)* is paradoxically a defiant refusal to be broken up,
reduced to the threatened living dead condition ('You will have nothing').

Shortly after receiving Daniel Cosway's letter, the husband hunts out a volume
on native superstitions. To understand the significance of the extract he reads to
himself is to understand how the contrast between two countries and two people
(which *Wide Sargasso Sea* may be said, at one level, to be about) becomes a
lament for the divided self; and how subtly Miss Rhys has defined at last the crude
duality with which her earlier works were partly concerned. From the chapter on
'Obeah' in the fictitious (?) *The Glittering Coronet of Isles*, the husband reads that
'A zombi is a dead person who seems to be alive or a living person who is dead'
*(p. 107)*. Antoinette's husband is left deliberately nameless because he is a
necessary part of herself which she must digest (her early dream, *pp. 59-60*: 'I
follow him, sick with fear but I make no effort to save myself; if anyone were to
try to save me, I would refuse. This must happen'). Antoinette is a ghost to her
husband also. Although he decides to return to his familiar landscape of steel and
stone where he hopes a day will come 'when she's only a memory to be avoided,
locked away, and like all memories a legend. Or a lie. . .', the novel tells us
something more liberating. The zombi of modern civilisation can still, *if he
wishes*, turn back spiritually and vitalise himself upon those neglected natives of
the psyche.

Footnotes:

1 See Critical Reading.
2 See Works by Jean Rhys.
3 See Critical Reading.
4 See Critical Reading.
5 From *Rights of Passage* (1967).

# DARK SMILE, DEVILISH SAINTS

*by John Updike*

"Smile Please," by Jean Rhys (Harper & Row; $10.95), and "Port of Saints," by William S. Burroughs (Blue Wind; $15.95 cloth, $5.95) paper), are about the same size and shape, have spooky brownish dust jackets, and might both be catalogued as fragmentary autobiographies. The publication attached to Miss Rhys's name, indeed, is forthrightly subtitled "An Unfinished Autobiography." It consists of a completed memoir of her childhood bound in with scattered recollections of her later life, including portions of diary; the book has been assembled, edited, and introduced with especial affection and tact by the novelist's English editor, Diana Athill. Miss Athill briskly begins, "Jean Rhys began to think of writing an autobiographical book several years before her death, on May 14th, 1979. The idea did not attract her, but because she was sometimes angered and hurt by what other people wrote about her, she wanted to get the facts down." Though many facts seem not so much got down as left discreetly floating, this truncated effort at self-revelation is attractive, to us if not to its author, in part because of its slim, provocative fragmentariness. In truth, the fragment, the sketch, the unfinished canvas, and the shattered statue are all congenial to an age of relativity, indeterminacy, and agnosticism. Most of the oppressively complete books that labor for our attention would benefit, we suspect, from a few reductive blows of the hammer. In the case of "Smile Please," the hammer was applied by Miss Rhys's habitual reticence and perfectionism, and by the furies that made all her attempts at composition in later life difficult.

Even so, admirers of Jean Rhys's amazing fiction — amazing in its resolute economy of style and in its illusionless portrait of a drifting heroine, a portrait that the recent gush of female confessionalism has not rendered any less stunningly honest and severe — will find much to surprise and delight them. The laconic sketch of her growing up as a member of the white minority of Dominica has the emotional fibre without the exotic coloring of the doomed heroine's girlhood in her novel "Wide Sargasso Sea." In both versions, the unreachable mother is a cruel keystone, a hard absence: "Even after the new baby was born there must have been an interval before she seemed to find me a nuisance and I grew to dread her. . . . Yes, she drifted away from me and when I tried to interest her, she was indifferent." Over seventy years after the event — for Jean Rhys wrote these paragraphs in the three years before her death at eighty-six — she looks with the eyes of a little girl toward a mother who is hardly there:

> Just before I left Dominica she was ill and unable to come
> downstairs for some time. I went up to see her but walked softly and
> she didn't hear me. . . . Behind her silence she looked lonely, a
> stranger in a strange house . . . lonely, patient and resigned. also
> obstinate. "You haven't seen what I've seen, haven't heard what I've
> heard.". . . I wanted to run across the room and kiss her but I was too
> shy so it was the usual peck.

The blackness all around them seems to drain this essential relationship of blood.
"Once I heard her say that black babies were prettier than white ones. Was this
the reason why I prayed so ardently to be black, and would run to the looking glass
in the morning to see if the miracle had happened? And though it never had, I tried
again. Dear God, let me be black." In "Wide Sargasso Sea," the mother's curse
is beauty and madness, passed on to the daughter. In the autobiography, lassitude
and indifference seem to be the inheritance — a zombielike, parasitic resignation
to being not fully alive. "Every night someone gave a dance; you could hear the
drums. We had few dances [The blacks] were more alive, more a part of the place
than we were."

Not merely indifference but hate was early woven into the soul of Ella
Gwendolen Rees Williams, as she was christened. Children in their brutal
frankness dramatize the socioeconomic secrets of a place. A nightmare recognition about the Caribbean, vividly dramatized in "Wide Sargasso Sea," was that
the blacks hated whites among them. In "Smile Please," Jean Rhys remembers
admiring a lightly colored black classmate seated next to her at convent school:

> I tried, shyly at first, then more boldly, to talk to my beautiful
> neighbour.
> Finally, without speaking, she turned and looked at me. I knew
> irritation, bad temper, the "Oh, go away" look; this was different. This
> was hatred — impersonal, implacable hatred. I recognized it at once
> and if you think that a child cannot recognise hatred and remember it
> for life you are most damnably mistaken.
> I never tried to be friendly with any coloured girls again. I was
> polite and that was all.
> They hate us. We are hated.
> Not possible.
> Yes it is possible and it is so.

An authenticity early conceded to negative emotion gives a macabre tinge to
"Smile Please." The narrator explicitly "hates" many things: her own appearance
in the mirror at the age of nine; sewing; a photograph of her mother when young
and pretty; her father when he gets a short haircut; the unknown persons who
years later knock down the cross over his grave. "I hated whoever had done this
and thought, 'I can hate too.'" From a black nurse, Meta, who "didn't like me
much anyway," she imbibes fear and voodoo superstition: "Meta had shown me
a world of fear and distrust, and I am still in that world." In an incident that gets
a chapter to itself the little girl smashes the face of a doll with a rock: "I remember

vividly the satisfaction of being wicked. The guilt that was half triumph."
Reading "Paradise Lost," she is fascinated by Satan; at a later age, "an unconscious Manichee," she arrives "at the certainty that the Devil was quite as
powerful as God, perhaps more so. . . . I was passionately on the side of God,
but it was very difficult to see what I could do about it." After the dreadful death
of their fox terrier Rex from distemper, she decides that "the Devil was undoubtedly stronger than God, so what was the use?" The strikingly combined intensity
and apathy of Miss Rhys's world view have their seeds in the black/white, fear-
riddled atmosphere of Dominica. She was infected by the macabre in the
Caribbean, these threadbare economies perched on a sea of plangently lovely
days. She became a European but saw it all with slitted eyes. As a writer, she
startles us with what it does not occur her to overlook.

In the second half of this unfinished autobiography, artfully titled by Miss
Athill "It Began to Grow Cold," the narrator as a young woman in England
continues to hate things, including the London zoo and landladies, and turns with
her newly bloomed looks to life in a chorus line. This genial demimonde and the
proximate worlds of money and sex ("It seems to me now that the whole business
of money and sex is mixed up with something very primitive and deep") are
glancingly, even flirtatiously described, and constitute, of course, the well-
tracked terrain of her first four novels, all written before 1939. Her beginnings as
a writer are presented, characteristically, as a triumph of drift and whim.
Displeased by the ugly bareness of a table in a newly rearranged room in Fulham,
she passes a stationer's shop "where quill pens were displayed in the window, a
lot of them, red, blue, green, yellow. Some of them would be all right in a glass,
to cheer up my table, I thought. I went into the shop and bought about a dozen.
Then I noticed some black exercise books on the counter. . . . I bought several
of those, I don't know why, just because I liked the look of them. I got a box of
J nibs, the sort I liked, an ordinary penholder, a bottle of ink and a cheap inkstand.
Now that old table won't look so bare, I thought." Then, as in a trance, she
employs these so accidentally purchased implements to write late into the night.
The notebooks she filled in a few days — before penning the concluding
sentence, "Oh God, I'm only twenty and I'll have to go on living and living and
living" — were carried unread in her luggage for seven more years, before they
became the basis for her novel "Voyage in the Dark." After the Second World
War, she herself was to be mislaid and her small reputation had dwindled to
almost nothing, before a radio adaptation of "Good Morning, Midnight" in 1957
uncovered her existence in a Devonshire cottage and prompted her revival as a
functioning writer and a recognition that "as Miss Athill puts it, came "too late
to give her much lively pleasure." She finished out her surprisingly long life in
a country that she hated, England, and in a cottage that she and her third husband
accepted sight unseen and that, upon first sight, she "took a dislike to." No
modern writer of note presents a career less purposeful in its appearance. Yet she
wrote in her diary, "If I stop writing my life will have been an abject failure," and
of herself as a child remembered, "Before I could read, almost a baby, I imagined

that God, this strange thing or person I heard about, was a large book standing upright and half open and I could see the print inside but it made no sense to me. Other times the book was smaller and inside were sharp flashing things." Later, when she could read, she lost herself "in the immense world of books, and tried to blot out the real world which was so puzzling to me. Even then I had a vague, persistent feeling that I'd always be lost in it, defeated." So writing, which Jean Rhys carried out with such fanatic control and noble candor, was for her a kind of ascent out of a Devil-dominated world into the Godly half, abounding with "sharp flashing things," of the Manichaean equation.

# BIBLIOGRAPHY

Reference to articles written about Rhys is unfortunately not centralized and the researcher finds himself having to comb several bibliographical sources in order to know what is being published, not only outside the United States, but even within. Jean Rhys's reputation since the publication of *Wide Sargasso Sea* in 1967 is ever increasing. Elgin Mellown's 1984 *Jean Rhys: A Descriptive and Annotated Bibliography of Works and Criticism*, a volume of two hundred pages of entries, indicates that between 1939 and 1966 little was written about Rhys; only nine pages of Mellown's bibliography are devoted to this early criticism. Twenty-nine pages are required, however, for the period between 1966 and 1982. A recent computer information search of the Modern Language Bibliography from 1980 to 1987 yielded one hundred thirteen entries. Considering that this survey is incomplete, since it is conducted by themes, one can measure the extent of Jean Rhys's popularity.

Although material may have eluded this personal search because some titles may remain unindexed to this date, this bibliography represents as diligent an inquiry as possible. It is hoped that it, together with Elgin Mellown's annotated bibliography, will be of service to anyone looking for a convenient source of information on Jean Rhys. Due to the extent of material written on Rhys, the author of this collection chose to present a survey of writing by and about Rhys as complete as possible instead of a selective annotated bibliography, the composition of which would be highly subjective.

## I. PRIMARY SOURCES

### A. Books by Jean Rhys

*The Left Bank and Other Stories*. Pref. Ford Madox Ford. London Jonathan Cape, 1927; New York: Harper & Brothers, 1927; as *Rive Gauche*, Paris: Mercure de France, 1981.

*Postures*. London: Chatto & Windus, 1928; as *Quartet: a Novel*, New York: Simon and Schuster, 1929; as *Quartet*, London: André Deutsch, 1969; New York: Harper and Row, 1971; Harmondsworth: Penguin, 1973, 1977, 1981; New York: Vintage Books, 1974; New York: Perennial Library, Harper & Row, 1981; as *Quatuor*, Paris: Les Lettres Nouvelles, 1973; as *Kvartett*, Stockholm: Tiden, 1980; as *Quartetto*, Milan: Sperling & Kupfer.

*After Leaving Mr. Mackenzie*. London: Jonathan Cape, 1931; New York: Knopf, 1931; London: André Deutsch, 1969; Harmondsworth: Penguin, 1971; New

York: Harper & Row, 1972; 1982; New York: Vintage Books, 1974; New York: Harper & Row, 1982; as *Dopo l'addio, Milan: Bomiani, 1975*; as *Na Meneer Mackenzie*, Utrecht: Bruna, 1977; as *Efter Mr. Mackenzie*, Göteborg: Stegeand, 1977; as *Despúes de dejar al Señor Mackenzie*, Barcelona: Noguer, 1978; as *Quai des Grands-Augustins*, Paris: Denoël, 1979.

*Voyage in the Dark*. London: Constable, 1934, 1936; New York: Morrow, 1935; London: André Deutsch, 1967; New York: Norton, 1968, 1982; New York: Popular Library, 1975; Harmondsworth: Penguin, 1969, 1975, 1978, 1980; as *Mélodie in Mineur*, Amsterdam: Uitgeveriu de Steenuil; as *Reis Door Het Duister*, Antwerp: A.W. Bruna & zoon; Utrecht: Bruna & zoon, 1975; as *Voyage dans les ténèbres*, Paris: Denoël, 1974; as *A Sötétség Utasa*, Budapest: Europa, 1974.

*Good Morning Midnight* London: Constable, 1939; London: André Deutsch, 1967; Harmondsworth: Penguin, 1969; New York: Harper & Row, 1970; New York: Vintage Books, 1974; New York: Perennial Library, 1973, 1975; as *Goodemorgen, Middernacht*, Antwerp: A. W. Bruna, 1969; Utrecht: Bruna & Zoon, 1975; as *Bonjour Minuit*, Paris: Les Lettres Nouvelles, 1969; as *Guten Morgen, Mitternacht*, Hamburg: Hoffman & Campe, 1969; Munich: Deutscher Tashenbuch Verlag, 1971; as *Günaydin Geceyarisi*, Istanbul: Dilek Matbaasi, 1972; as *Buongiorno, Mezanotte*, Milan: Bompiani, 1973; as *Jó reggelt, éjfél!* Budapest: Európa, 1974; as *Buenos Dias, Medianoche*, Barcelona, 1975; as *Godmorgon, Midnattl!* Götenborg, Stegeland, 1977.

*Wide Sargasso Sea* London: André Deutsch, 1966; New York: Norton, 1967, 1982; Harmondsworth: Penguin, 1968; 1969, 1970, 1975, 1976, 1977, 1979, 1980; New York: Popular Library, 1973, 1975; as *Langt Over Havet*, Copenhagen: Fremad, 1967; as *Siintää Sargassomer*, Helsinki: Werner Söderström, 1968; as *Kreolerinnen på Thornfield Hall*, Oslo: H. Aschehoug, 1969; as *La Prisonnière des Sargasses*, Paris: Gallimard, 1977; as *Széles Sargasso-Tenger*, Budapest: Európa, Kiadó, 1971; as *Il Grande Mare dei Sargassi*, Milan: Adelphi, 1971, 1980; as *Široko Sargaško Morje*, Mrska Sobota: Pomurska Zalozba, 1971; as *Hiroi Mo No Umi*, Tokyo: Shobô Shinsa, 1972; as *Sire Sargasové More*, Bratislava: Smena, 1973; as *Sargasso Zee*, Utrecht: Bruna & Zoon, 1974; as *Ancho Mar de los Sargazos*, Barcelona: Noguer, 1976; as *Sargasso-Meer*, Munich: Rogner & Bernhard, 1980.

*Tigers Are Better Looking with a Selection from The Left Bank*. London: André Deutsch, 1968; Harmondsworth: Penguin, 1973, 1977, 1981, 1982; New York: Harper & Row, 1974; New York: Popular Library, 1973, 1975; as *Les Tigres sont plus beaux à voir, Mercure de France*, 1969; as *Die Dicke Fifi: Geschichten aus London und Paris*, Hamburg: Hoffman & Campe.

*My Day*. New York: Frank Hallman, 1975; as *Ma journée, Vogue*, 1975.

*Sleep it Off, Lady*. London: André Deutsch, 1976; New York: Harper & Row, 1976; New York: Popular Library, 1978; Harmondsworth: Penguin, 1979, 1980, 1981; as *Mens, Slaap Je Roes Uit: Verhalen*, Utrecht: A. W. Bruna &

Zoon, 1977; as *Il ne faut pas tirer les oiseaux au repos*, Paris: Denoël, 1978; as *Sov AvSig Ruset, Damen!*, Götenborg: Stegeland, 1978.

*Smile Please, and Unfinished Autobiography*. London: André Deutsch, 1979; New York: Harper & Row, 1979; Harmondsworth: Penguin, 1981, 1982; Berkeley: Donald S. Ellis/Creative Arts, 1983; as *Souriez s'il vous plait, autobiographie inachevée*, Paris: Denoël, 1980.

*Jean Rhys Letters 1931-1966* Ed. Francis Wyndham and Diana Melly. London: André Deutsch, 1984; as *The Letters of Jean Rhys*, New York: Viking. 1984.

### B. Collected Works

*Jean Rhys: The Complete Novels*. Intro. Diana Athill. New York: W.W. Norton & Co., 1985.

*Penguins Modern Stories*. By Jean Rhys, Ed. Judith Burnley. Harmondsworth: Penguin Books Ltd., 1969.

*Voices*. By Jean Rhys. Ed. Robert Ruben. London: Michael Joseph. 1963.

*Winter's Tales*. By Jean Rhys. ed. A. D. Maclean. London: Macmillan & Co. 1960.

### C. Translations by Jean Rhys

Carco, Francis. *Perversity* (French title, *Perversité*) Chicago: Pacal Covici, 1928 (Although the translator's name is given as Ford Madox Ford, the translation is attributed to Jean Rhys in a letter from Ford to Isabel Paterson in *Letters of Ford Madox Ford*. Ed. Richard M. Ludwing. Princeton: Princeton University Press, 1965, March 5, 1928.

De Nève, Edward. *Barred* (translated from *Sous les verrous*) London: Harmsworth, 1932.

### D. Stories and Poems by Jean Rhys

The stories which appear below are not included in the contents of *the Left Bank and other Stories, Tigers Are Better Looking*, and *Sleep It Off, Lady*.

"Four Poems (Night on the River, All through the Night, A Field Where Sheep Were Feeding, To Toni.)" *London Observer*, 20 February 1977.

"Night Out, 1925." *Planet (Wales)* 33 (August 1976): 32-34.

"Our Gardener." *The New Review* 4, 41 (August 1977): 30.

"Passage from a Diary." *New York Times Book Review* 85 (25 May 1980): 16.

"Q. and A.: Making Bricks without Straw." *Harper's* (July 1978): 70-1.

"The Christmas Presents of Mynheer van Rooz." *Time and Tide* 12 (28 November 1931): 1360-1361.

"The Joey Blagstock Smile." *New Statesman* 94 (23-30 December 1977): 890.

"The Tinsel November." *Growing Point* 14 (May 1975): 2654.

"Whatever Became of Old Mrs. Pearce?" *The Times* (London) 21 May 1975.

"The Whistling Bird." *New Yorker* 54 (11 September 1978): 38-40.

## II. SECONDARY SOURCES

A few of the early reviews of Jean Rhys's books criticize Rhys for the prevailing despair in her stories and the passivity of her heroines. Most, however, praise Rhys as a superb stylist. The sharpness and intensity of her prose and the sheer poetry of her language are often commented upon. Recognition is also given to her gift of insight into the problems which affect modern man, whose sense of isolation and loss she understood well. In a prose free of sentimentality, with the cool detachment of irony, Rhys captures the truth of moment, the reality of experience that shapes the sensibility of heroines. For these qualities, she is acclaimed by fellow writers such as V.S. Naipaul, Joyce Carol Oates, John Updike, John Hearne, Wilson Harris and given a place among the ranks of the best West Indian and British writers. The number of reviews and articles which follow attests to her popularity.

**A. Book Reviews** (The title of the book reviewed is given only when that book is specifically reviewed; when more than one of her works are addressed, no title is mentioned).

Rev. of *The Left Bank. Saturday Review of Literature* 4 (5 November 1927): 287.

"A Choice of Paperbacks." Rev. of *Quartet. British Book News.* October 1981: 581.

"A Fairy-Tale Neurotic." Rev. of *Wide Sargasso Sea. Times Literary Supplement* 3377 (17 November 1966): 1039.

Aiken, Conrad. Rev. of *The Left Bank. New York Evening Post* (1 October 1927): 10.

Allen, Bruce. Rev of *Tigers Are Better Looking. Library Journal* 99 (15 November 1974): 2983.

Allen, Walter. "Bertha the Doomed." Rev. of *Wide Sargasso Sea* New York Times Book Review (18 June 1967): 5.

Annan, Gabriele. "Turned Away by the Tropics." Rev. of *Smile Please. Times Literary Supplement* 4005 (21 December 1979): 154.

Alvarez, A. "Books of the Year." *New Leader* (59 (6 December 1976): 26. A review of *Sleep It Off, Lady* and E. L. Doctorow's *Ragtime*.

"A Mistress of the Conte." Rev. of *The Left Bank. New York Herald Tribune Books* 4 (6 November 1927): 16.

"A Selection of Recent Titles." Rev. of *Quartet. New York Times Book Review* 6 June 1971: 3.

"A Selection of Recent Titles." Rev. of *Good Morning, Midnight. New York Times Book Review* (7 June 1970): 2.

Auchincloss, Eve. "Jean Rhys. Voyage Through the Dark." Rev. of *Smile Please. Book World* [Washington Post] 10 (8 1980: 4.

Auchincloss, Eve. "Lighting up the Inner Dark." Rev. of *Sleep It Off, Lady. Washington Post Book World* 10 (7 November 1976): G1-G2.

Bailey, Paul. "Bedrooms in Hell." *Observer* 9279 (18 May 1969): 30.

____. "True Romance." Rev. of *Sleep It Off, Lady. Times Literary Supplement.* 3893 (22 October 1976): 1321.

Baker, R. Rev. of *Tigers Are Better Looking. Books and Bookmen* 13 (June 1968): 34.

Balliett. Whitney. "Books: Talking on Paper." *New Yorker* 10 December 1984: 184.

Bell, Pearl. "Letter from London." *New Leader* 59 (6 December 1976): 3-5.

____. "Writers and Writing: Women Cast Adrift." Rev. of *After Leaving Mr. MacKenzie. New Leader* 55 (29 March 1972): 14015.

Blackburn Sarah. "Women's Lot." Rev. of *Good Morning, Midnight. Book World* [*Chicago Tribune* and *Washington Post*] 4 (5 April 1970): 6.

Blythe, Ronald. "A Girl from Dominica." Rev. of *Smile Please. Listener* 102 (6 December 1979): 789.

"Books in Brief." Rev. of *Quartet. Nation and Anthenæum* 44 (6 October 1928): 26.

"Books of the Month." Rev. of *Quartet .Bookman* 75 (November 1928): 144.

Braybrooke, Neville. "Between Dog and Wolf." *Spectator* 219 (21 July 1967): 77-78.

____. "Shadow and Substance." Rev. of *Wide Sargasso Sea. Spectator* 217 (28 October 1966): 560-561.

"Briefly Noted." Rev. of *Sleep It Off, Lady. New Yorker* 52 (10 January 1977): 98.

Britten, Florence Haxton. Recent Leading Fiction." Rev. of *Voyage in the Dark, New York Herald Tribune Books* 1 (17 March 1935): 10.

Broyard, Anatole. "A Difficult Year for Hats." Rev. of *Good Morning Midnight New York Times* 123 (26 March 1974): 39.

Byatt, A.S. "Trapped." *New Statesman* 75 (29 March 1968): 421-422. (Rev. of *Tigers Are Better Looking* with five other novels).

Casey Geneviève M. Rev. of *Wide Sargasso Sea.* Best Sellers 27 (15 May 1967): 75.

Clap, Susannah. "Bleak Treats." Rev. of *Sleep It Off, Lady. New Statesman* 92 (22 October 1976): 568-569.

Clemons, Walter. Rev. of *After Leaving Mr. MacKenzie. Newsweek* 79 (6 March 1972): 77.

Collier, Carmen P. Rev. of *Voyage in the Dark. Best Sellers* 28 (1 May 1968): 58-59.

Cooke, Michael. "Recent Fiction." Rev. of *After Leaving Mr. MacKenzie. Yale Review* 61 (June 1972): 607-609.

Corke, Hilary. "New Fiction." Rev. of *Wild Sargasso Sea. Listener.* 77 (19 January 1967): 103.

Core, George. "Current Books in Review. Wanton Life, Importunate Art." Rev. of *Sleep It Off, Lady. Sewanee Review* 85 (Winter 1977): ii-x.

Crane, Peggy. "Writers in an Alien Land." *Books and Bookmen* 22 (February 1977): 60-61.

Davis, Hunter. "Atticus; Rip van Rhys." Rev. of *Wide Sargasso Sea. Sunday Times* 7465 (6 November 1966): 13.

Dawson, Margaret Cheney. "Unbearable Justice. Rev. of *After Leaving Mr. MacKenzie. New York Herald Tribune Books* 28 June 1931: 7.

Dick, Kay. "Wife to Mr. Rochester." *Sunday Times* 7474 (3 October 1966): 50.

Doherty, Gail and Paul. "Spring Paperback Parade." Rev. of *Voyage in the Dark. America* 134 (20 March 1976): 230.

Fabre-Luce, Anne. "Incandescences." Rev. of *Quartvor. Critique* (Paris) 29 (July 1973): 674-675.

"Felicitous Fiction." *Book World* [*Chicago Tribune* and *Washington Post*] 12 December 1976: H5. Rev. of *Sleep It Off, Lady* and of books by Anthony Powell and Kurt Vonnegut.

"Fiction Reprint." Rev. of *Sleep It Off, Lady. Publishers Weekly* 213 (13 February 1978): 126.

Frazer, Elizabeth W. Rev. of *Voyage in the Dark. Library Journal* 93 (1 May 1968): 1919.

____. Rev. of *Wide Sargasso Sea. Library Journal* 92 (15 May 1967): 1951.

Gilman, Lelde. Rev of *After Leaving Mr. MacKenzie. Best Sellers* 31 (1 March 1972): 532.

Gorman, Herbert, Rev. of *Quartet. New York Herald Tribune Books* 10 February 1929: 7.

Grumbach, Doris. "Jean Rhys: Pleasure and Regrets." Rev. of *The Letters of Jean Rhys. Washington Post* 7 October 1984.

Gould, Gerald. "New Novels. All Sorts of Societies." Rev. of *After Leaving Mr. Mackenzie. Observer* 7289 (8 February 1931): 6.

Gould, Tony. "In a Dark Wood." Rev. of *Sleep It Off, Lady. New Society* 38 (28 October 1976): 209.

Graham, Gladys. "A Bedraggled Career." Rev of *After Leaving Mr. MacKenzie. Saturday Review of Literature* 8 (25 July 1931): 6.

Haltrecht, Montague, "More from Jean Rhys." Rev. of *Tigers Are Better Looking. Sunday Times* 7556 (24 March 1968): 52.

Harcourt, Joan. Rev. of *Sleep It Off, Lady. Queen's Quarterly* 84 (1977): 512-513.

Hawthorne, Hazel. "Some Spring Novels." Rev of *Voyage in the Dark. New Republic* 82 (10 April 1935): 260.

Hazzard, Shirley. Rev. of *Quartet. New York Times Book Review* 11 April 1971: 6.

Heidenry, John. Rev. of *Sleep It Off, Lady. Commonweal* 104 (30 September 1977): 632-634. *Sleep It Off, Lady* is reviewed with Philip Larkin's *A Girl in Winter.*

Heppenstall, Rayner. "Bitter-sweet." Rev. of *Tigers Are Better Looking. Spectator* 220 95 April 1968): 446-447.

Hope, Francis, "Did You Once See Paris Plain?" Rev. of *Tigers Are Better Looking. Observer* 9220 (31 March 1969): 29.

____. "The First Mrs. Rochester." Rev. of *Wide Sargasso Sea. New Statesman* 72 (28 October 1966): 638-639.

____. "Women Beware Everyone." *Observer* 9178 (11 June 1967): 26.

Hynes, Samuel. Rev. of *Smile Please. New Republic* 182 (31 May 1980): 28-31.

Jebb, Julian. "Painful Eye." *Financial Times* 14 June 1967.

Jefferson Margo, "Anatomy of Melancholy." Rev. of *Sleep It Off, Lady." Newsweek* 88 (6 December 1976): 90, 93.

Johnson, Diane. "Overdrawn at the Left Bank of the World." *Book World [Chicago Tribune* and *Washington Post], 3 November 1974: 1-2.*

____. "Sensitive Survivors." Rev. of *Tigers Are Better Looking. Times* 57, 214 (30 March 1968): 21.

Kakutani, Michiko. Books of the Times." Rev. of *The Letters of Jean Rhys. The New York Times* 10 September 1984: C22.

Kersh, Gerald. "The Second Time Around." Rev. of *Wide Sargasso Sea. Saturday Review* 50 (1 July 1967): 23.

Klein, Mary Ann. "Autobiography." Rev. of *Smile Please. World Literature Today* 55 (Spring 1981): 324-325.

Knight, Norman G. "Caribbean Bookshelf." Rev. of *Tigers Are Better Looking. West Indies Chronicle* 83 (June 1968): 288.

Knowler, John. "Return of Jean Rhys." Rev. of *Wide Sargasso Sea. Books and Bookmen* 12 (December 1966): 84, 96.

Kullman, Agnes M. Rev. of *Smile Please. Best Sellers* 40 (July 1980): 140.

Kyria, Pierre. "Jean Rhys, In Memoriam." Rev. of *Souriez, s'il vous plaît. Le Monde (des livres)* 11036 (25 July 1980): 11, 14.

Lane, Margaret, "Life and Hard Times." *Spectator* 222 (16 May 1969): 649-650.

Laski, Marghanita. "Books of the Year. Some Personal Choices." Rev. of *Wide Sargasso Sea. Observer* 9154 (18 December 1966): 23.

Latin Quarter Rotters Characters of this Yarn." Rev. of *Quartet. New York World* 69 (10 February 1929: 11.

Leiter, Robert. Rev. of *Tigers Are Better Looking. New Republic* 171 (7 December 1974): 22-24.

Leonard, John. "What Men Don't Know about Woman. . . Rev. of *Good Morning, Midnight. New York Times* 119 (12 May 1970): 37.

Levin, Martin. "New & Novel." Rev. of *After Leaving Mr. MacKenzie. New York Times Book Review* 27 (February 1972): 52.

_____. Rev. of *Good Morning, Midnight. New York Times Book Review* 22 March 1970: 39.

Loercher, Diana. "When a gel must cut loose." Rev. of *Quartet. Christian Monitor* 63 (20 May 1971): 4.

"Losing Battles." Rev. of *Tigers Are Better Looking. Times Literary Supplement* 3453 (2 May 1968): 466.

"Lost Years." Rev. of *Good Morning, Midnight. Times Literary Supplement* 1942 (22 April 1939): 231.

Lovett, Robert Morss. Rev. of *Quartet. Bookman* (New York) 69 (April 1929): 193.

Lynd, Sylvia. "Tales of Long Ago in New Novels." Rev. of *Voyage in the Dark. News Chronicle* 27630 (12 November 1934): 4.

Macauley, Robie. "Things Unsaid and Said too Often." Rev of *Sleep It Off, Lady. New York Times Book Review* 21 November 1976: 7, 50.

Mair, John. "New Novels." Rev. of *Good Morning, Midnight. New Statesman* 17 (22 April 1939): 614.

Matthews, T.S. "The Cocktail Hour." *New Republic* 58 (17 April 1929): 258-259.

MacInnes, Colin. "Nightmare in Paradise." Rev. of *Wide Sargasso Sea. Observer* 9147 (30 October 1966): 28.

McBride, Mary G. Rev. of *My Day. Library Journal* 100 (1 December 1975): 2243.

McNeil, Helen. "Broken Heart." Rev. of *Smile Please. New Statesman* 99 (15 Feb. 1980): 253-254.

Mellors, John. "World Shrinkers." Rev. of *Sleep It Off, Lady. Listener* 96 (23 December 1976): 854.

Meyers, Jeffrey. "Sense of Evil." Rev. of *Smile Please*. *Spectator* 243 (22 December 1979): 31-32.

Mitchell, Lucy Sprague. Rev. of *The Left Bank*. *New Republic* 52 (16 November 1927): 345.

"Miss Rhys's Short Stories." *New York Times Book Review* 11 December 1927: 28, 30.

Moss, Howard. "Going to Pieces." Rev. of *Tigers Are Better Looking*. *New Yorker* 50 (16 December 1974): 161-164.

"Nonfiction." Rev. of *Smile Please*. *Publishers Weekly* 217 (4 April 1980): 68.

"Notes on Current Books." Rev. of *Sleep It Off, Lady*. *Virginia Quarterly Review* 53 (Summer 1977): 103.

"Noted by the Editors." Rev. of *Smile Please*. *Antioch Review* 39 (Spring 1981): 264.

Naipaul, V.S. "Without a Dog's Chance." *New York Review of Books* 18 (18 May 1972): 29-31.

"Nation Book Marks." Rev. of *Wide Sargasso Sea*. *Nation* 205 (2 October 1967): 317.

"Neurotic Women." *Times Literary Supplement* 3412 (20 July 1967): 644.

"New Books: A Selected List." Rev. of *Voyage in the Dark*. *London Mercury* 31 (December 1934): 189.

"New Fiction." Rev. of *Wide Sargasso Sea*. *Times* 56, 791 (17 November 1966): 16.

"New in Paperback." Rev. of *Voyage in the Dark*. *Book World [Chicago Tribune and Washington Post]* 12 (28 February 1982): 12.

Norton, G. Rev. of *Sleep It Off, Lady*. *West Indies Chronicle* 17 April 1977, 19 May 1977.

Nye, Robert. "Women in a Man's World." *Guardian* 15 (May 1969): 9; *Manchester Guardian Weekly* 100 (22 May 1969): 15.

Oates, Joyce Carol. "Books." Rev. of *Smile Please*. *Mademoiselle* 86 (June 1980): 50.

O'Brien, Kate. "Fiction." Rev. of *Good Morning, Midnight*. *Spectator* 162 (16 June 1939): 1062.

"Paperback Choice." Rev. of *Quartet*. *Observer* 9920 (11 October 1981): 32.

"Paperback Choice." Rev. of *Smile Please*. *Observer* 9929 (13 December 1981): 31.

"Paperbacks: Fiction." Rev. of *Quartet*. *Books and Bookman* 18 (August 1973): 137.

"Paperbacks: New and Noteworthy." *New York Times Book Review* 83 (2 April 1978): 41. Publication announcement: *Sleep It off, Lady*.

"Paperbacks." Rev. of *Good Morning, Midnight. Observer* 9608 (28 September 1975): 22.

"Paperbacks." Rev. of *Voyage in the Dark. Observer* 9608 (28 September 1975): 22.

"Paperbacks." Rev. of *Voyage in the Dark. Times* (London) 57586 (14 June 1969): 23.

"Paperback Short List." Rev. of *Quartet. Sunday Times* 7820 (29 April 1973): 40.

Phillips, Robert. "Pearls on a String." Rev. of *Smile Please. Commonweal* 107 (29 August 1980): 474-475.

Piazza, Paul. "The World of Jean Rhys." *Chronicle of Higher Education* 14 (7 March 1977): 19. Introduction to Rhys's writing career and her life. Rev. of *Sleep It Off, Lady.*

"Poignant Tragedy." Rev. of *Quartet. New York Times Book Review* 10 February 1929: 8.

Pollit, Katha. *Books in Brief.* Rev. of *Sleep It Off, Lady. Saturday Review* 4 (13 November 1976): 40-41.

Pool, Gail. "Jean Rhys: Life's Unfinished Form." Rev. of *Smile Please. Chicago Review* 32 (Spring 1981): 68-74.

Pritchett, V.S. "Displaced Person." Rev. of *Smile Please. New York Review of Books* 27 (14 August 1980): 8, 10.

Raskin, Barbara. Rev. of *Good Morning, Midnight. New Republic* 163 (4 July 1970): 27.

Raynor, Vivien. "Woman as Victim." Rev. of *Quartet. Book World [Chicago Tribune* and *Washington Post]* 5 (23 May 1971): 9.

"Recommended Novels." Rev. of *Voyage in the Dark. Saturday Review* (London) 158 (1 December 1934): 568.

Reedy, Gerard C. "Fiction." *America* 136 (7 May 1977): 422. Rev. of *Sleep It Off, Lady* among other books.

R.M.C. "Books, Books, Books." Rev. of *After Leaving Mr. MacKenzie.* New Yorker 4 July 1931: 53.

Rev. of *After Leaving Mr. MacKenzie. Boston Evening Transcript* 29 August 1931: 1

Rev. of *After Leaving Mr. MacKenzie. New Republic* 68 (16 September 1931): 124.

Rev. of *After Leaving Mr. MacKenzie. New Yorker* 48 (8 April 1972): 130.

Rev. of *Voyage in the Dark. Nieuwe Rotterdamsche Courant* 20 October 1934: 2.

Rev. of *After Leaving Mr. MacKenzie. Times Literary Supplement* 1518 (5 March 1931): 39.

Rev. of *Good Morning, Midnight. Dublin Magazine* 15 (January-March 1940): 58-59.

Rev. of *Good Morning, Midnight. Manchester Guardian* 97 (21 December 1967): 11.

Rev. of *Good Morning, Midnight. Publishers Weekly* 197 (26 January 1970): 268.

Rev. of *Quartet. Boston Evening Transcript* 20 March 1929: 2.

Rev. of *Quartet. New York Times Book Review* 13 October 1974: 44

Rev. of *Quartet. Saturday Review of Literature* 5 (20 April 1929): 936.

Rev. of *Quartet. Springfield Republican* 24 March 1929: 7

Rev. of *Quartet. Times Literary Supplement* 1392 (4 October 1928): 706.

Rev. of *Sleep It Off, Lady. Booklist* 73 (1 November 1976): 392-393.

Rev. of *Sleep It Off, Lady. Choice* 14 (March 1977): 65.

Rev. of *Smile Please. Atlantic* 245, 92 (June 1980): 92.

Rev. of *Smile Please. Times* 116 (7 July 1980): 69.

Rev. of *The Left Bank. Boston Evening Transcript* 9 November 1927: 7.

Rev. of *The Left Bank. Nation and Athenæum* 41 (25 June 1929): 90.

Rev. of *The Left Bank. New Statement* 29 (30 April 1927): 90.

Rev. of *The Left Bank. Spectator* 138 (30 April 1927): 772.

Rev. of *The Left Bank. Times Literary Supplement* 1318 (5 May 1927): 320.

Rev. of *The Letters of Jean Rhys. The Economist* 19 May 1984: 101.

Rev. of *Tigers Are Better Looking. Booklist* 71 (1 December 1974): 367.

Rev. of *Tigers Are Better Looking. Kirkus Review* 42 (15 August 1974): 299.

Rev. of *Tigers Are Better Looking. New York Times Book Review* 20 October 1974: 5-6.

Rev. of *Tigers Are Better Looking. Publishers Weekly* 206 (26 August 1974): 299.

Rev. of *Voyage in the Dark. New Yorker* 44 (24 August 1968): 119.

Rev. of *Voyage in the Dark. Publishers Weekly* 193 (8 January 1968): 65.

Rev. of *Voyage in the Dark. Saturday Review of Literature* 11 (16 March 1935): 556.

Rev. of *Voyage in the Dark. Times Literary Supplement* 1709 (1 November 1934): 752.

Rev. of *Wide Sargasso Sea. Booklist* 63 (15 July 1967): 1182.

Ricks, Christopher. "Female and Other Impersonators." Rev. of *Good Morning, Midnight. New York Review of Books* 15 (23 July 1970): 12-13.

Rinaldi, Angelo. "Etranger. La vieille Dame du Devonshire." Rev. of *Quatuor. L'Express* (Paris) 12-18 February 1973: 77-78.

Ringer, Agnes. Rev. of *Quartet. Library Journal* 96 (August 1971): 2547.

Rose, Phyllis. "Jean Rhys in Fact and Fiction." Rev. of *Smile Please. Yale Review* 69 (Summer 1980): 596-602.

Ross, Alan. Rev. of *Wild Sargasso Sea. London Magazine* 6 (November 1966): 99, 101.

Sage, Lorna. "Phantom Returns." Rev. of *Sleep It Off, Lady. Observer* 9665 (31 October 1976): 28.

Sarraute, Anne. "Une femme à la dérive." Rev. of *Quai des grands-Augustins. La Quinzaine Littéraire* 298 (1979): 11-12.

Scannell, Vernon, "The Destruction of Innocence." *Sunday Times* 7615 (11 April 1969): 57.

Seltzer, Hara L. Rev. of *Sleep It Off, Lady. Library Journal* 101 (15 November 1976): 2395.

"Short Review." Rev. of *Smile Please. Atlantic* 245 (June 1980): 92.

"Shorter Notices." Rev. of *Quartet. New Statesman* 31 (6 October 1928): 806.

Shrapnell, Norman. "The Gift and Some Skills." Rev. of *Wide Sargasso Sea. Guardian* 28 (October 1966): 9.

Shuttleworth, Martin. "Mrs. Micawber." *Punch* 253 (16 August 1967): 253.

Smyser, Phyllis A. T. "Poignant Vignettes of Jean Rhys's Early Life." Rev. of *Smile Please. Saint Louis Globe Democrat* July 19-20, 1980: 4B

Southron, Jane Spence. "A Girl's Ordeal." Rev. of *Voyage in the Dark. New York Times Book Review* 17 March 1935: 7.

Stone, Geoffrey. Rev. of *After Leaving Mr. MacKenzie. Bookman* (New York) 74 (September 1931): 84.

Spurling, Hilary. "Werewolves and Zombies." Rev. of *Smile Please. Observer.* 9821 (18 November 1979): 40.

Straus, Ralph. "New Fiction. Black and White." Rev. of *Good Morning, Midnight. Sunday Times* 6061 (11 June 1939): 8.

_____. "New Fiction: Some Feminine Portraits. Rev. of *Voyage in the Dark. Sunday Times* 5822 (11 November 1934): 9.

Sullivan, Walter. "Erewhon and Eros. The Short Story Again." Rev. of *Tigers Are Better Looking. Sewanee Review* 83 (July 1975): 539-540.

Theroux, Paul. "Novels." Rev. of *After Leaving Mr. MacKenzie. Book World* [*Chicago Tribune* and *Washington Post*] 6 (13 February 1972): 6.

Thorpe, Michael. "Current Literature 1977. Ill. Commonwealth Literature. Caribbean." *English Studies* 60 (1979): 63-64.

Totton, Nick. "Speak, Memory." Rev. of *Sleep It Off, Lady. Spectator* 237 (30 October 1976): 22.

Trilling, Diana. "The Odd Career of Jean Rhys." Rev. of *Smile Please. New York Times Book Review* 85 (25 May 1980): 1, 17.

"Twice as Naturalism." Rev. of *After Leaving Mr. MacKenzie. New York Times Book Review* 28 June 1931: 6.

Tyler, Anne. "Boundaries and Bonds. Concerning Strangers in Strange Lands." *National Observer* 15 (11 December 1976): 18. Rev. of *Sleep It Off, Lady* and Ruth Prawer Jhbvala's *How I became a Holy Mother.*

Tyler, Ralph. "Luckless Heroines, Swinish Men." Rev. of *Tigers Are Better Looking. Atlantic* 235 (January 1975): 81-84.

Updike, John. "Books: Dark Smile, Devilish Saints." Rev. of *Smile Please. New Yorker* 56 (11 August 1980): 82, 85-89.

Usabel, Frances Esmonde de. Rev. of *Smile Please. Library Journal* 105 (15 April 1980): 983.

Warner, Marina. "Jean Rhys: A Voyage in to the Dark." Rev. of *Smile Please. Sunday Times* 8108 (18 November 1979): 41.

____. "The Art of Survival." Rev. of *Jean Rhys Letters 1931-1966. The Sunday Times* 13 May 1984.

Water, Van de. Rev. of *Quartet. New York Evening Post* 2 February 1929: 9.

Weigle. Edith. "Books." Rev. of *After Leaving Mr. MacKenzie. Daily Telegraph* (no date).

Williams, Sally. "Mr. Rochester's First Wife." Rev. of *Wide Sargasso Sea. Evening Standard* 15 November 1966: 14.

Wimers, Mary-Kay. "Some Must Cry." Rev. of *Sleep It Off, Lady. New Review* 3 (November 1976): 51-52.

"Window on the Fall," Rev. of *Sleep It Off, Lady. Book World* [*Chicago Tribune* and *Washington Post*] 29 August 1976: M2.

Wood, Michael. "Endangered Species." *New York Review of Books* 23 (11 November 1976): 30-32. Rev. of Muriel Spark's *The Takeover,* Francine Gray's *Lovers and Tyrants,* and *Sleep It off, Lady.*

Wolff, Geofrey. Rev. of *Good Morning, Midnight. Newsweek* 75 (1 June 1970): 91-92.

Wyndham-Lewis D.B. "Hinterland of Bohemia." Rev. of *The Left Bank. Saturday Review* (London) 143 (23 April 1927): 637.

### B. Books about Jean Rhys

Angier, Carole. *Jean Rhys.* Harmondsworth: Penguin Books, Co., 1985. 126pp.

Codaccioni, Mari-José. *L'autre vie de Bertha Rochester.* Paris: Didier Erudition, 1984. 701 pp.

Davidson, Arnold E. *Jean Rhys.* New York: Ungar Press. 1985. 165 pp.

Gardiner, Judith Kegan. *Rhys, Stead, Lessing and the Politics of Empathy.* Bloomington: University of Indiana Press, 1989. 200 pp.

Givner, Joan. "Charlotte Brontë, Emily Brontë and Jean Rhys: What Rhys's Letters Show about that Relationship." Westport, CT: Greenwood, 1988. 350 pp.

Harrison, Nancy. *Jean Rhys and the Novel as Women's Text.* Chapel Hill: University of North Carolina Press, 1988. 289 pp.

Hemmerechts, Kristien. *A Plausible Story and a Plausible Way of Telling It: A Structuralist Analysis of Jean Rhys's Novels.* Frankfurt/M. Berne, New York: European University Studies: Series 14, Anglo-Saxon Language and Literature, Vol 163, 1986.

James, Louis. *Jean Rhys.* London: Longman. 1978. 74 pp.

Mellown, Elgin W. *Jean Rhys: A Descriptive and Annotated Bibliography of Works and Criticism* New York, London: Garland Publishing, Inc., 1984. 218 pp.

Nebeker, Helen. *Jean Rhys, Woman in Passage. A Critical Study of the Novels of Jean Rhys.* Montreal, Canada: Eden Press Women's Publications, 1981. 224 pp.

O'Connor, Teresa F. *Jean Rhys: The West Indian Novels.* New York: New York University Press, 1987. 256 pp.

Staley, Thomas. *Jean Rhys: A Critical Study.* Austin: University of Texas Press: London: Macmillan, 1979. 140 pp.

Wolfe, Peter. *Jean Rhys.* Boston: Twayne Publishers; G.K. Hall & Co. 1980. 186 pp.

## C. Interviews

Bernstein, Marcelle. "The Inscrutable Miss Jean Rhys." *Observer Magazine* (London) - [color supplement] 1 June 1969; 40-42, 49-50.

Burton, Peter. "Jean Rhys Interviewed by Peter Burton." *Transatlantic Review* 36 (Summer 1970): 105-109.

Cantwell, "A Conversation with Jean Rhys, the Best English Novelist." *Mademoiselle* 79 (October 1974): 170-171, 206, 208, 210, 213.

Campbell, Elaine. "Apropos of Jean Rhys." *Kunapipi* 2 (1980): 152-157.

Carter, Hannah. "Fated to Be Sad. Jean Rhys Talks to Hannah Carter." *Guardian* 8 August 1968: 5

Froshaug, Judy. Jean Rhys: 'I have always been afraid of people'." *Nova* (UK) Sept. 1967: 45.

Parkin. "Everything makes you want pretty clothes." *Sunday Times* 7811 (25 February 1973): 33.

Pree, Barry. "Meet . . . Sargasso Lady." *The Observer Magazine* (London) [color supplement] 3 October 1976: 8-9.

Thomas, Ned. "Meeting with Jean Rhys." *Planet* (Llangeitho, Tregaron, Wales) 33 (August 1976: 29-31.

Vreeland, Elizabeth. "Jean Rhys. The Art of Fiction. LXIV." *Paris Review* 21 (Fall 1979): 219-237.


**D. Critical Studies**

Abel, Elizabeth. "Women and Schizophrenia: The Fiction of Jean Rhys." *Contemporary Literature* 20 (Spring 1979): 155-177.

Abbot, Keith. "Some Thoughts on Jean Rhys's Fiction," *The Review of Contemporary Fiction* 5, 2 (Summer 1985): 112-114.

Alvarez, A. "The Best Living English Novelist." *New York Times Book Review* 17 March 1974: 6-7.

Amiram, Minda Rae. "What Women's Literature?" *College English* 39 (1978): 653-661.

Amuso, Teresa Rose. "Crisis of Survival: The Precarious 'I' in the Works of Elizabeth Bowen and Jean Rhys." *DAI* 48, 2 (August 1987): 395A. U. of Michigan, Ann Arbor.

Ashcom, Jane Neide. "The Novels of Jean Rhys: Two Kinds of Modernism." *DAI* 42, 12 (June 1982): 5125A. U of Michigan, Ann Arbor.

Athill, Diana. "Jean Rhys, and the Writing of *Wide Sargasso Sea*" *Booksellers* 3165 (20 August 1966): 1378-1379.

Baer, Elizabeth Roberts. "The Pilgrimage Inward." The Quest Motif in the Fiction of Margaret Atwood, Doris Lessing and Jean Rhys." *DAI* 42, 8 (Feb. 1982): 3606. U. of Michigan, Ann Arbor.

Baer, Elizabeth; Abel, Elizabeth; Hirsch, Marianne; Langland, Elizabeth. Eds. The Sisterhood of Jane Eyre and Antoinette Cosway." *The Voyage in: Fictions in Female Development* Hanover, NH: UP of New England for Dartmouth College, 1983: 131-148.

Baldanza. "Jean Rhys on Insult and Injury." *Studies in the Literary Imagination* 11, 2 (Fall 1978): 55-65.

Bamber, Louis. "Jean Rhys." *Partisan Review* 49 (1982): 92-100.

Baybrooke, Nelville. "Jean Rhys." *Contemporary Novelists*. Ed. James Vinson. London: St. James Press, 1972, 1976: 1061-1064.

____. "The Return of Jean Rhys." *Caribbean Quarterly* 16, 4 (December 1970): 43-46.

Bender, Todd. "Jean Rhys and the Genius of Impressionism." *Studies in the Literary Imagination* 11, 2 (Fall 1978)" 43-53.

Berger, Gertrude. "Rhys, de Beauvoir and the Woman in Love." *The Review of Contemporary Literature* 5, 2 (Summer 1985): 139-145.

Blodgett, Harriet. "Enduring Ties: Daughters and Mothers in Contemporary English Fiction by Women." *South Atlantic Quarterly* 80 (Autumn 1981): 441-453.

___. "Tigers Are Better Looking to Jean Rhys." *Arizona Quarterly* 32 (1976): 226-244.

Bogataj, Katarina. "Nekdanja in danasnja Jane Eyre (Ob romanih Charlotte Brontë in Jean Rhys)." *Proster in Cas* (Yugoslavia) 5 (1973): 640-656.

Bon, Adriano. Jean Rhys: Dominatori e devianti." *Uomini e Libri: Periodico Bimestrale di Critica ed Informazione Letteraria* 20, 22 (Sept.- Oct. 1980): 28.

Borinsky, Alicia. "Jean Rhys: Poses of a Woman as Guest." *Poetic Today* 6 (1-2) (1985): 229-243.

Brown, Beverly. "Mansong and Matrix: A Radical Experiment." *SPAN: Newsletter of the South Pacific Association for Commonwealth Literature and Language Studies* 21 (Oct. 1985): 56-74.

Brown, Nancy Hemond. "Aspect of the Short Story: A Comparison of Jean Rhys's 'The Sound of the River' with Ernest Hemingway's 'Hills Like White Elephants.'" *Jean Rhys Review* 1, 1(Fall, 1986): 2-13.

___. "England and the English in the Works of Jean Rhys." *Jean Rhys Review* 1, 2 (Spring 1987): 8-20.

___. "On Becoming a Butterfly: Issues of Identity in Jean Rhys's *After Leaving Mr. MacKenzie.*" *Jean Rhys Review* 2, 1 (Fall 1987): 6-15.

Brune, Charlotte H. A Caribbean Madness: Half Slave and Half Free." *Canadian Review of Contemporary Literature* 11, 2 (June 1984): 235-248.

Campbell, Elaine. "A Report from Dominica, BWI." *World Literature Written in English* 17 (April 1978): 305-316.

___. "Jean Rhys, Alec Waugh, and the Imperial road." *Journal of Commonwealth Literature* 14 (August 1979): 58-63.

___. "Reflections of Obeah in Jean Rhys' Fiction." *Kunapipi* 4, 2 (Winter 1982): 42-50.

___. "The Unpainted Pastel Portrait." *Jean Rhys Review* 1, 1 (Fall 1986): 13-15.

Casey, Nancy. "Jean Rhys's *Wide Sargasso Sea*: Exterminating the White Cockroach." *Revista Interamericana Review* 4 (Fall 1974): 340-349.

___. "Study in the Alienation of a Creole Woman: Jean Rhys's Voyage in the Dark." *Caribbean Quarterly* 19 (September 1973): 95-102.

___. "The 'Liberated' Woman in Jean Rhys's Later Short Fiction." *Revista Interamericana Review* 4 (Summer 1974): 264-272.

Chartier, Delphine. "Jean Rhys: L'auto-Censure créatrice: Analyse des version successive de la nouvelle 'Rapunzel, Rapunzel'." *Jean Rhys Review* 1, 1 (Fall 1986): 15-29.

Codaccione, Maria-José. "L'Erreur chez Jean Rhys." *L'Erreur dans la littérature et la pensée anglaise*. Actes du Centre aixois de Recherches Anglaises. Aix-en-Provence: University of Provence, 1980: 127-141.

Cole, Laurence. "Jean Rhys." *Books and Bookmen* 17 (January 1972): 20-21.

Connolly, Cyril. "Three Shelves." *New Statesman* 11 (4 January 1936): 25-26.

Cummins, Marsha. "Point of View in the Novels of Jean Rhys: The Effect of a Double Focus." *World Literature Written in English* 24, 2 (Autumn 1984): 359-373.

Curtis, Jan. "Jean Rhys' Voyage in the Dark: A Re-Assessment." *The Journal of Commonwealth Literature* 22, 1 (1987): 144-158.

____. "The Room and The Black Background: A Re-Interpretation of Jean Rhys's *Good Morning, Midnight.*" *World Literature Written in English* 25, 2 (Autumn 1985): 264-270.

Dash, Cheryl M.L. "Jean Rhys." *West Indian Literature* Ed. Bruce King. London: Macmillan; Hamden, Conn.: Archon Books, 1979: 196-209.

Davidson, Arnold E. "The Art and Economics of Destitution in Jean Rhys' *After Leaving Mr. Mackenzie.*" *Studies in the Novel* 16, 2 (Summer 1984): 215-227.

____. "The Dark is Light Enough: Affirmation of Despair in *Good Morning, Midnight.*" *Contemporary Literature* 24, 3 (Fall 1983): 349-364.

Defromont, Françoise. "Mémoires hantées "de *Jane Eyre à Wide Sargasso Sea.*" *Revue du Centre d'Etudes et de Recherches Victoriennes et Eduardiennes de l'Université Paul Vale* 27 (April 1988): 149-157.

Delany, Paul. "Jean Rhys and Ford Madox Ford: What 'Really' Happened?" *Mosaic* 16, 4 (Fall 1983): 15-24.

Delourme, Chantal. "Jean Rhys: Perte, retour. Egarements." *Fabula* (France) 3 (Mar. 1984): 65-76.

Dias, Selma Vaz. "In Quest of a Missing Author." *Radio Times* 3 May 1957: 25.

Emery, Mary Lou. *Modernism and the Marginal Woman: A Sociocritical Approach to the Novels of Jean Rhys. DAI* 42, 11 (May 1982): 4823A. U Michigan, Ann Arbor.

____. "The Paradox of Style: Metaphor and Ritual in *Good Morning, Midnight.*" *The Review of Contemporary Literature* 5, 2 (Summer 1985): 145-150.

____. The Politics of Form: Jean Rhys's Social Vision in *Voyage in the Dark* and *Wide Sargasso Sea.*" *Twentieth Century Literature* 28, 4 (Winter 1982): 418-430.

Erwin, Linda Lee. *"Gender, Time, and Narrativity in the Novels of Jean Rhys. DAI* 49, 1 (July 1988): 90A. U of Michigan, Ann Arbor.

Fayad, Mona. "Unquiet Ghosts: The Struggle for Representation in Jean Rhys's *Wide Sargasso Sea".Modern Fiction Studies* 34, 3 (Autumn 1988): 437-452.

Ferracane, Kathleen K. *Images of the Mother in Caribbean Literature: Selected*

*Novels of George Lamming, Jean Rhys, and V.S. Naipaul. DAI* 48, 2 (Aug. 1987): 398A. U of Michigan, Ann Arbor.

Fromm, Gloria G. "Making up Jean Rhys." *The New Criterion* 4, 4 (1985): 47-50.

Ford, Madox Ford. Preface. *The Left Bank and Other Stories*. By Jean Rhys. London: Jonathan Cape; New York: Harper & Row, 1927.

Gaines, Nora. "Bibliography." *Jean Rhys Review*. 2, 2 (Fall 1987): 15-20.

Ganner, Heidemarie. "Jean Rhys: Eine Studie zur Rezeption ihres Werkes." *Arbeiten aus Anglistik und Amerikanistik* 8, 1 (1983): 55-65.

Gardiner, Judith Kegan. "Good Morning, Midnight; Good Night, Modernism." *Boundary* 11, 1-2 (Fall-Winter 1982-1983): 233-251.

____. "The Grave, "On not Shooting Sitting Birds," and the Female Esthetic." *Studies in Short Fiction* 29, 4 (Fall 1983): 265-270.

____. "Rhys Recalls Ford: *Quartet* and *The Good Soldier.*" *Tulsa Studies in Women's Literature* 1, 1 (Spring 1982): 67-81.

Gregg, Veronica Marie. "Jean Rhys and Modernism: A Different Voice." *Jean Rhys Review* 1, 2, (Spring 1987): 30-46.

Groves, Robyn Kaye, *Fiction on the Self: Studies in Female Modernism: Jean Rhys, Gertrude Stein and Djuna Barnes. DAI* 49, 5 (Nov. 1988): 1138A. U of Michigan, Ann Arbor.

Hagley, Carol R. "Ageing in the Fiction of Jean Rhys." *World Literature Written in English* 28, 1 (Spring 1988): 115, 125.

Hall, John. "Jean Rhys." *Guardian* 10 (January 1972): 9.

Hampson, John. "Movements in the Underground." *Penguin New Writing*. 27 (April 1946): 133-151.

Hanson, Clare. "Each Other: Images of Otherness in the Short Fiction of Doris Lessing, Jean Rhys, and Angela Carter." *Journal of the Short Story in English* 10, 67 (Spring 1988): 67-82.

Harris, Wilson. "Carnival of Psyche: Jean Rhys's *Wide Sargasso Sea.*" Kunapipi 2, 2 (1980): 142-150.

____. "Jean Rhys's 'Tree of Life'." *The Review of Contemporary Literature* 5, 2 (Summer 1985): 114-117.

Harrison, Nancy Rebecca. *An Introduction to the Writing Practice of Jean Rhys: The Novel as Women's Text. DAI* 44, 9 (Mar. 1984): 2763A. U of Michigan, Ann Arbor.

Hearne, John. "The Wide Sargasso Sea: A West Indian Reflection." *Cornhill Magazine* 1080 (Summer 1974): 3230333.

Hochstadt, Pearl. "Connais-tu le pays? Anna Morgan's Double Voyage." *Jean Rhys Review* 1, 2 (Spring 1987): 2-7.

Huang, Yaunshen. "The portrayal of Women in the Flight from the Enchanter and

After Leaving Mr. Mackenzie." *Yaiguoyu* (Shanghai) 2, 48 (Apr. 1987): 36-40.

____. "From Vulnerability to Selfhood: The Pain-Filled Affirmations of Jean Rhys." *Jean Rhys Review* 2, 1 (Fall 1987): 2-6.

Jackson, Joe and Kim Connell. "Gigolos: The Last of the Courtly Lovers." *Journal of Popular Culture* 15, 2 (Fall 1981): 130-141.

James, Louis, "Sun Fire — Painted Fire: Jean Rhys as a Caribbean Novelist." *Ariel* 8, 3 (July 1977): 111-127.

"Jean Rhys." Ed. Carolyn Riley. *Contemporary Authors*. 25-28. Detroit: Gale Research Co., 1971: 608.

"Jean Rhys." *Current Biography Yearbook*. Ed. Charles Moritz. New York: H.W. Wilson Co., 1972: 364-367.

"Jean Rhys." *Who's Who 1973*. London: Adam and Charles Black, 1973: 2711.

Jordis, Christine, "Jean Rhys ou la Perspective de l'Exil." *Nouvelle Revue Française* July-Aug.. 1983: 366-367; 157-167.

Kapper-den Hollander, Martien. "Jean Rhys and the Dutch Connection." *Journal of Modern Literature* 11, 1 (Mar. 1984): 159-173; *Maatstaf* BO-4 (1982): 30-40.

____. "A Gloomy Child and Its Godmother: Jean Rhys, *Barred, Sous les verrous, In de Strik*." Jean Rhys Review 1, 2 (Spring 1987): 20-29; *Autobiographical and Biographical Writing in the Commonwealth*. Ed. Doireann MacDermott. Barcelona: Editorial AUSA, 1984: 123-130.

Kerchove, Arnold. "John Updike, Jean Rhys, André Gide." *Revue Générale Belge* 1970-1973: 91-97.

Klein, Eva. *"Ancho Mar de los Sargazos*. Las Antillas dese dentro." *Plural: Revista Cultural de Excelsior* (Mexico) 16, 12, 192 (Sept. 1987): 49-51.

Kloepfer, Deborah Kelly. *"Voyage in the Dark:* Jean Rhys's Masquerade for the Mother." *Contemporary Literature* 26, 4 (Winter 1985): 443-459.

Knapp, Bettina L. "Jean Rhys: *Wide Sargasso Sea* Mother/Daughter Identification and Alienation." *Journal of Evolutionary Psychology* 7, 3, 4 (Aug. 1986): 211-226.

Kraft, Elaine, "Jean Rhys: The Men in Her Novels (Hugh Heidler, 'The Gigolo', and Mr. Mackenzie)." *The Review of Contemporary Literature* 5, 2 (Summer 1985): 118-128.

Kubitschek, Missy Dehn. "Charting the Empty Spaces of Jean Rhys's *Wide Sargasso Sea*." *Journal of Women's Studies* 9, 2 (1987): 23-28.

Leigh, Nancy J. "Mirror, Mirror: The Development of Female Identity in Jean Rhys's Fiction. *World Literature Written in English* 25, 2 (Autumn 1985): 270-285.

Lai, Wally Look. "The Road to Thornfield Hall. An Analysis of Jean Rhys's *Wide Sargasso Sea*." *New Beacon Reviews. Collection One*. Ed. John La Rose. London: New Beacon Books Ltd., 1968: 38-52.

Lindroth, Collette. "Whispers outside the Room: The Haunted Fiction of Jean Rhys." *The Review of Contemporary Literature* 5, 2 (Summer 1985): 135-139.

Lindroth, James R. "Arrangement in Silver and Grey: The Whistlerian Moment in the Short Fiction of Jean Rhys." *The Review of Contemporary Literature* 5, 2 (Summer 1985): 128-134.

"Londoner's Diary." *Evening Standard* 12 June 1967: 6; 21 June 1967: 6.

Luengo, Anthony. "*Wide Sargasso Sea* and the Gothic Mode." *World Literature Written in English* 15 (April 1976): 220-245.

Margary, Kevin. "The Sense of Place in Doris Lessing and Jean Rhys." In *A Sense of Place in the New Literature in English*. St. Lucia: U of Queensland Press, 1986. 152 pp.

Marroni, Francesco. "*Voyage in the Dark*: Jean Rhys e le stanze dell 'esilio." *It Lettore di Provincia* 17, 67 (Dec. 1986): 78-91.

Meckier, Jerome. "Distortion versus Revaluation: Three Twentieth-Century Responses to Victorian Fiction." *Victorian Newsletter* 73 (Spring 1988): 3-8.

Mellown, Elgin. "Character and Themes in the Novels of Jean Rhys." *Contemporary Literature* 13 (1972): 458-475; *Contemporary Women Novelists*. Ed. Patricia Meyer. Englewood Cliffs, N.J.: Prentice Hall, Inc., 1977: 118-136.

Meyers, Robert A. "The Theme of Identity in the Works of Jean Rhys." *Revista Interamericana* 13, 1, 4 (1983): 15-158.

Morrell, A.C. *The Rhetoric of Space and Place: A Study of the Use of Symbolic Analogy, Circular Patterning, and Romance Conventions as Persuasion in Certain Modern Commonwealth Fictions. DAI* 45, 6 (Dec. 1984): 1749A. U of Michigan, Ann Arbor.

____. "The World of Jean Rhys's Short Stories." *World Literature Written in English* 18 (April 1979): 235-244.

Moss, Howard. "Books. Going to Pieces." *New Yorker* 50 (16 December 1974), 161-162, 165-166.

Mossin, "The Existentialist Dimension in the Novels of Jean Rhys." *Kunapipi* 3, 1 (1981): 143-150.

Naipaul, V.S. "Without a Dog's Chance." *New York Review of Books*. 18 (18 May 1972): 29-31.

Nebeker, Helen. "Jean Rhys's *Quartet*. The Genesis of Myth." *International Journal of Women's Studies* 2 (1979): 257-267.

Nelson, Barbara. *The Anatomy of the Madwoman. DAI* 47, 12 (June 1987): 4399A. U of Michigan, Ann Arbor.

Nève, Edouard de. "Jean Rhys, romancière inconnue." *Les Nouvelles Littérairres* 880 (26 August 1939): 8.

Nielsen, Hanne and Brahms, Flemming. "Retrieval of a Monster: Jean Rhys's *Wide Sargasso Sea" Enigma of Values.* Ed. Anna Rutherford and Kristen Peterson. Aarhus: Dangeroo Press 1975: 139-162.

Niesen de Abruna, Laura. "Jean Rhys's Feminism: Theory against Practice." *World Literature Written in English* 28, 2 (Autumn 1988): 326-336.

Nudd, Donna Maria. "The Uneasy Voyage of Jean Rhys and Selma Vaz Dias." *Literature i Performance* 4, 2 (Apr. 1984): 20-32.

Nunes, Maria Luisa. "Becoming Whole: Literary Strategies of Decolonization in the Works of Jean Rhys, Franz Fann, and Oswald de Adrade." In *Proceedings of the Xth Congress of the International Comparative Literature Association.* New York: Garland, 1985: 28-33.

Oates, Joyce Carole. "Romance and Anti-Romance; from Brontë's *Jane Eyre* to Rhys's *Wide Sargasso Sea." Virginia Quarterly Review* 61, 1 (Winter 1985): 44-58.

O'Connor, Teresa F. *The Meaning of the West Indian Experience for Jean Rhys.* DAI 46, 3 (Sept. 1985): 709A. U of Michigan, An Arbor.

Plante. "Jean Rhys: A Remembrance." *Paris Review* 76 (1979): 238-284. Rep. in *Difficult Women: A Memory of Three.* New York: Atheneum, 1983.

Pool, Gail. "Jean Rhys: Life's Unfinished Form." *Chicago Review* 32, 4 (Spring 1981): 68-74.

Porter, Dennis. "Of Heroines and Victims: Jean Rhys and *Jane Eyre." Massachusetts Review* 17 (Autumn 1976): 540-552.

Raban, Jonathan. "Opinion: Living with Loose Ends." *New Review* 2, 19 (October 1975): 51-56.

Ramchand, Kenneth. "Terrified Consciousness." *Journal of Commonwealth Literature* 7 (July 1969)" 8-19. Rep. in Kenneth Ramchand. *The West Indian Novel and Its Background.* New York: Barnes and Noble, Inc., 1970: 230-235; London: Heinemann Educational Books Ltd., 1983: 223-236.

Rodriguez, Maria Cristina. "Men and Women Interacting in the Novel and in the Film Version of Jean Rhys' *Quartet." Imagenes* (PR) 3,1: 24-27.

Roe, Sue. Ed. "The Shadow of Light: The Symbolic Underworld of Jean Rhys." In *Women Reading Women's Writing.* Brighton, Eng.: Harvester, 1987: 227-262.

Ruben, Robert. "Introduction and Biographical Notes." *Voices.* Ed. Robert Ruben. London: Michael Joseph, 1963: 9-10, 263.

Sage, Lorna. "The Available Space." *In Women's Writing: A Challenge to Theory.* New York: Harvester; St. Martin's, 1986: 15-33.

Scharfman, Ronnie. "Mirroring and Mothering in Simone Schwarzbart's *Pluie et*

*Vent sous Télume Miracle* and Jean Rhys's *Wide Sargasso Sea*." *Yale French Studies* 62 (1981): 88-1006.

Souza, Eunice de. "Four Expatriate Writers." *Journal of the School of Language* (Jawaharial Nehru University) 4, 2 (Winter 1976-1977): 54-60.

Smilovitz, Erika. "Childlike Women and Paternal Men: Colonization in Jean Rhys's Fiction." *Ariel* 17, 4 (Oct. 1986): 93-103.

____. *Expatriate Women Writers from Former British Colonies: A Bio-Critical Study of Katherine Mansfield, Jean Rhys, and Una Marson. DAI* 48, 6 (Dec. 1987): 1453A. U of Michigan, Ann Arbor.

Spivak, Gayatri Chakravorty. "Three Women's Texts and a Critique of Imperialism" *Critical Inquiry* 12, 1 (Autumn 1985): 143-261.

Stacey-Doyle, Michele. *Jean Rhys: A Sense of Place. DAI* 48, 3 (Sept. 1987): 656A. U of Michigan, Ann Arbor.

Staley, Thomas F. "The Emergence of a Form: Style and Consciousness in Jean Rhys's *Quartet*." *Twentieth Century Literature* 24 (Summer 1978): 202-224.

Summers, Marcia A. "Victimization, Survival and Empowerment in *Wide Sargasso Sea*" In *Woman's Place. 6*. Vermillion: University of South Dakota Conf., 1985: 79-85.

Thomas, Clara. "Mr. Rochester's First Marriage: *Wide Sargasso Sea* by Jean Rhys." *World Literature Written in English* 17 (April 1978): 342-357.

Thompson, Irene. "The Left Bank Apéritifs of Jean Rhys and Ernest Hemingway." *Georgia Review* 35, 1 (Spring 1981): 94-106.

Thorpe, Michael. "'The Other Side'; *Wide Sargasso Sea* and *Jane Eyre*." *Ariel* 8, 3 (July 1977): 99-110.

Thurman, Judith. "The Mistress and the Mask: Jean Rhys's Fiction." *MS* 4 (January 1976): 51-52, 91.

Tiffin, Helen. "Mirror and Mask: Colonial Motifs in the Novels of Jean Rhys." *World Literature Written in English* 17 (April 1978): 328-341.

Tracy, Laura. "Jean Rhys: The Daughter's Revenge." *"Catching the Drift." Authority, Gender, and Narrative Strategy in Fiction*. New Brunswick; Rutgers University Press, 1988.

Turner, Alice. "Paperbacks in the News: Jean Rhys Rediscovered: How It Happened." *Publishers Weekly* 206 (1 July 1974): 56, 58.

Updike, John. "An Armful of Flowers." *New Yorker* 56 (29 December 1980): 69-72.

____. "Books: Dark Smile, Devilish Saints." *New Yorker* 56, 82 (11 August 1980): 84-85.

Vanouse, Evelyn Hawthorne. "Jean Rhys' Voyage in the Dark: Histories Patterned and Resoloute." *World Literature Written in English* 28, 1 (Spring 1988): 125-13.

Vriesland, Victor van. Preface. *Melodie in Mineur*. By Jean Rhys. Trans. Edouard de Nève. Amsterdam: Uigeveriu de Steenuil, 1935.

Waugh, Alec. *The Sugar Island*. A Caribbean Travelogue. New York: Farrar, Straus & Co., 1949. Gives valuable information on Dominica, Rhys's home island.

Webb, Ruth. "Swimming the Wide Sargasso Sea: The Manuscripts of Jean Rhys's Novel." *The British Library Journal* 14, 2 (Autumn 1988): 165-177.

Wilson, Lucy. "Women Must Have Spunks: Jean Rhys's West Indian Outcasts." *Modern Fiction Studies* 32, 3 (Autumn 1986): 439-448.

William, Angela. "The Flamboyant Tree: The World of the Jean Rhys Heroine." *Planet* (Llangeitho, Tregaron, Wales) 33 (August 1976): 35-41.

Winnett, Susan, et al. Eds. "Aesthetische Innovationen." In *Frauen-Literatur-Geschichte: Schreibebde Frauen vom Mittelalter bis zu Gegenwart*. Stuttgart: Metzler, 1985: 318-337.

Wyndham, Francis. "An Inconvenient Novelist." *Tribune* 721 (15 December 1950): 16. 18.

____. [Biographical note]. *Art and Literature, an International Review* 8 (Spring 1966): 212-213.

____. "Introduction." *Art and Literature, an International Review* 1 (March 1964): 173-177.

____. Introduction. *Wide Sargasso Sea*. By Jean Rhys. London: André Deutsch, 1966: 5-13.

____. "Introduction to Jean Rhys." *London Magazine* 7 (January 1960): 15-18.

____. "Jean Rhys." *Concise Encyclopedia of Modern World Literature*. Ed. Geoffrey Grigson. New York: Hawthorn Books, Inc.: 369-370.

____. "Twenty-Five Years of the Novel." *The Craft of Letters in England*. Ed. John Lehmann. London: Cresset Press, 1956: 44-59.

# CONTRIBUTORS

Bender, Todd
Professor of English at the University of Wisconsin at Madison. Author of *Gerard Manley Hopkins: The Critical Reception and Classical Background of his Works*. Co-author of *A Hopkins Concordance* and *Concordance to Conrad's Heart of Darkness*. Principal editor of *Modernism in Literature*. Wrote and published numerous critical essays.

Campbell, Elaine
Lecturer in writing at the Massachusetts Institute of Technology. A long-term resident of Tortola, British Virgin Islands. Wrote her doctoral dissertation on "West Indian Fiction: A Literature of Exile." Has published articles on Caribbean culture and literature in scholarly journals throughout the world.

Gregg, Veronica
Assistant Professor of English at Spelman College. Received her Ph.D. from the University of Kent. Wrote her dissertation on Jean Rhys. Author of "Jean Rhys and Modernism: A Different Voice," published in the spring, 1987 issue of *Jean Rhys Review*.

Hearne, John
Novelist, historian, teacher, commentator, and journalist. Was the recipient of the Rhys Memorial Prize (1956) and the Institute of Jamaica's Siver Musgrave Medal (1964). Author of five novels, *Voices under the Window* (1955), *The Faces of Love* (1957), *A Stranger at the Gate* (1956), *Autumn Equinox* (1959), *The Land of the Living* (1961), a number of short stories, and two plays, *Freedom Man* (1957), *The Golden Savage* (1968).

James, Louis
Senior Lecturer at the University of Kent at Canterbury. Taught at universities in Africa. the Caribbean, and the United States. Published *Fiction for the Working Man, Print and the People*, and *Islands in Between* (edition of essays on West Indian Literature, *Jean Rhys* (1978).

Kappers-den Hollander, Martien.
Has taught English and American Literature at the University of Amsterdam

233

for more than a decade. Has a special interest in women's literature. Published on Jean Rhys in the United States and in Holland. Is currently doing research on "The Dutch Dimension" in Jean Rhys' life and works.

Lindroth., Colette
Professor of English at Caldwell College in Caldwell, N.J. Researches and publishes on American Literature and contemporary fiction, in particular the relationship between cinema and literature.

Luengo, Anthony
Born in Trinidad. Studied at McGill University, UCLA, and McMaster University. Taught in the West Indies, Canada, and the United States. Published studies on West Indian and fourteenth century literature. For the past ten years, has been involved in textbook publishing and is currently Vice-President of Language-Arts publishing at a major Canadian textbook publisher in Toronto, Canada.

Mellown, Elgin
Has taught English at Duke University since 1965. Published on Edwin Muir and Jean Rhys and is the author of *Jean Rhys, A Descriptive and Annotated Bibliography of Works and Criticism (1984)*.

Morrell, Carol A.
Ph.D., Assistant Professor of English at the University of Saskatchewan in Saskatoon, Canada. Teaches, researches, and publishes in the areas of Commonwealth Literature, Canadian Literature, and Women's Studies. Published articles on Jean Rhys in major journals.

Naipaul, V.S.
Born in Trinidad, an internationally renowned novelist, historian, and social critic. Won the John Llewellyn Rhys Memorial Prize, the Somerset Maugham Award, the Hawthornden Prize, the W.H. Smith Award, and the Phoenix Trust Award. Published over twenty books of fiction and nonfiction, including *A House for Mr. Biswas* (1961), *An Area of Darkness* (1965), *A Bend in the River* (1980).

Nebeker, Helen
Professor of English and assistant department chair at Arizona State, Tempe. Specializes in contemporary British and American literature. Published articles on the works of James Joyce, Katherine Mansfield, Shirley Jackson, Jean Rhys, William Faulkner, Matthew Arnold and Mark Twain. Her works have appeared in *Studies in Short Fiction, Modern Fiction Studies, International Journal of Women's Studies*. Is the author of *Jean Rhys, Woman in Passage* (1981).

Ramchand, Kenneth
Teaches West Indian Literature at the University of the West Indies in St. Augustine,Trinidad. Critic of West Indian Literature and author of *West Indian Narrative, an Introductory Anthology* (1966), *The West Indian Novel and Its Background* (1970), *West Indian Poetry* (1971), *An Introduction to the Study of West Indian Literature* (1976).

Staley, Thomas
Presently Director of the Harry Ransom Humanities Research Center at the University of Texas at Austin, Chancellor's Council Centennial Professor in the Book Arts and Professor of English. Founding editor of the *James Joyce Quarterly*. Recently initiated *Joyce Studies*. Wrote or edited eight books on Joyce. Author of several books on modern British women novelists, including Jean Rhys and Dorothy Richardson. Published essays on modern literature in journals in this country and abroad. Has written and spoken widely in the United States and Europe on literary subjects, libraries and on the state of the humanities in the contemporary culture. Author of *Jean Rhys* (1979).

Thorpe, Michael
Teaches English at Mount Allison University. Has taught in Turkey, Nigeria, Singapore, and Holland. Author of two books, *By the Niger and Other Poems* and *Doris Lessing's Africa* . Also published essays on V.S. Naipaul, Doris Lessing. Contributes an annual "Commonwealth Literature " survey to *English Studies*.

Updike, John
Novelist, critic and poet with three books of poetry, eight short- story collections and more than ten novels. Among his novels are *Rabbit Run* (1960); *The Centaur* (1963), awarded the National Book Award for Fiction; *Rabbit Redux* (1972); *Rabbit Is Rich* (1982), awarded the Pulitzer Prize; *The Witches of Ipswich*. Winner of the 1983 National Book Critics Circle Award for Criticism for *Hugging the Shore* (1983).

Van Houts, Jan
A Dutch secondary school teacher and writer of poetry and short stories. Visited Jean Rhys in Cheriton Fitz Paine, where he spent five days in her company. Became a long-time friend and correspondent of Rhys. Wrote "Het gaatje in het gordijn" (translated as "The Hole in the Curtain), a companion piece to Rhys's story, "Who Knows What's Up in the Attic."

Wilson, Lucy
Teaches English at Loyola Marymount University, Los Angeles.